The Hell-Bound Train

Glenn Ohrlin

The Hell-Bound Train

A Cowboy Songbook

*With a Foreword by Archie Green
and a Biblio-Discography by Harlan Daniel*

UNIVERSITY OF ILLINOIS PRESS

Urbana and Chicago

Illini Books edition, 1989
© 1973 by the Board of Trustees of the University of Illinois
Manufactured in the United States of America
P 5 4 3 2 1
This book is printed on acid-free paper.

Acknowledgments are made to the following persons and organizations for permission to use copyrighted material.

John B. Baker, the copyright owner, for "Average Rein," copyright 1965; for "Ballad of Billy the Bull Rider," copyright 1965; for "Blue Bell Bull," copyright 1964; for "Circuit Rider's Home," copyright 1965; for "Tradin' Out Blues," copyright 1966. Used by permission.

Bit and Spur, for "The Strays." Used by permission.

M. M. Cole Publishing Company, for "The Strawberry Roan," by Curley Fletcher. Used by permission.

Gail I. Gardner, for "The Sierry Petes." Copyright 1935; copyright renewed 1963. Used by permission.

Ginn and Company, for "The Cowboy" ("My Home's in Montana"), from *Singing Days* of The World of Music series. Used by permission.

Houghton Mifflin Company, for "Walking John" and "The Bosky Steer" ("Jake and Roanie"), by Henry Herbert Knibbs, from *Songs of the Last Frontier.* Copyright 1930; copyright renewed 1958. Used by permission.

Westerners International, for "The Glory Trail" ("High Chin Bob"), by Badger Clark, from *Sun and Saddle Leather.* By special permission.

Library of Congress Cataloging-in-Publication Data

The Hell-bound train.

   (Music in American life)
   Unacc. melodies, transcribed from recordings by
Glenn Ohrlin, with notes by him on the songs.
   Reprint. Originally published: Urbana : University
of Illinois Press, 1974.
   Includes index.
   1. Cowboys—West (U.S.)—Songs and music. 2. Folk
music—United States. 3. Folk-songs, English—United
States. I. Ohrlin, Glenn, 1926-   . II. Series.
M1629.6.W5H44 1989   88-753440
ISBN 0-252-06071-7

Contents

Foreword

Within the chronology of American occupations, cowboys are on a middle plateau neither as old as colonial silversmiths nor as new as today's astronauts, and, accordingly, they share the temporal attributes of ancient and modern craftsmen. Because cowboys are not so remote as to be antiquated, we can accept them comfortably as contemporaries in rodeos and on ranches. Because cowboys are not so contemporary as to be antiseptic or technological, we can accept them comfortably as old-timers around whom folklore properly clusters. It is this intertwined skein of time that marks most cowboy songbooks simultaneously hoary and fresh. A reader cannot turn the pages of such an anthology without finding some material as familiar as "Yankee Doodle" or as challenging as "Jesus Christ Superstar."

When continental growth is viewed in terms of craft skill as a complement to geographic expansion, one becomes sensitive to the fact that drovers of cattle, sheep, and hogs tended domestic animals for several centuries before cowboys were isolated and identified as a distinct occupational category. It is obvious that the term *cowboy* has been used more metaphorically than the term *drover;* hence, an important concern for delineators of American identity is to ask how this specific work group drew to itself song and story, poetry and drama, history and folklore. Fortunately, the published literature about cowboying is ample. If to this writing is added the handful of documentary films made in recent decades as well as the group of long-playing discs recorded by traditional singers, the reader/viewer/listener has an excellent set of tools at hand to measure the cowboy as a national culture hero.

In this foreword to Glenn Ohrlin's songbag I shall report something of how it came to be, as well as its position in the procession of western songbooks. To begin on a personal note — how does a folklorist prepare himself for the act of "discovering" a folksinger? Like most urban children who grew up during the era of silent films, I was acquainted with Tom Mix, Hoot Gibson, and Ken Maynard as Saturday friends. Soon after elementary school I discovered Will James's *Smoky, the Cow Horse* (1926), to learn that matinee excitement could be complemented by books that were close at hand for rereading under the loneliest circumstance. Between the years of movie and novel I listened to Harry K. McClintock ("Haywire Mac"), a pioneer radio star in California. His renditions of "Trail to Mexico" and

"Bury Me Not on the Lone Prairie" seemed to be quintessential American folksongs, even though it would have been impossible for me at that time to define the term or bound the genre. Countless persons in the past had come to cowboy lore through Wild West dime novels or tent shows. My own children know more about "Bonanza" and "Gunsmoke" than about Tom Mix or "Haywire Mac." The key point is that for a century Americans have had available tales — literary, visual, aural — of frontiersmen, buffalo hunters, and range riders. None of us has escaped preparation for accepting cowboy imagery.

My first meeting with Glenn Ohrlin occurred during the fall of 1963 at Eureka Springs, Arkansas. Previously, as a University of Illinois librarian, I had become involved with the Campus Folksong Club, one of the many student groups to emerge in the folksong "revival" of the 1960s. Club members, whether concert-goers or performing interpreters, were caught up mainly by Anglo-American or Afro-American ballads, bluegrass, and blues material. It is unlikely that anyone at the university would have reached out to a cowboy musician but for an invitation by Jimmie Driftwood to attend an Ozark folk festival. I traveled to Eureka Springs in the company of Dick Adams, John Schmidt, and Judith McCulloh; actually, our quartet met Glenn simultaneously and shared the pleasure of a new friend.

Ohrlin appeared on stage early in the festival, characteristically in Levi's, work shirt, and Stetson; accompanying himself on the guitar, he sang Woody Guthrie's "Hard Traveling." My immediate reaction was one of disdain. Glenn looked as if he had been sketched by Will James — there was no question that he was a working cowboy. Why did he feature a "revival" song? After the concert I introduced myself as a folklorist and asked him bluntly whether or not he knew any cowboy songs. My demeanor must have betrayed that I had already heard numerous levi-clad collegians who idealized and imitated Woody. Glenn's response to my challenge was equally blunt: People at festivals didn't like cowboy songs but would accept Guthrie compositions as "the real thing." I tried to cajole him into performing at least one traditional piece. He was adamant but relented to the extent that he might do so at an informal session. That dark night in a Eureka Springs hillside park I heard Glenn sing "The Hell-Bound Train" — understated and pensive. I became the troubled cowboy, I was scorched by sulphur, I was awakened from my dream, I returned to life. Folklorists as scholars are strongly drawn to obscure or unusual ballads; but the appeal of "The Hell-Bound Train" was much stronger than intellectual curiosity, for, in effect, Glenn had pulled me back to the childhood ambience of Mix and McClintock.

In December, 1963, Ohrlin was invited to present a concert at the University of Illinois. *Daily Illini* critic Roger Ebert recalled that many students had already deserted the campus for the holidays and that the remaining folksong enthusiasts were dubious about cowboy lore. On a stage cluttered with empty music stands and scattered folding chairs, Glenn held a student audience spellbound not only with song but with flamenco music, salty tales, and wry anecdotes. He was accepted by his auditors because he was experientially real and was also hailed as a fresh addition to the "revival" roster. All of us that night sensed that Ohrlin would place his brand on the college and festival circuit.

In the summer of 1964 the Campus Folksong Club released Glenn Ohrlin's first LP, *The Hell-Bound Train,* which held eighteen songs, a tale, and a guitar instrumental, complemented by an illustrated brochure. This record served to introduce Glenn to folksong enthusiasts throughout the United States. Following his appearance at the 1964 Newport Folk Festival, *Sing Out* (May, 1965) presented an article excerpted from several of his letters. Editor Paul Nelson suggested that in Glenn's life two worlds (work and "revival") had interacted yet remained separate. It is my feeling that Ohrlin was able to function in these two realms partly because of his personal strength and integrity, but also because he had already learned to move back and forth between the prosaic life of ranch-hand cowboy and the dramatic life of rodeo rider.

The commercial rodeo itself evolved out of informal or "folk" entertainments at late nineteenth-century cattle roundups. Not until 1936 did tourney participants organize in Boston as "turtles" (the Cowboys Turtle Association was the forerunner of the present professional rodeo contestants' Rodeo Cowboys Association). Today, the rodeo synthesizes many disparate American scenes: cowboy workaday skill, tent show flamboyance, circus mystique, sports competitiveness, wealth to the brave (top prizewinner Phil Lyne won more than $60,000 in 1972). Glenn's years "back of the chutes" were typical of the lives of his fellows: incessant travel, hard times, close friendships, frequent injury, lonely hospital stays, rough practical jokes, special lingo, rigorous behavior codes. The subculture of the rodeo professional — its congruence with and departure from "straight" cowboy life — is still unstudied by folklorists.

Students who wish to use Ohrlin's songbook as a partial introduction into either range or rodeo life may enjoy as background reading an early interview with such a figure in Edward and Eleanor Aveling's *The Working-Class Movement in America* (1888). Here the daughter of Karl Marx described her meeting with Broncho John, an entertainer at a Cincinnati dime museum. John, "of singularly handsome face and figure," told how cowboys engaged in arduous and dangerous toil, were poorly paid, and were exploited or blacklisted by ranchers. The Avelings were conscious that to literate readers in the 1880s cowboys were not known as proletarians so much as flamboyant personalities. While Glenn in no way uses the word *proletarian*, he is careful to point out that cowboys continue to labor on ranches and at rodeos. His major criticism of folklorists is in response to their view of cowboys as riders in the past, when it should be obvious that work continues today and therefore cowboy music is functionally alive. I would formulate his animating belief in this way: Work, a centripetal force, bonds individuals into folk-like societies, and work songs, broadly defined, encode the behavior of members of such societies. In his remarks on the one hundred songs and poems gathered in this anthology Ohrlin tells much of his life story in terms of work. Here a brief outline is in order.

Glenn Ohrlin was born October 26, 1926, in Minneapolis, Minnesota. His father, a Swedish immigrant, had drifted from farm labor to work as a house painter in the Twin Cities, and his mother was a Minnesota girl whose parents had come from Norway. Many years were to pass before anyone queried Glenn about musical influences. Both parents knew Scandinavian and American songs alike. Glenn learned the rudiments of guitar technique from his father's sister, Anna Molinder, as well as a number of ballads from his mother's sister, Irene Eraker. From earliest childhood he wanted to be a rider; at twelve he frequented stables and stockyards in order to be near horses. Work and adventure always seemed more important than school. His family moved to California when he was fourteen; two years later he left home to buckaroo in Nevada. Glenn's memory of his apprenticeship is clear, and his warm letters convey the feel and movement of his life as adequately as his stories underline his songs.

Writing to me late in 1963, Ohrlin reported: "When July 4th [1943] rolled around all the cowboys went to Caliente, Nevada, for the annual rodeo. So I got started rodeoing then. I started riding bareback broncs for $2.50 a head mount money. The other events were contest, and I thought I'd like the bareback best. During '43 and '44 I cowboyed on ranches in Nevada, Arizona, Montana, Wyoming, and California. Also entered an occasional rodeo when possible. '45 and '46 was in the Army, from '47 through '50 I rodeoed full time as a contestant in the bareback riding, and starting in '49 in the saddle bronc. I have always made a few rodeos every year since, mainly in the saddle bronc riding. I joined the Cowboys Turtle Association at the Tucson, Arizona, rodeo in 1944. . . . The last rodeo I made [before University of Illinois] was at Andalusia, Alabama, October 4-6, [1963]. I placed in the bronc riding there."

Only ten weeks elapsed between the Andalusia meet and the Illinois concert which resulted in Ohrlin's debut LP. Following the Campus Folksong Club's disc, Glenn appeared on three other records. *Traditional Music at Newport 1964* (Vanguard VRS 9183) included "Montana Is My Home" and "The Chickens They Grow Tall"; *Stone County Singing* (Shoestring label, Clifton Hill, Missouri), a "private" disc produced by folklorist Keith Cunningham, included four songs by Glenn, two of them self-accompanied on fiddle; on *Folk Festival of the Smokies*, 2 (Traditional Records FFS 529), Glenn contributed "Jake and Roaney and the Bald Faced Steer" and accompanied his wife, Kay, on "The Hanging of Eva Dugan." Together these four LPs represent a fair cross section of Glenn's repertoire: traditional ballads, bawdy pieces rare in print, popular folksongs known to GIs during World War II, hobo ditties, jukebox western hits, songs out of folios and newspapers. The records also display Glenn's unadorned laconic vocal style and his simple rhythmic guitar technique, which generally serves to color the narrative thread in his songs. Glenn's departure from instrumental simplicity is seen in his pleasure in flamenco. While in Japan he began to learn flamenco from a Chicano soldier buddy. (Not giving himself over entirely to exotic music, he participated in several Nipponese rodeos.) Back home, he purchased Spanish records, continued to teach himself flamenco style, and augmented his self-education by listening to traditional songs from Mexican cowboys in the Southwest. He speaks with nostalgia about such music: "I try to play a lot of Spanish music. Maybe it isn't logical but the cowboys all seem to like it."

A question asked frequently of Ohrlin is why he lives in the Ozarks rather than the Great Plains or the Southwest. His answer is largely a matter of economics: Rodeo people dream of settling down on little ranches of their own when they retire. In 1954 Glenn bought 166 acres near Mountain View, in Stone County, Arkansas, and, in time, a small Angus herd. He followed other cattlemen to this area because land was cheap and taxes low. Of his chosen region Ohrlin wrote: "We have had, and still have to this day, free range in this county. There are many people who range their cattle out the biggest part of the year in herds from a few head to 200 or more. These cattle are generally branded or ear marked, sometimes belled so they can be found in the woods. The fenced areas merely dot the country. . . . My neighbor Hub Willis ran a lot of cattle and hogs on the range west of here in the Murphy and Bull Pen Holler country. Hub rode a mule for 20 years in that area, a place as rough and wild as you could find. I was several years finding the old road over the rim and into Bull Pen Holler. The approaches are now grown up in timber and brush. Row crop farming has nearly passed out of the picture here in the Ozarks and livestock and feed crops has taken over. . . . As far as free range, the easy going ways of the people, the general interest in cattle and riding, this is a sort of last frontier."

Here Glenn built his own stone dwelling. Indicative of his skill is the massive elm beam that supports his ranch house roof; the timber was hand hewn and squared by Glenn from a tree on his mountainside. His facility in construction is paralleled by his artistic skill; some of his drawings are found in this book. Over the years he has supplemented ranch and rodeo income by making saddles and chaps or painting signs. When the Stone County Saddle Club, for example, commissioned him to advertise their annual festival rodeo, he "wandered with a box of paints from store window to store window painting pictures of cowboys, brahma bulls and bucking horses" (*Stone County Leader*, April 13, 1972). Glenn has described one of his "murals" in a Mountain View livestock auction barn as "Arkansas Western": It "showed two cowboys on horseback looking down into a deep holler for cattle and a cow and calf looking back up at them." Of his esthetic for this book Glenn stated: "On the drawings I tried to get the exact styles of clothes and gear to fit the era and areas involved. For instance, in the drawings of Pete Knight and Fritz Truan it shows their actual chaps and other gear plus their riding styles on broncs. Same with the other stuff. Styles change for cowboys just like anybody else."

Because of preoccupation in establishing his ranch, the relative isolation of Stone County, and his personal independence, Ohrlin escaped immersion in the early "folk boom" of the 1950s. Even after "The Battle of New Orleans" drew national attention to composer Jimmie Driftwood and Stone County folksong wealth, Glenn remained apart. He was not a native Ozarkian; he had yet to establish himself as belonging to that particular corner of the land. In the spring of 1963 the Rackensack Folklore Society, organized by Driftwood, staged a Mountain View festival at which Glenn sang. He drew no special attention from the out-of-town folklorists in attendance. Nothing much happened to make him aware of his own values to folksong enthusiasts until his encounter late in 1963 with a University of Illinois advance guard. (I have already touched on Glenn's subsequent adjustment to the "revival" scene, but without noting the variety of his audiences: for example, the Old Town School of Folk Music at Chicago, the Smithsonian Institution Festival of American Folklife on the National Mall, the Philadelphia Folk Festival, the UCLA Folk Festival. Here I might also mention some of the "stars" with whom Glenn has swapped songs: Joan Baez, Seamus Ennis, Sarah Gunning, Mississippi John Hurt, Jean Ritchie, Mary Travers, Merle Travis. Of special note is the fact that the Newport Folk Foundation, by a 1968 grant, encouraged Glenn to complete this anthology.)

When Ohrlin picked the Arkansas site of his Rafter O ranch, he was unaware that he had moved into a rich pocket of American songlore. In 1960, while browsing in the Batesville Public Library for art books, he discovered Vance Randolph's superb four-volume collection, *Ozark Folksongs*. These books made Glenn conscious that his personal songbag had special merit and that pieces which his neighbors took for granted were much like Randolph's material. Now he began "collecting" from his friends Sam Hess and Raymond Sanders. The combination of Randolph's classic volumes and Glenn's chance to learn from neighbors steeped in mountain tradition, as well as his exposure to folklorists during "revival" years, gave him a sophisticated knowledge of folksong and a desire to make his own folkloric contribution. For example, Glenn has collected and deposited ten rolls of tape in the Archives of Traditional Music at Indiana University. It would be naive to assert at this juncture that Glenn does not know the main thrust of cowboy song scholarship in the United States.

In essence, a new body of traditional material was shaped in a relatively short period (1875-1925) out of old balladry carried west, mid-nineteenth-century sentimental pieces, and journalistic poetry. Seemingly, the earliest published "collection" of cowboy songs was by Clark Stanley in 1897; proprietor of a snake-oil liniment factory, he issued a pamphlet that coupled song texts and ads. In 1901 "Oh, Bury Me Not on the Lone Prairie," text and tune, appeared in the *Journal of American Folklore,* collected by Mrs. Annie Laurie Ellis at Uvalde, Texas; it was the first academic appearance of any cowboy piece. During 1908 Jack Thorp printed a fifty-page booklet in Estancia, New Mexico, of items he had collected as well as poems of his own composition (some of which were to enter tradition). A year later the *JAF* accepted a "full" article by G. F. Will, "Songs of the Western Cowboy," collected in North Dakota.

However, the work that was to capture the public mind was John A. Lomax's *Cowboy Songs and Other Frontier Ballads* (1910). This book, with piano accompaniments for eighteen items, was hailed by Theodore Roosevelt and Texas rawhiders alike. Revised in 1916 and again in 1938, it precipitated a scholarly controversy that elicited comment by Louise Pound, Cecil Sharp, Alice Corbin Henderson, D. K. Wilgus, and Alan Lomax. The useful musical transcriptions in Lomax's book were supplemented during the 1920s and 1930s by the incidental printing of cowboy music in numerous mountain and hillbilly song folios. The first major anthology to include tunes for every song was Margaret Larkin's *Singing Cowboy* (1931). Needless to say, collecting, publishing, and contention continue to this day; recent articles and books by John I. White, Richard Lingenfelter, and Austin and Alta Fife are especially valuable. The biblio-discography by Harlan Daniel which supplements this anthology will direct readers to further sources.

Hopefully, Ohrlin's book will introduce many new readers to cowboy songlore. Because it was put together after he met a number of academic scholars, it benefits from the skill of his friends Harlan Daniel and Judith McCulloh. That such a collaboration by cowboy, discographer, and musicologist is possible in the 1970s is itself one of the best consequences of the present-day fluidity in American life. To those familiar with previous compilations, this anthology will also be understood as drawing upon diverse models. Like Jack Thorp before him, Glenn is a workingman who perceives a tradition from within. Because there are relatively few folksong collections by members of folk societies, his book should be of special value to students of culture. That a book put together in the era of space exploration can contain some recent cowboy songs is testimony to the continuous ability of Glenn Ohrlin and his fellows to give fresh expression to their time-tested craft.

Archie Green

A Note on the Music

The tunes in this book are all transcribed from a tape of Glenn Ohrlin's singing, with the following exceptions: Mrs. Nellie Westerskow's "My Old Pinto Pal" (no. 89) and George B. German's "I Learned about Horses from Him" (no. 71) and "The Chuck Wagon's Stuck" (no. 98) are included in Glenn and Kay Ohrlin's field tapes now on deposit in the Archives of Traditional Music, Indiana University. Johnny Baker's contributions (nos. 93-97) come from his LP, *Songs of the Rodeo,* Audio Arts 705. To give a general notion of each tune, I have transcribed the opening stanza, sometimes also the second stanza. While I would not automatically rely on the first part of any traditional performance to be representative of what follows — a variant or new melody may take over, a singer may have to settle into his tune — in this case I think it sufficient. For points of Ohrlin's style beyond the scope of these transcriptions, such as variation in pickups and passing tones, subtler anticipation of the beat, or the way he pauses between stanzas in certain songs, I recommend listening to any of the LPs on which he appears.

JUDITH McCULLOH

The Hell-Bound Train

1

My Home's in Montana

Among my very earliest memories are the Montana broncs my grandparents farmed with all through the thirties at Winger, Minnesota, in the Red River Valley of the North, where the northern prairies begin. Somewhere along in those years I learned this song, "My Home's in Montana," from my aunt Irene (now of Minot, North Dakota) and other neighbor kids who learned it in school from Ginn and Company songbooks. It was a favorite song and very common in that area. Boys from that country often went to the Dakotas and Montana to work the wheat harvests and some just naturally got a start on the cow and horse ranches in the same states. At that time most any farm boy could handle horses, and many were accustomed to some real snakey ones. My uncle Raymond Eraker (now residing in North Dakota also) and I used to practice roping every day. We rode an old buckskin horse called Bud, who could work cows and also wore half a dozen brands. Bud belonged to some neighbors named Christensen. Grandpa's broncs were too big a chaw for us till we got to be about thirteen or fourteen.

When we had a chance to see a rodeo or Wild West show at local county fairs we came home full of details of what we had seen. Then we tried to copy most of the rope tricks and had many a wild ride on a big stout heifer, to emulate the bull riders we saw. These rides on cattle were secret for the most part, except once, when I rode a heifer right through a big lawn party celebrating my uncle Arnold's wedding. I was thirteen at the time.

There was one ex-cowboy named Art Wang nearby who ran some Hereford cattle on the White Earth Reservation, a short distance to the south. Art had punched cows in Montana and was glad to show a kid what he could. He was a dally-style roper (he took a turn around the saddle horn rather than tie). The dally style of roping, which in early years held sway west of the Rockies, came into Montana with trail herds from Oregon some twenty years before the Texans, with their tied ropes, brought the longhorns up from Texas. The upshot of all this was that both styles of cowboying were common on the northern plains where you would think the Texas style would predominate, being east of the Rockies. However, I don't suppose Art ever gave much thought to the history of roping styles.

Anyway, "My Home's in Montana" painted a vivid picture for us then and is still among my favorites. There were many cowboy songs that nearly everyone knew at that time, for most radio stations had their own cowboy singer. We could hear George B. German, who broadcast from Yankton, South Dakota, and sang lots of genuine cowboy songs. The Yankton station

MY HOME'S IN MONTANA

was heard in parts of Nebraska, Iowa, Minnesota, the Dakotas, and eastern Montana. So I soaked up songs along with all the rest and had a list of about one hundred that I knew while still in grade school. Some of them I learned working with horses around Minneapolis, where there were stables and one dude ranch. There are many cowboys moving around through every kind of riding job: at stockyards, stables, training establishments, ranches, rodeos, movies, and what have you. When my parents and I moved to the state of Washington in '42 and to California a little later the same year, I could get along pretty well with lots of riding jobs. When I started punching cows and rodeoing in Nevada in '43 at age sixteen, all I had learned stood me in good stead. Riding my first bareback bronc at a rodeo at Caliente, Nevada, July 4, 1943, reminded me a lot of nodding it out with the big heifer at my uncle's party.

I continued to learn songs wherever I worked, but still I liked and sang this one. The tune of "My Home's in Montana" is the same as the usual old tune of "The Cowboy's Lament" before they started calling the "Lament" "The Streets of Laredo." Ginn and Company took the words "my home's in Montana, I wear a bandana" from "The Cowboy's Lament" in Margaret Larkin's book *The Singing Cowboy* and wrote the rest of the first verse and all of the second and third verses to make a good cowboy song for kids. Larkin reports her version of the "Lament" as given by a Montana cowboy. My friend Bill Ramsey of Mountain View, Arkansas, tells me they had a song that started the same way when he was a boy near Billings, Montana. Bill doesn't sing but says his father's hands made up numerous unprintable verses to sort of round it out. So there were probably other songs that started with the words "my home's in Montana," though Bill Ramsey's mention of

4

hearing a version is as close as I've come to finding a third variant. He has forgotten the rest of the verses; he just remembers about it. Bill is a retired railroad man who is known locally as the Mayor of Beach Fork, Beach Fork being in a wild and nearly inaccessible part of Stone County.

MY HOME'S IN MONTANA

My home's in Montana, I wear a bandana,
My spurs are of silver, my pony is gray.
While riding the ranges my luck never changes,
With foot in my stirrup I gallop for aye.

When valleys are dusty my pony is trusty,
He lopes through the blizzards, the snow in his ears.
The cattle may scatter but what does it matter,
My rope is a halter for pig-headed steers.

When far from the ranches I chop the pine branches
To heap on my campfire as daylight grows pale.
When I have partaken of beans and of bacon
I'll whistle a merry old song of the trail.

5

2

My Friends and Relations

This is another song with the same tune as "My Home's in Montana." The first half of the first verse occurs in some versions of "The Cowboy's Lament." I have been familiar with this song since the early forties, but the only individual I can remember for certain who sang it was Powder River Jack Lee; that was in Arizona in early 1944. Dane Coolidge gives a version of this song in his book *Texas Cowboys*, which is about Texans working for Henry Boice's Chiricahua Cattle Company on the San Carlos Apache Reservation in Arizona before World War I. He collected it from a cowboy called "Outlaw Tom." Coolidge doesn't give or say anything about the melody. In Arizona in '43 and '44 I worked with a few old-timers who bragged of working for the "Cherrycows," as it was called. According to them, if you hired on with that outfit you'd better be able to cowboy some. It was rough country, rank horses and wild cattle. There are still some outfits in that country that haven't changed much in terms of a cowboy's work. Nowadays a cowboy might haul his horse in a pickup truck as far as the road goes, but when they unload and hit for the rocks and cactus and wild cattle it's about the same thing.

MY FRIENDS AND RELATIONS

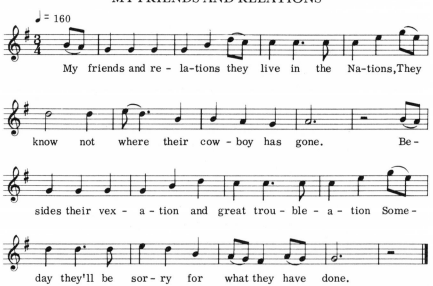

My friends and re-la-tions they live in the Na-tions, They know not where their cow-boy has gone. Be-sides their vex-a-tion and great trou-ble-a-tion Some-day they'll be sor-ry for what they have done.

My friends and relations they live in the Nations,
They know not where their cowboy has gone.
Besides their vexation and great trouble-ation
Someday they'll be sorry for what they have done.

My fortune is small, I am quick to confess it,
But what I have got it is all of my own.
I might have lived long in this world and enjoyed it
If my cruel friends could have left me alone.

Farewell to this country, I now must leave it
And make my way to some far distant land.
My horse and my saddle's the source of all pleasure,
And when I meet friends I'll join heart and hand.

For money is said to be the source of all evil
And gossip a thing that the ladies adore.
I've money aplenty to bear all expenses,
And when it is gone I know how to get more.

I won't drown my sorrow in no bottle of wine,
But away on my pony forever I'll roam
And ride through the wild to pass away time,
And when death calls me I'll follow him home.

3

The Mowing Machine

Still another song with the same tune for the verses is "The Mowing Machine." This was written by "Haywire Mac" McClintock, who wrote it for Charlie Marshall. Charlie in turn recorded it about 1934. The recording was sent to me by D. K. Wilgus of the John Edwards Memorial Foundation at UCLA. Dr. Wilgus is a walking encyclopedia on this sort of thing. In 1967 I described to him a cowboy singer I heard once in 1939 or '40, and all I remembered was that he was from Eagle Pass, Texas. Wilgus said, "Oh! That's old So-and-so (I forget who he said it was), he lives in L.A. now!"

THE MOWING MACHINE

Oh, once in the sad-dle I used to go dash-ing, Oh, once in the sad-dle I used to go gay. But that was be-fore they in-vent-ed wire fenc-es And

CHORUS

start-ed the cow-boys to shov-el-ing hay. And it's shov-el-ing hay, it's shov-el-ing hay, I toil and I sweat through the long sum-mer day. I ain't near so dash-ing and I don't feel so gay 'Cause I

8

can't get a - way from this shov-el-ing hay.

Oh, once in the saddle I used to go dashing,
Oh, once in the saddle I used to go gay.
But that was before they invented wire fences
And started the cowboys to shoveling hay.

 And it's shoveling hay, it's shoveling hay,
 I toil and I sweat through the long summer day.
 I ain't near so dashing and I don't feel so gay
 'Cause I can't get away from this shoveling hay.

When I rode an old cayuse the grass looked so green,
But it ain't quite the same from a mowing machine.
And we don't sing no songs at the end of the day,
We just sit and talk about shoveling hay.

 And the mowing machine, the mowing machine,
 I hate the durn clatter, you know what I mean.
 Instead of a horse and a job that was clean,
 Well, here I am driving that mowing machine.

Oh, once we could ride o'er the country so straight
Without ever stopping to open a gate.
And somewhere there must be a special hot fire
Preserved for the man that invented barbwire.

 We're digging postholes, and digging postholes,
 Cuttin' posts, stringin' barbwire, and diggin' postholes.
 Across the wide valleys and over the knolls
 They got all the cowboys a-diggin' postholes.

Now somewhere there must be a land that is free
That'd fit an old bowlegged cowpoke like me,
Where neither a fence or a hayfork is seen
And you can't hear the noise of a mowing machine.

 So when I'm gone, boys, here's all I require:
 Round my grave build a fence that is made of barbwire,
 Plant me out on a hill where the west wind blows keen,
 For a tombstone just put up a mowing machine.

4

Cowboy Jack

About the time I was learning "My Home's in Montana" a lot of folks were singing "Cowboy Jack." Aunt Irene and Uncle Clarence Eraker sang it, while Uncle Raymond only hummed the tune. "Cowboy Jack" is kind of sad and sweet and typical of what people liked in a less complicated time. Recently I passed this one along to Loretta Pitts in Mountain View, Arkansas. Loretta learned to sing it but thinks it's a mite sad.

COWBOY JACK

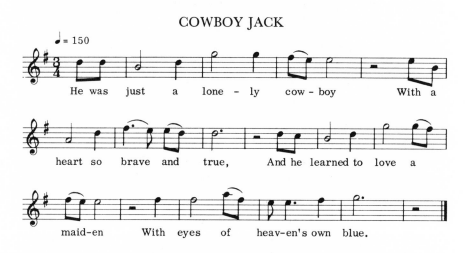

He was just a lone - ly cow - boy With a
heart so brave and true, And he learned to love a
maid-en With eyes of heav-en's own blue.

He was just a lonely cowboy
With a heart so brave and true,
And he learned to love a maiden
With eyes of heaven's own blue.

They learned to love each other
And named their wedding day.
But a quarrel came between them
And Jack he rode away.

He joined a band of cowboys
And tried to forget her name.
But on the lonely prairie
She waits for him the same.

One night when work was finished,
Just at the close of day,

10

Someone said, "Sing a song, Jack,
Will drive dull care away."

When Jack began his singing
His mind did wander back,
For he sang of a maiden
Who waited for her Jack.

> Your sweetheart waits for you, Jack,
> Your sweetheart waits for you
> Out on the lonely prairie,
> Where the skies are always blue.

He left the camp next morning,
Breathing his sweetheart's name.
"I'll go and ask forgiveness,
For I know that I'm to blame."

But when he reached the prairie
He found a new-made mound.
His friends they sadly told him
They'd laid his loved one down.

They said as she was dying
She breathed her sweetheart's name
And asked them with her last breath
To tell him when he came.

> Chorus:

5

Windy Bill

"Windy Bill" is a real cowboy song with a story that is interesting and funny to cowboys to this day. More cowboy friends who know about my song collecting have asked about "Windy Bill" and "The Sierry Petes" ("Tying the Knots in the Devil's Tail") (no. 27) than about any other songs. Many know it as a poem, and it is often recited as well as sung. At a Yankton, South Dakota, rodeo in '49 or '50, where I was entered in the bareback and saddle bronc riding, I heard the old champion steer roper Ike Rude recite "Windy Bill" for a bunch of the boys. Ike started roping in contests in 1910 and was champion steer roper in 1941 and 1953. When Ike had finished reciting "Windy Bill," one young cowboy asked, "Gosh! Where did you learn that?" Ike said, "Well, I was raised as sorta half a cowboy, you know!" I was a bit proud that I, too, had known "Windy Bill" for some years. As far as I know, Ike Rude is punching cows in California and roping steers occasionally, almost sixty years after his first rodeo. Late in 1946, just out of the army, I went to Tucson, Arizona, to see Ike Rude rope steers in a match roping against Carl Arnold for $10,000. Carl Arnold won the match; Ike had bad luck on one steer.

I learned "Windy Bill" as a song from Powder River Jack in Arizona in 1944. At the time I thought it was a real fine song that brought out the

work of Arizona rock-hoppers working wild cattle. The mention of *malpais* (black volcanic rock) and the meeting of the Spanish-style dally-ropers and a typical Texas roper with his maguey tied hard and fast seem to suggest the action took place in Arizona. The *Sam Stack tree* mentioned in the song was an old style of saddletree (the frame a saddle is constructed on), and *magee* is a maguey rope, but pronounced so it rhymes with *tree*. *Dally-welter* (*dally welta*) is an Americanization of the Spanish *dale vuelta*, meaning "take a turn."

While movies, fiction, and television stress gunfights and lead flying in all directions, most of the stories cowboys tell in their bull sessions concern these roping wrecks like Windy Bill's, or rough horses they rode, or the outfits they worked for. Cowboying, after all, has mainly to do with livestock. I knew a few guys who got shot, but the same thing happens to people in the rest of the general population — probably about in the same ratio.

WINDY BILL

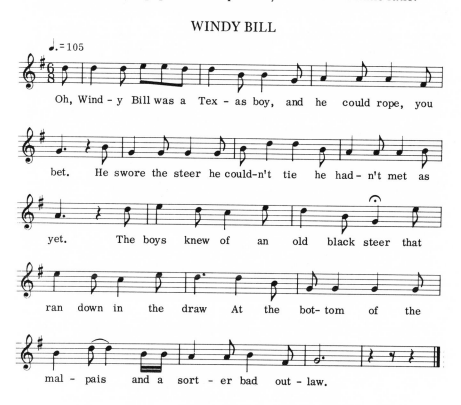

Oh, Wind-y Bill was a Tex-as boy, and he could rope, you bet. He swore the steer he could-n't tie he had-n't met as yet. The boys knew of an old black steer that ran down in the draw At the bottom of the mal-pais and a sort-er bad out-law.

Oh, Windy Bill was a Texas boy, and he could rope, you bet.
He swore the steer he couldn't tie he hadn't met as yet.
The boys knew of an old black steer that ran down in the draw
At the bottom of the malpais and a sorter bad outlaw.

Now, many a boy had tried the steer but he got away for fair.
We bet old Bill at two to one he couldn't quite sit there.
He saddled up his old gray hoss, his back and withers raw,
And he started after the old black steer that ran down in the draw.

With his Sam Stack tree and his new magee and his spurs and chaps to boot,
And his rope tied to the saddle horn, he tackled that old brute.
But when he caught the old black steer the cinches broke like straw,
And his Sam Stack tree and new magee went drifting down the draw.

Now, Bill lit in a flintrock pile, his face and his head was scratched.
We got him up and dusted him off and sorter got him patched.
He just stood there a-cussing, maddest man I ever saw,
While his Sam Stack tree and new magee went drifting down the draw.

There's a moral to my story, boys, as you can plainly see.
Don't ever tie your catch-rope to your saddletree,
But take your dallywelters to the California law,
And your Sam Stack tree and new magee won't go drifting down the draw.

6

Ten Thousand Cattle

When I sang this song in 1963 for the first academic folklorists whose acquaintance I made, Archie Green and Judy McCulloh of the University of Illinois, I couldn't tell them much about it except that I'd known it a long time. Archie and Judy and Harlan Daniel got to digging around, and Harlan came up with an old sheet music copy of "Ten Thousand Cattle Straying." We learned that the words and music were by Owen Wister, author of *The Virginian* (1902). The song was written to be sung in a 1904 stage production of *The Virginian*. Wister gathered the material and background for his famous novel in Wyoming ranch country. My version is a lot different in both words and music. The folklorists say my tune is, by comparison to all the others, very much simplified.

Anyway, I have a hunch that Owen Wister built his song on something sung in Wyoming around the turn of the century. The terrible winter of 1886–87 that killed thousands of cattle all over the northern cow country would have been fresh in many minds. The famous Montana cowboy artist Charlie Russell first drew wide attention with his watercolor *The Last of Five Thousand,* or *Waiting for a Chinook.* The picture showed a starving snow-bound cow surrounded by wolves. Russell sent the picture to his employers to answer their queries about the state of their cattle in the terrible winter. He was eventually known to all cowboys for his art, and prints and postcards of his works have been long popular all over the West. I mention this picture of Russell's, for it reminds me of this song. Russell's art and philosophy have had such an impact on all who love western things. Though he died October 24, 1926, he is still the cowboy's cowboy artist. On one occasion when I was a kid I was looking at a whole wall full of Russell prints in a Montana bar, when some customers got in a fight and one guy emptied a six-shooter in another for kicking the third party to the fracas in the head. Needless to say, I hit the door breaking all previous track records.

I have a young female cousin in Minot, North Dakota, who loves this song because it mentions *chinooks,* a familiar feature in the northern plains. A chinook is a warm winter wind that can melt a lot of snow in a short time. To a rancher short of hay a chinook can be a real blessing. When the winter of '86–87 had the range covered with ice and snow along with terrible cold, there were few ranchers who had put up hay. Cattle were expected to rough it through the winter. For a contrast, the logical song to

15

sing after "Ten Thousand Cattle" would be "The Mowing Machine" (no. 3).

TEN THOUSAND CATTLE

Ten thousand cattle gone astray,
Left my range and traveled away,
The sons of a guns I'm here to say
Have left me broke, dead broke today.

Ten thousand cattle straying,
As the ranger sang of old,
The warm chinook's delaying,
The aspen shakes with cold.

16

Now my girl has gone away,
Left my cabin and gone astray
With a son of a gun from Ioway,
Left me alone, alone today.

Ten thousand cattle straying,
As the ranger sang of old,
The warm chinook's delaying,
The aspen shakes with cold.

7

Cowboy in Church

"Cowboy in Church" is another song I learned as a kid, probably from a booklet of cowboy songs. Before World War II a lot of singers sold booklets containing the words to their songs. You got the tune listening to them sing it over the air, or you made up a tune. I never learned the last verse of this song but had a vague idea of it, so I cribbed a little on Robert Service and put the last verse together myself.

Judging from the story, this song would seem to be from the trail-driving days, and it seems to picture a town not used to cowboys. In some areas not accustomed to men from the livestock, ranch, and rodeo environment people think it odd to see a cowboy. Most cowboys who have traveled a lot have had some smart aleck pop off and say, "Hey, Tex! Where's your horse?" I have been a few places where people start swinging when they see a big hat. Maybe people are becoming better informed or more sophisticated, for this sort of thing seems mostly to have died out.

COWBOY IN CHURCH

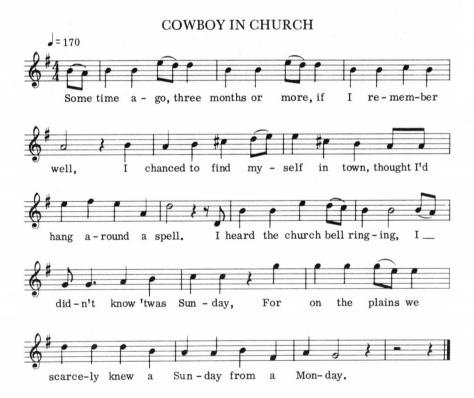

Some time a - go, three months or more, if I re - mem - ber well, I chanced to find my - self in town, thought I'd hang a - round a spell. I heard the church bell ring - ing, I did - n't know 'twas Sun - day, For on the plains we scarce - ly knew a Sun - day from a Mon - day.

Some time ago, three months or more, if I remember well,
I chanced to find myself in town, thought I'd hang around a spell.
I heard the church bell ringing, I didn't know 'twas Sunday,
For on the plains we scarcely know a Sunday from a Monday.

I started by the chapel door, but something urged me in
And told me not to spend God's day in revelry and sin.
I never gave a single thought to my not being dressed
In Sunday rig, but carelessly I went in with the rest.

You should have seen the shrugs and nods as I came walking in,
As though my honest clothing were some kind of worldly sin,
Although the goodly parson in his vestry garb arrayed
Was dressed the same as I was in the trappings of his trade.

The good man prayed for all the world and all its motley crew —
Hindu, Chinee, heathen Turk, and unbelieving Jew —
Though the congregation doubtless thought that cowboys as a race
Were a kind of mortal outlaw with no good claim to grace.

It's very strange that cowboys are a wild and reckless crew.
Their garb forbids them doing good as Christian people do.
They frequent scenes of revelry where death is bought and sold,
Where at least they get a welcome, though it's prompted by their gold.

But at that last great roundup when before the throne we stand,
When it is decided what will be our final brand,
I have a hunch that we'll be judged by what we are inside,
And He alone shall judge His own, so I His judgment bide.

8

The Swede from North Dakota

As long as I can remember, my father, the late Bert Ohrlin, sang this song.
Dad was a Swede who left home after World War I. He worked as a sailor
and then, during his first years in the States, as a harvest hand, lumberjack,
and boxer. He worked some in North Dakota, where he met both cowboys
and farmers. Dad picked up songs easily, and this is one he sang often. He
knew many that the working stiffs sang, like this one and "Hallelujah, I'm
a Bum" (no. 13). Later in life he composed many songs in the popular
vein, but without financial success. He wrote one cowboy song, "I'm a
Working Cowboy," which begins "I'm a working cowboy, have no time to
play guitar, / I've never seen the inside of a cocktail bar." Though Dad
never cowboyed any himself, he knew a good many cowboys, particularly
in California. Somehow he had the idea that they were a rollicky bunch.
Looking over his old snapshots from his sailing days, I have a hunch that
he ran with a salty bunch at one time himself.

The first two verses of "The Swede from North Dakota" given here I
learned from Dad, and the rest I've gathered here and there over the years.

THE SWEDE FROM NORTH DAKOTA

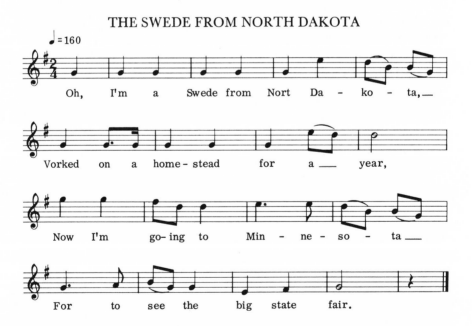

Oh, I'm a Swede from Nort Da - ko - ta, —
Vorked on a home - stead for a — year,
Now I'm go- ing to Min - ne - so - ta —
For to see the big state fair.

Oh, I'm a Swede from Nort Dakota,
Vorked on a homestead for a year,
Now I'm going to Minnesota
For to see the big state fair.

I landed down in Minneapolis,
Dere I vent on one big spree.
Now all the Swedes in Minnesota
Look a little bit like me.

I vent down to Seven Corners,
Vere Salvation Army play.
Dere a voman come up to me,
Dis is vat the voman say.

She said, "Vill you vork for Yesus?"
I said, "How much Yesus pay?"
She said, "Yesus don't pay nothing."
I said, "I von't vork today."

I vent down to Vashington Avenue,
Dress me up all out of sight.
Got me a suit and got me a bottle,
Yesus Christ, I feel for fight.

I voke up the very next morning
In the town they call Saint Paul.
I voke up vit an awful headache,
Guess I get some alcohol.

Going back to Nort Dakota,
Get me a yob on a farm somewhere.
Going back to Nort Dakota,
Oh, to hell vit the big state fair.

9

Dakota Land

While "Dakota Land," like some other pieces in this collection, is not strictly a cowboy song, it is about a land that has plenty of cowboys. The biggest part of North and South Dakota west of the Missouri River is ranchland. The Dakotas have produced some top-hand rodeo cowboys and have been especially strong on saddle bronc riders. It would be difficult for city folk, particularly eastern city folk, to realize how deeply steeped in cowboy, rodeo, and bronc-riding tradition much of this country is. "Dakota Land" is more a farmer's song than anything else, but a lot of yesterday's small homesteaders are today's family ranchers, and from their ranks came plenty of boys who took to western ways and turned to cowboying in the arena and on the range. Many areas that were completely filled with homesteaders from 1910 to the dirty thirties have been returned to grass and cattle. By nature, this west river country was better suited for ranching.

"Dakota Land" also reminds me that North Dakota is the home of the majority of my own relations; I have four uncles and one aunt and their families in that state. I have known this song since childhood and can give no clear sources for it.

DAKOTA LAND

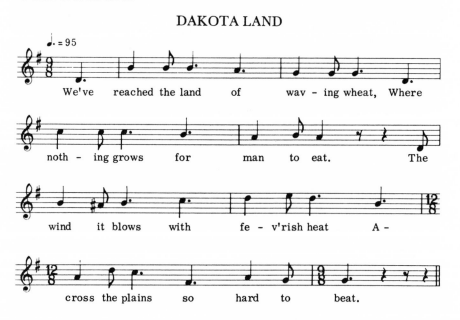

We've reached the land of wav-ing wheat, Where
noth - ing grows for man to eat. The
wind it blows with fe - v'rish heat A -
cross the plains so hard to beat.

CHORUS

Da - ko - ta land, sweet Da - ko - ta land, As
on your fier - y soil I stand, I
look a - way a - cross the plains And I
won - der why it nev - er rains, Till
Ga - briel blows his trum - pet sound And
says the rain's just gone a - round.

We've reached the land of waving wheat,
Where nothing grows for man to eat.
The wind it blows with feverish heat
Across the plains so hard to beat.

    Dakota land, sweet Dakota land,
    As on your fiery soil I stand,
    I look away across the plains
    And I wonder why it never rains,
    Till Gabriel blows his trumpet sound
    And says the rain's just gone around.

We have no wheat, we have no oats,
We have no corn to feed our shoats.
Our horses are of bronco race,
Starvation stares them in the face.

    Chorus:

23

Our neighbors are the rattlesnakes
That crawl up from the badlands' breaks.
We do not live, we only stay,
We are too poor to get away.

Chorus:

Left, prairie town: Winger, Minnesota; *right,* ranch country town: Kildeer, North Dakota.

10

Saskatchewan

Another area that knows both the cowboy and the farmer is the prairie province of Saskatchewan in Canada. This song is one more version of "Dakota Land," "Kansas Land," and I don't know how many others modeled on the gospel song "Beulah Land." I learned "Saskatchewan" listening to Alan Nixon, a former Canadian now ranching in Stone County, Arkansas, and while working as an announcer for Cliff Claggett calling chuck-wagon races in 1968. Cliff would sometimes entertain the crowd by taking over the mike and singing this song. Both men were from the same part of Saskatchewan. These chuck-wagon races, by the way, are a pretty wild event. You hook four racehorses to a chuck wagon and start by driving a figure eight around two barrels on the infield close to the track. The barrels are placed in such a way that each wagon should run the same distance to reach the track. When three or four wagons hit the track at the same time and pour it on things get pretty western. The summer with Cliff we were racing on small fairground tracks in Iowa, Nebraska, and Kansas. This was the same country I had rodeoed all over twenty years before. There were some awful tight squeaks on odd-shaped, rough tracks and a few overturned wagons. What Alan Nixon and Cliff Claggett lacked in beautiful, pear-shaped tones in their singing of this song they made up in fervor, especially when partying!

In this version of "Saskatchewan" the second line of the chorus is dropped, so it comes out a little different than "Dakota" or "Beulah Land." It also ends on an optimistic note.

SASKATCHEWAN

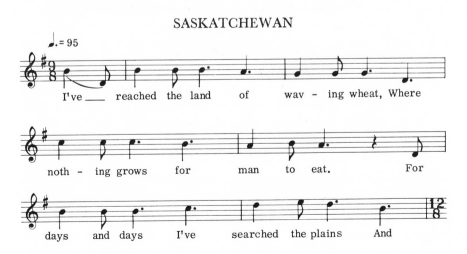

I've ___ reached the land of wav - ing wheat, Where

noth - ing grows for man to eat. For

days and days I've searched the plains And

won - der why it nev - er rains. Sas -

katch - e - wan! Sas - katch - e - wan! I

look a - way a - cross the plains And

won - der why it nev - er rains, Till

Ga - briel blows his trum - pet sound And

says the rain has gone a - round.

I've reached the land of waving wheat,
Where nothing grows for man to eat.
For days and days I've searched the plains
And wonder why it never rains.

Saskatchewan! Saskatchewan!
I look away across the plains
And wonder why it never rains,
Till Gabriel blows his trumpet sound
And says the rain has gone around.

Our turkey-hens they lay no eggs,
We feed them on grasshopper legs.
Our horses are of bronco race,
Starvation stares them in the face.

Chorus:

We have no corn to feed our shoats,
We have no bills to pay our notes.
We do not live, we only stay,
We are too poor to get away.

    Chorus:

But still I love Saskatchewan,
I'm proud to be its native son.
And after all, no need to fret,
Next year may be the best year yet.

    Chorus:

11

Wonderful Watford

Mrs. Tiny Johnson, a ranch lady from Watford City, North Dakota, sang this song for me at the Johnson ranch in October of 1965. Tiny Johnson entertains locally with her singing and yodeling. She starts her local programs with "Wonderful Watford," which she made to the tune of "Beautiful Texas." Watford City is the center of a fine ranching area, McKenzie County. This prairie and badlands area was settled by ranchers after the Sioux were subdued, and it still has a last-frontier flavor. Some of the better-known ranches in the area are Brooks Keogh's *T* Up and *T* Down and the old Long *X*, which began in trail-driving days. There was Anders Madsen's Birdhead ranch. Several local ranchers ran cattle on the Big Lease on the Fort Berthold Indian Reservation. However, the government dam on the Missouri River at Garrison backed water over much of the bottoms and hay lands that these ranches depended on. Other cow towns in the area are Kildeer (near Kildeer Mountain), Halliday, Grassy Butte, and Trotters. Top bronc riders from the same country in recent years have been Pete Fredericks and Joe Chase of Halliday, North Dakota. The Fettig string of rodeo stock from Kildeer has sent great buckers, such as Red Pepper, Funeral Wagon, Bear Den (named for Bear Den Creek), and Figure Four (named for the old Figure Four ranch), to Montana and Dakota rodeos and also as their tops to the National Finals Rodeo each year.

WONDERFUL WATFORD

all that makes it so. You can
ride o'er the plains and the cou-lees _____ Or
down where the wil - low ____ grows ____ And
still be in won - der - ful Wat - ford, ___ The most
won - der - ful place that I ___ know. ____

Wonderful, wonderful Watford,
Where the Little Missouri flows,
We're proud of all our Norwegians
And all that makes it so.
You can ride o'er the plains and the coulees
Or down where the willow grows
And still be in wonderful Watford,
The most wonderful place that I know.

12

Bonny Black Bess

"Bonny Black Bess" is an old, old song I learned as a boy from Leo Burroughs. Leo was a family friend who worked with my dad on jobs in Minnesota, Washington, and California. He was originally from the Flint Hills of Kansas, a great grazing area famed for fattening steers on its native bluestem grass. He knew many old songs and we "sang at each other" when I was just a button. Leo passed away in California in 1949.

Though this song about the outlaw Turpin and his mare, Bonny Black Bess, appears in several published folksong collections, including Vance Randolph's *Ozark Folksongs,* Leo Burroughs is the only one I ever heard sing it. There was an old-timer at the Clemens's Chandler, Arizona, feedlot and ranch in late 1943 who said he'd heard it a lot when he was young. I don't recall this cowboy's name, but I remember he often spoke of the famous "Cherrycow" outfit on the San Carlos Reservation (also called the "Cherries," with the brand "CCC"). In his book *Texas Cowboys,* which has its setting on the CCC in Arizona, Dane Coolidge tells of getting the words to "Bonny Black Bess" from cowboy Sam White, who'd come from Toyah, Texas.

BONNY BLACK BESS

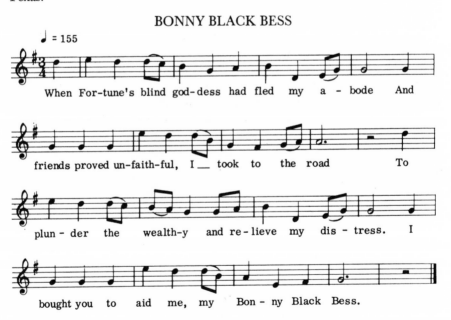

When For-tune's blind god-dess had fled my a - bode And friends proved un-faith-ful, I __ took to the road To plun - der the wealth-y and re-lieve my dis - tress. I bought you to aid me, my Bon - ny Black Bess.

When Fortune's blind goddess had fled my abode
And friends proved unfaithful, I took to the road
To plunder the wealthy and relieve my distress.
I bought you to aid me, my Bonny Black Bess.

When dark able Midnight her mantle had thrown
O'er the bright face of Nature, many times we have gone
To the famed Hounslow Heath, though an unwelcome guest
To the minions of Fortune, my Bonny Black Bess.

How gentle you'd stand as the stages I'd stop
And down to me their money and jewelry they'd drop.
We'd never rob a poor man or ever oppress
Any widows or orphans, my Bonny Black Bess.

When auger-eyed Justice did hot me pursue,
From Yorktown to London like lightning we flew.
No tollgates would stop us, high waters you'd breast.
In eight hours we made it, my Bonny Black Bess.

But hate darkens o'er me, despair is my lot.
The law does pursue me for the many I've shot.
To save me, dumb friend, you have done your best.
You are worn out and weary, my Bonny Black Bess.

Oh, hark, hear the hounds — but they never shall have
A beast like thee, so noble and brave.
You must die, my dumb friend, though it does me distress.
There, there, I have shot you, my Bonny Black Bess.

But they never can say that ingratitude dwelt
In the breast of Dick Turpin — there it never was felt.
I now am surrounded, will soon be at rest.
Once more I will be with my Bonny Black Bess.

13

Hallelujah, I'm a Bum

Another of the earliest songs I picked up from my dad is this hobo classic. At one time everybody I knew could sing this. Rancher Dick Smith of Buffalo, South Dakota, rode the Harding County range with an old-timer who came to South Dakota with a trail herd from Texas. Smith reports that while riding along this old-timer would sing "the old 'Bum Song.'" Railroad and bum songs like "Haywire Mac" McClintock's "Big Rock Candy Mountain" were once popular with the farmer, the cowboy, and like groups. On the other hand, genuine railroader and entertainer "Mac" McClintock could sing a cowboy song as straight as anybody.

HALLELUJAH, I'M A BUM

Oh, why don't you work like other men do?
How the hell can I work when there's no work to do?

Hallelujah, I'm a bum. Hallelujah, bum again.
Hallelujah, give us a handout to revive us again!

Oh, springtime has come, oh, won't we have fun,
We'll throw up our jobs and we'll go on the bum.

Chorus:

32

Oh, springtime has come, I'm just out of jail,
Without any money, without any bail.

Chorus:

Oh, I love my boss, my boss he loves me,
And that is the reason I'm so hungry.

Chorus:

Oh, why don't you save all the money you earn?
If I didn't eat I'd have money to burn.

Chorus:

I went to a house, I asked for some bread.
A lady came out, said, "The baker is dead."

Chorus:

I went to a house, I knocked on the door.
A lady came out, said, "You've been here before!"

Chorus:

14

My Love Is a Rider

I'd known parts of this song and bawdy songs modeled after it since grade school days. I put the rest of it together from the singing of Powder River Jack and Kitty Lee in Arizona in 1944. The cowboy in the song skips out in the spring after romancing the maid all winter. When the silver-haired Powder River Jack finished this song he would turn to Kitty Lee and say, "Well, here's one that didn't get away!"

MY LOVE IS A RIDER

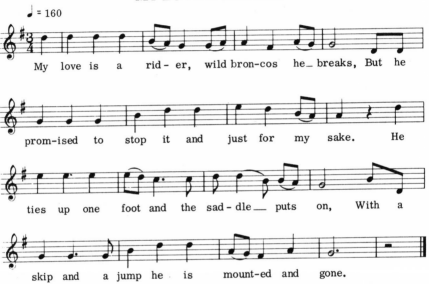

My love is a rid-er, wild bron-cos he_ breaks, But he prom-ised to stop it and just for my sake. He ties up one foot and the sad-dle _ puts on, With a skip and a jump he is mount-ed and gone.

My love is a rider, wild broncos he breaks,
But he promised to stop it and just for my sake.
He ties up one foot and the saddle puts on,
With a skip and a jump he is mounted and gone.

The first time I saw him was early one spring,
He was riding a bronco, a high-headed thing.
He tipped me a wink as he gaily did go,
For he wished me to look at his bucking bronco.

The next time I saw him was late in the fall,
He was swinging the ladies at Tomlinson's hall.

We laughed and we talked as we danced to and fro.
He promised never to ride on another bronco.

He made me a present, among them a ring,
But that which I gave him was a far better thing.
'Twas a young maiden's heart, and I want you to know
He won it while riding his bucking bronco.

Come all you young maidens, where'er you reside,
Beware of the cowboy who swings the rawhide.
He'll court you and then he will leave you and go
Up the trail in the spring on his bucking bronco.

15

The Hell-Bound Train

I learned "The Hell-Bound Train" from my aunt Irene when I was a small boy. Irene doesn't remember it at all now, but I remember we even made up a parody that was a cross between "The Hell-Bound Train" and "The Eastbound Train." I'd always supposed Irene got it from listening to George B. German sing it on radio or from his song folio we had. However, when I finally met Mr. German in 1968, he said he never sang this song. "So," as the folklorists say, "we have a minor mystery." Some of my early cowboy buddies liked this song and would sometimes get me to sing it. It was especially effective at a rip-roaring party. Even some of the wild guys would have a reflective moment over this one!

THE HELL-BOUND TRAIN

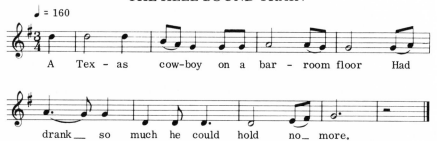

A Tex - as cow-boy on a bar - room floor Had drank __ so much he could hold no __ more.

A Texas cowboy on a barroom floor
Had drank so much he could hold no more.

He fell asleep with a troubled brain
To dream he rode on the Hell-bound train.

The engine with murderous blood was damp
And the headlight was a big brimstone lamp.

The imps for fuel were shoveling bones
And the furnace rang with a thousand groans.

The boiler was filled full of lager beer
And the Devil himself was the engineer.

The passengers they were a mixed-up crew,
Church member, atheist, Gentile, and Jew.

36

There were rich men in broadcloth and poor in rags,
Handsome girls and wrinkled hags.

With red men, yellow men, black, and white,
All chained together, a fearful sight.

The train rushed on at an awful pace,
The sulphurous fumes scorched their hands and face.

Faster and faster the engine flew,
And wilder and wilder the country grew.

Brighter and brighter the lightning flashed,
And louder and louder the thunder crashed.

Hotter and hotter the air became
Till the clothes were burned from each shrinking frame.

Then out of the distance there rose a yell:
"Ha, ha," said the Devil, "the next stop is Hell."

Then oh, how the passengers shrieked with pain
And begged the Devil to stop the train.

But he capered about and danced with glee
And he laughed and mocked at their misery.

"My friends, you have paid for your seats on this road,
The train goes through with a complete load.

"You've bullied the weak, you've cheated the poor,
The starving brother turned from your door.

"You've laid up gold till your purses bust
And given free play to your beastly lusts.

"The laborer always expects his hire,
So I'll land you safe in a lake of fire.

"Your flesh will scorch in the flames that roar,
My imps torment you forevermore."

Then the cowboy awoke with an anguished cry,
His clothes were wet and his hair stood high.

He prayed as he'd never prayed before
To be saved from Hell's front door.

His prayers and pleadings were not in vain,
For he never rode on the Hell-bound train.

16

The Gol-Darned Wheel

While many writers remark on the "sadness" of cowboy songs, it seems to me there are more that are comical. "The Gol-Darned Wheel" is a fine example of the "funny" cowboy song. I was familiar with the poem when I heard Powder River Jack sing it in Arizona in '44. Cowboys I worked with knew parts of this and other pieces, and I knew a good many songs myself at that time. However, Powder River Jack was unusual in that he seemed to know them all, and all the words, too. Maybe he was apt to stretch it a bit about the authorship of some songs (I heard him claim he wrote "Red River Valley" for his wife, Kitty Lee), but he could sure sing and looked like he was having such a heck of a good time. As my friend Roy Mack of Leslie, Arkansas, and Capoosa, Oklahoma, who had spent thirty years in Arizona, remarked, "Powder River Jack Lee was the kind of guy if he walked in a bar everybody wanted to buy him a drink."

In *Texas Cowboys*, Dane Coolidge tells of getting cowboy Jess Fears to write "The Gol-Darned Wheel" down for him in Arizona in 1909. Coolidge wrote further, "This was hot stuff and the boys all wanted a copy of it. They were like housewives exchanging recipes, only a cowboy hates to write." I know what he meant!

THE GOL-DARNED WHEEL

38

hair,— And I've had a live - ly tus - sle with a
tar - nal griz-zly bear. I can rope and throw a
long – horn of _ the wild - est Tex - as brand, And at
In - jun dis - a - gree-ments I _ can take a lead-ing
hand. But I fin' - ly met my mas - ter and he
real - ly made me squeal _ When the boys got me a-
rit. _
strad - dle of that gol - darned wheel.

I can ride the wildest bronco in the wild and woolly West,
I can rake him, I can break him, let him do his level best.
I can handle any cattle ever wore a coat of hair,
And I've had a lively tussle with a tarnal grizzly bear.
I can rope and throw a longhorn of the wildest Texas brand,
And at Injun disagreements I can take a leading hand.
But I finally met my master and he really made me squeal
When the boys got me astraddle of that gol-darned wheel.

'Twas a tenderfoot who brought it while he was on his way
From this land of freedom out to San Francisco Bay.
He tied it at the ranch house to get outside a meal,
Never dreaming that us cowboys would monkey with his wheel.
There was old Arizona and there was Jack Magill,
They said I'd been a-braggin' way too much about my skill.

They said I'd find myself against a different kind of deal
If I would get astraddle of that gol-darned wheel.

Such a slam against my talent made me madder than a mink,
And I swore that I would ride it for amusement or for chink,
That it was just a plaything for the kids and such about,
And they'd have their idees shattered if they'd lead the critter out.
They held it while I mounted and I gave the word to go.
The shove they gave to start me warn't unreasonably slow,
But I never spilt a cussword and I never give a squeal,
I was buildin' reputation on that gol-darned wheel.

Well, the grade was mighty sloping from the ranch down to the creek,
And I went a-gallyflutin' like a crazy lightning streak,
Just a-whizzing and a-dartin', first this way and then that,
The darned contrivance wobbling like the flying of a bat.
I pulled up on the handles but I couldn't check it up,
I yanked and sawed and hollered, but the darn thing wouldn't stop.
And then a sort of meechin' in my brain began to steal
That the Devil had a mortgage on that gol-darned wheel.

I've a sort of dim and hazy remembrance of the stop,
With the world a-goin' round and the stars all tangled up.
Then there came an intermission that lasted till I found
I was lying at the bunkhouse with the boys all gathered round.
And a doctor was a-sewing on the skin where it was ripped,
And old Arizona whispered, "Well, old boy, I guess you're whipped."
I said that "I am busted from sombrero down to heel."
He grinned and said, "You ort to see that gol-darned wheel!"

17

Old-Time Cowboy

This is also known as "Come All Ye Melancholy Folks" and, in Jack Lee's version, "Come All Ye Solemncholy Folks." I got this set of words from a sheepman who lived for a spell at Alco, Arkansas, in the west end of Stone County. This was the colorful John Hobbs, who had run sheep at times in Minnesota, South Dakota, Wyoming, Colorado, and God knows where else before coming to Arkansas. John was some storyteller and entertaining to swap stories with. In his day he had cowboyed, broken horses, prospected, and claims to have hoboed with the late "Yodeling Brakeman," Jimmie Rodgers. All in all, Hobbs is about as salty an old boy as you'd hope to meet. He has since moved to the Lake Chelan country in Washington state. Here is John Hobbs's version of the words. The tune is as I remember it without hearing it for over twenty-five years. Hope I got it right.

OLD-TIME COWBOY

Come all you melancholy folks, wherever you may be,
I'll sing you a song of the cowboy whose life is wild and free.
He roams the prairie over, and at night when he lies down
His heart's as gay as the flowers in May in his bed upon the ground.

41

They're a little bit rough, I must confess, most of them at least.
But if you do not hunt a quarrel you can live with them in peace.
For if you do you're sure to rue the day you joined their band.
They will follow you up and shoot it out with you, just man to man.

Did you ever go to a cowboy whenever you were hungry and dry,
Asking for a dollar and have him you deny?
He'll just pull out his pocketbook and hand to you a note.
They are the fellows to help you whenever you are broke.

Go to their ranches and stay awhile, they never ask a cent.
And when they go to town their money is freely spent.
They walk right up and take a drink, paying for everyone.
And they never ask your pardon for anything they've done.

When they go to their dances, some dance while others chat.
They ride their bucking broncos and wear their broad-brimmed hats.
With their California saddles and their pants stuck in their boots
You can hear their spurs a-jinglin', and perhaps some of them shoots.

Come all soft-hearted tenderfeet, if you want to have some fun.
Go live among the cowboys, they'll show you how it's done.
They'll treat you like a prince, my boys, about them there's nothing mean.
But don't try to give them too much advice, for all of them ain't green!

18

The Old Scout's Lament

All I can say about "The Old Scout's Lament" is that John Hobbs gave me this set of words. I have no idea about the tune, nor have I found any folklorist who has heard it. So perhaps this should go as poetry rather than a song. Could it be the work of "The Poet Scout," "Captain Jack" Crawford?

THE OLD SCOUT'S LAMENT

Come all of you, my brother scouts,
And join me in a song.
Come, let us sing together,
Though the shadows be long.

Of all the old frontiersmen
That used to scout the plain
There are but few of them
That with us remain.

Day after day they're dropping off,
They're going one by one.
Our clan is fast decreasing,
Our race is almost run.

There were many of our number
That never wore the blue.
But faithfully they did their part
As brave men, tried and true.

They never joined the army
But had other works to do,
In piloting the coming folks
To help them safely through.

But brothers, we are falling,
Our race is almost run.
The day of elk and buffalo
And beaver traps are gone.

Oh, the days of elk and buffalo!
It fills my heart with pain
To know these days are past and gone,
To never come again.

We fought the redskin rascals
Over valley, hill, and plain.
We fought him in the mountaintops
And fought him down again.

These fighting days are over,
The Indian yells resounds
No more along the border.
Peace sends for sweeter sounds.

But we found great joy, old comrade,
To hear and make it die.
We won great homes for gentle ones,
And now, our West, good-bye.

19

Cowboy's Life

Another song from my earliest working days is "Cowboy's Life" (also known as "The Tenderfoot" and "The Horse Wrangler"). I have sung two slightly different tunes to this one. The tune given here seems the most usual, but I have also used the tune to the old song that went "She's a pretty little girl, she lives up town, / Her daddy is a butcher, his name is Brown." Early radio singer John White dug up the dope on this song. The verses first appeared as a poem entitled "D2 Horse Wrangler" in a livestock journal printed in Miles City, Montana. It was written by cowboy poet D. J. O'Malley. John Hobbs, who gave me "The Old Scout's Lament" and "Old-Time Cowboy," also gave me a set of words to "Cowboy's Life." It is the same story as given here, but a few words are changed around.

COWBOY'S LIFE

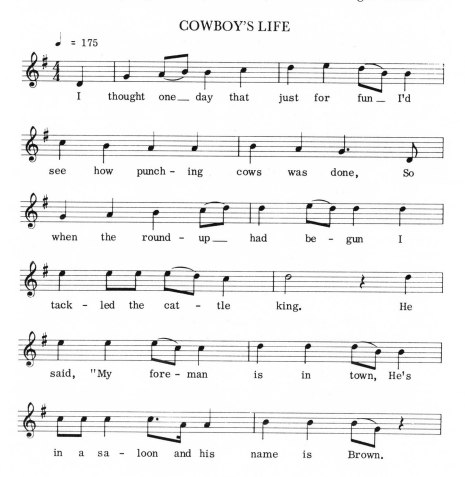

I thought one day that just for fun I'd
see how punch-ing cows was done, So
when the round-up had be-gun I
tack-led the cat-tle king. He
said, "My fore-man is in town, He's
in a sa-loon and his name is Brown.

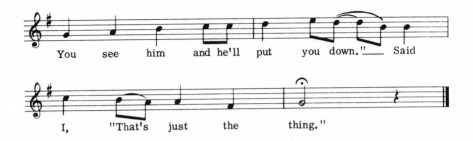

You see him and he'll put you down." Said
I, "That's just the thing."

I thought one day that just for fun
I'd see how punching cows was done,
So when the roundup had begun
I tackled the cattle king.
He said, "My foreman is in town,
He's in a saloon and his name is Brown.
You see him and he'll put you down."
Said I, "That's just the thing."

They took me to the ranch next day,
Brown argued me most all the way.
He said that punching cows was play,
It was no work at all,
That all you had to do was ride,
Was only drifting with the tide.
The son of a gun, oh, how he lied,
I'll say but he had his gall.

They put me in charge of the cavyyard
And told me not to work too hard.
All I had to do was guard
The horses from getting away.
I had one hundred and fifty head.
Sometimes I wish that I was dead.
When one got loose Brown's head turned red,
And there was the Devil to pay.

Oh, sometimes one would make a break.
Across the prairie he would take
As though running for a stake,
It seemed to them but play.
Sometimes I couldn't head 'em at all.
Sometimes my horse would take a fall,
And I'd shoot on like a cannonball
Till the earth came in my way.

They saddled me up an old gray hack
With two big setfasts on his back.
They padded him down with a gunnysack,
They used my bedding and all.
When I got on he left the ground,
Went straight up and turned around.
Then I came down and busted the ground,
I sure had a hell of a fall.

They picked me up and carried me in
And rubbed me down with a rolling pin.
"Oh, that's the way they all begin,
You're doing fine," said Brown.
"And in the morning, if you don't die,
I'll give you another horse to try."
"Oh, say, can't I walk?" says I.
Said he, "Yeah, back to town!"

Well, I've traveled up and I've traveled down,
I've traveled this country up and down.
I've been in the city and I've been in town,
And I've got this much to say:
Before you try the cowboy's life
Take heavy insurance upon your life.
Then shoot yourself with a butcher knife,
It's easier that way!

20

Roundup in the Spring

"I'd like to be in Texas for the roundup in the spring" — these words and the tune were familiar and popular, as I recall, in the late thirties. I remember very well one cowboy who sang this in the late forties. He was a bareback bronc and bull rider, cartoonist, and movie stunt man, Walt Larue of North Hollywood, California. There were two cowboy bars in the River-bottom section of Burbank, California, during that era. They were the meeting places and hangouts for rodeo cowboys contesting in or passing through southern California. These bars were also a mecca for horsemen of all sorts and movie riders and stunt men. One of these bars was the Hitching Post, owned by the Olmstead brothers, and the other was the Pickwick, owned at that time by the 1946 world champion saddle bronc rider, Jerry Ambler, and the 1947 champion bull rider, Wag Blessing. Among the regular customers when they were in that section of the country were the great rodeo champions, the late Bill and Bud Linderman of Red Lodge, Montana. One of the all-time great bareback riders, the 1948 champ in the event, Sonny Tureman, then of John Day, Oregon, was often seen at the Pickwick. Also Gene Pruett, the '48 saddle bronc champ, who is now with *Hoofs and Horns* magazine in Denver, and Carl Olson, '47 saddle bronc champ. If you were not a champion some people wondered what was wrong with you! Other rodeo hands in and out of there regularly in those days were Walt Larue, Dick Farnsworth, Carol Henry, Little Joe Lomax, Bill Callahan, Dick Slappert, George Yardley, Bill Williams (killed in a movie stunt), Gentleman Jim Goodman, Sandy Guymon, Zack McWiggins, Bob Hoke, Jack McCullar, Bob Burrows, Tom Knight, and Wayne Burson. Then there was me and my riding and traveling buddies, Bob Crowley, Red Wilson, Ray Anderson, Denny Krache, X Brands, and Stanley Atherton. There were more, but this will give you an idea of the wild bunch often present.

While the majority were reasonably quiet, gentlemanly fellows, there were some real scrappers, too. These bars hired no entertainers, but often someone felt the urge to sing, so a microphone and guitar were available. Sometimes the crowd listened and sometimes they didn't. However, if a customer kept gabbing through Walt Larue's rendition of "Roundup in the Spring," he usually found himself collared by a tough but sentimental cowboy who said something like "Shut up and listen, you son of a bitch!" There were others who sang when the spirit hit them, including a fellow known as "Dale," Buster Ford, "Cactus Mac" (who liked to sing "Zebra Dun"), and yours truly, when the sign was right. One night at the Post I'd finished a

"Old Riverbottom Gang," Burbank, California, June, 1948. *Left to right, standing:* X Brands, Denny Krache, Pat Burlson, Glenn Ohrlin; *kneeling:* Marvin, Johnny the Actor.

song, and four strangers walked over to me and said they'd kill me if my singing didn't improve. Fortunately, some friends of mine threw them out.

At that time my traveling buddies and I managed to contest at a rodeo or jackpot riding every weekend. We ranged far from the old home bar at times, to Kansas, Nebraska, South Dakota, Texas, Arizona, Nevada, Oregon, and other western states, and into the Midwest and Deep South. The guys who worked in pictures usually stayed in California. There were over a thousand horses in the Riverbottom, so there were other riding jobs, like breaking colts, putting a rein on green horses, wrangling dudes, and so on. In 1948, when recovering from a mashed vertebra picked up at Tucson, I had a job near Burbank exercising jumping horses. This got me back in shape in a few months. The Pickwick Bar usually kept a few crutches to loan out to banged-up bronc riders. After fifteen years ranching in Arkansas I still hear from Ray Anderson, who works with horses at Northridge, California. He says the only time he has seen many of the old buddies was at Bill Williams's funeral, about 1966. I see them often in the background of TV westerns.

49

ROUNDUP IN THE SPRING

♩ = 150
VERSE 1

In the lob-by of a big ho-tel in New York town one day A bunch of boys was spin-ning yarns to pass the time a-way. They told of plac-es they had been and cit-ies that they'd seen. They spoke a-bout Chi-ca-go___ and good old New Or-leans.

CHORUS

"I can see the cat-tle graz-ing on the hills at ear-ly morn, I___ can see the camp-fires smok-in' at the break-in' of the dawn. I can hear the bron-cos neigh-ing, I can hear the cow-boys sing. I'd like to be in Tex-as for the round-up in the spring."

In the lobby of a big hotel in New York town one day
A bunch of boys was spinning yarns to pass the time away.
They told of places they had been and cities that they'd seen.
They spoke about Chicago and good old New Orleans.

In the corner in an armchair sat a man whose hair was gray.
He was listening mighty eager to what they had to say.

50

When they asked him where he'd like to be, his poor old voice did ring,
"I'd like to be in Texas for the roundup in the spring."

"I can see the cattle grazing on the hills at early morn,
I can see the campfires smokin' at the breakin' of the dawn.
I can hear the broncos neighing, I can hear the cowboys sing.
I'd like to be in Texas for the roundup in the spring."

"I have seen the cattle stampeding when it seemed they'd never stop,
They'd run for miles and miles across the prairie till they'd drop.
I was foreman on a cow ranch, that's a calling for a king.
I'd like to be in Texas for the roundup in the spring."

Chorus:

21

Moonlight and Skies

The odds-on favorite singer of my old buddies of twenty years ago was the late Jimmie Rodgers, who died in 1933. Most of the Rodgers fans that I knew I met about ten years after his death. I know of no other singer who was so universally liked by cowboys and others who worked and knocked around the country. I've seen some tough guys choke up listening to the "Yodeling Brakeman" or "Blue Yodeler." Here in Stone County, Arkansas, most any adult is familiar with "the old Jimmie Rodgers songs." I have met many men over the years who claimed they either knew or saw him, and quite a few could give inside information on his life. If any entertainer ever reached the status of a true folk hero, it was Jimmie Rodgers. Reissues of his records still sell very well. This is one of his songs I learned as a kid working around horses. I now have a recording of this, but the tune I've always known doesn't quite jibe. Here is "Moonlight and Skies" as I know it.

MOONLIGHT AND SKIES

Oh, come hear my story of heartaches and sighs,
I'm a prisoner who's lonely for my moonlight and skies.
But I have a true love who is waiting for me
Back in old Oklahoma, not far from Shawnee.

Her lips like sweet cherries, her little heart cries,
"Oh, Daddy, don't leave me, my moonlight and skies."
I laughed at her pleading, youth must have its way.
I said I'd return in a couple of days.

My pal's name was Blackie, a lad with true heart.
A robbery we planned and decided to start.
I went to my darling, with tears in her eyes,
Saying, "Daddy, don't leave me, my moonlight and skies."

The next scene was fatal, a shot through the heart,
And Blackie died sending love to his sweetheart.
"Go tell her, go tell her I send my love,
And I'll meet her in Heaven with the angels above."

Next night I was captured out under the stars,
And now I must linger behind prison bars.
You'll find me at my window as day slowly dies,
A-dreaming of my darling and my moonlight and skies.

The pale moon is shining, it's shining so bright,
And lovers are strolling by my window tonight.
Their laughter so merry brings heartaches and sighs
To a prisoner who's lonely for his moonlight and skies.

22

Zebra Dun

Several folksong collectors have hashed over "Zebra Dun," and it's a great song, so I'll throw in my two cents' worth. First off, several city folks have assured me that it should have been "Z Bar Dun" instead of "Zebra Dun" because they have never heard of a zebra horse. Most dun or buckskin-colored horses, as well as grulla (mouse-colored) horses, particularly in the Southwest, have a dark stripe down their backs and horizontal zebra stripes on their legs. These stripes are common in some strains of modern Quarter horses. Old Zebra Dun must have been marked like this.

Another point, people hearing the song assume the stranger was a dude, while it's pretty clear he is a top-hand cowboy, though educated and dressed like a dude. Actually, this gag of a real top rider dressing like a dude and then showing everybody up after they've snickered is an old cowboy joke that has been pulled all over the country. A great bronc rider of the 1930s, Johnny Slater, would show up at a rodeo dressed in tweeds and cloth cap and smoking a pipe. He would enter the bronc riding, to the amusement of those who didn't know him. When his turn came around, they found he could write his name on a really rank bucking horse. Johnny Slater coached the late Fritz Truan, who became one of the greatest bronc riders of all time and was world all-around champion in 1940 and saddle bronc champion in 1939 and '40. Fritz rodeoed through an era of plentiful top bucking horses and rode all the rankest of his time.

Another bronc rider who occasionally pulled this "dude" stunt was Danny Wilder. The last time I saw Danny was at a Paul Long rodeo in Nebraska in 1949. He rode Paul Long's good bucking horse Ranger. Ranger bucked straight and hard and should have been a fine horse to ride, but he had a dirty trick. When he figured you'd been up there long enough, he rooted his head as far as he could reach and either took the rein away or sent you over his head. The first year I rode saddle broncs (I had started in bareback riding) I was on most of Paul Long's horses three or four times, but I never drew Ranger.

But back to the joke of dressing like a dude, I heard a good story on Paddy Ryan, who was a top bronc rider in the twenties and thirties. Paddy showed up at a big cow outfit in Nevada to ride the rough string (the spoiled saddle horses that were bad) and to break colts. He was wearing a cloth cap and pinchback coat and city shoes. All those Nevada buckaroos laughed up their sleeves till they saw Paddy Ryan ride. He was raised riding double-tough broncs in Montana and was a big money-winning contest rider

PADDY RYAN BRONC SPUR

for years. So you see, the dude-looking stranger that "sat there just like a camel's hump" while ole Dunny wiped 'er up isn't such a farfetched story at that.

The song "Zebra Dun" seemed to be well known or at least familiar enough since long before my first working days, and it seems I've always known the story to it. I remember a fellow called "Cactus Mac" singing it at the late Jerry Ambler's Pickwick Bar in California. While "Mac" sang "Zebra Dun" it was worth your front teeth to make too much noise, which would keep someone from hearing the words. The words are the main thing in this song, but it always seemed to me it was sung too fast, until I heard Raymond Sanders of Mountain View, Arkansas, sing "Zebra Dun" in 1963. That was when I really began to like the song and knuckled down to learn it thoroughly.

ZEBRA DUN

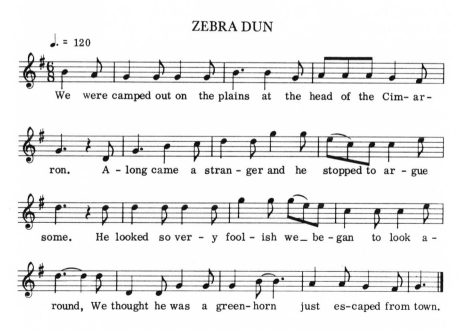

We were camped out on the plains at the head of the Cim-ar-ron. A-long came a stran-ger and he stopped to ar-gue some. He looked so ver-y fool-ish we _ be-gan to look a-round, We thought he was a green-horn just es-caped from town.

We were camped out on the plains at the head of the Cimarron.
Along came a stranger and he stopped to argue some.
He looked so very foolish we began to look around.
We thought he was a greenhorn just escaped from town.

We asked if he'd had breakfast, and he hadn't had a smear.
We opened up the chuck box and bade him have his share.
He took a cup of coffee, some biscuits, and some beans,
And he began to talk about them foreign kings and queens,

About the Spanish War and the fightin' o'er the seas,
With guns as big as steers, ramrods as big as trees,
About Paul Jones, a fightin' son of a gun,
Who was the grittiest cuss that ever pulled a gun.

Such an educated feller, his thoughts just come in herds.
He astonished all the cowboys with his jaw-breakin' words.
He just kept right on a-talkin' till he made the boys all sick.
Then we began to look around just how to play a trick.

He said he'd lost his job up on the Santa Fe,
Was a-goin' across the plains to strike the Seven D.
He didn't say how come it, some trouble with the boss.
Said he'd like to borrow a nice fat saddle hoss.

This tickled all the boys to death, they laughed right up their sleeves,
Said, "We'll loan you a saddle hoss, slick and fat as you please."
Shorty grabbed the lariat and roped ole Zebra Dun,
Hands him over to the stranger and waited for the fun.

Old Dunny was an outlaw, had grown so awful wild
He'd paw the white out of the moon every jump for a mile.
Old Dunny he just stood there as if he didn't know,
Till he was all saddled and ready for to go.

When the stranger hit the saddle old Dunny quit the earth,
And he traveled right straight up for all that he was worth.
A-pitchin' and a-squealin' and a-havin' wall-eyed fits,
His hind feet perpendicular, the front ones in the bits.

You could see the tops of mountains under Dunny every jump,
But the stranger he just sat there just like a camel's hump.
The stranger sat upon him and twirled his black mustache
Just like a summer boarder a-waitin' for his hash.

He thumped him in the shoulders and spurred him when he whirled
To show them flunky punchers he was the wolf of the world.

And when he had dismounted, once more upon the ground,
We knowed he was a Thoroughbred and not a gent from town.

The boss had been standin' round a-watchin' of the show,
Steps up to the stranger and he said, "You needn't go.
If you can throw the lasso like you rode old Zebra Dun
You're the man I've been a-looking for since the year of one."

Well, he could throw the lasso, and he didn't do it slow.
He'd catch those hind feet nine out of ten for any kind of dough.
And when the herd stampeded he was always on the spot
And set them all to millin' like the boiling of a pot.

Well, there's one thing and a sure thing I've learned since I been born,
Every educated feller ain't a plumb greenhorn!

23

Platonia

Another old familiar song, one of the earliest I learned, is "Platonia, the Pride of the Plains." I have heard it sung generally to one of two melodies, or maybe I should say to a "melody" and a "melody and a half." My friend Raymond Sanders of Mountain View, Arkansas, sings it variously as "Platonia" and "Black Beauty, the Pride of the Plains." In either case, he uses only the first half of the melody given here. Since it goes over and over, he thinks it a bit monotonous. The tune I always sing starts out the same for the first half of the verse but has a nice break in the tune (or "bridge," as my father called it) for the second half. This is the tune as Powder River Jack sang it, though I may have the words a bit different. "Platonia" is spelled several different ways; Margaret Larkin reports it as "Plantonio," and I have heard it as "Patonio." The story runs about the same in most versions.

PLATONIA

You gaze at this pic-ture with won-der-ing eyes And
then at the ar-row that hangs by its side. You
say, "Tell the sto-ry," you know there is one, "Of the
beau-ti-ful crea-ture with eyes like the sun." That
name ev-er haunts me wher-ev-er I go. I'll

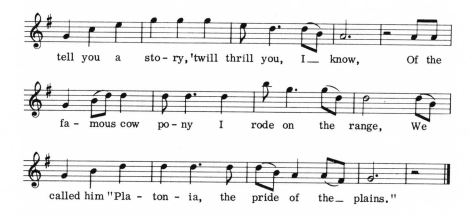

tell you a sto-ry, 'twill thrill you, I know, Of the

fa-mous cow po-ny I rode on the range, We

called him "Pla-ton-ia, the pride of the plains."

You gaze at this picture with wondering eyes
And then at the arrow that hangs by its side.
You say, "Tell the story," you know there is one,
"Of the beautiful creature with eyes like the sun."
That name ever haunts me wherever I go.
I'll tell you a story, 'twill thrill you, I know,
Of the famous cow pony I rode on the range,
We called him "Platonia, the pride of the plains."

The country was new and the settlers were scarce,
The Indians were savage, bloodthirsty, and fierce.
We sent out our scouts, but we got no report.
They were lost, for they never came back to the fort.
The captain spoke up and said, "Someone must go
Get help from the border of New Mexico."
A dozen brave cowboys at once answered, "Here!"
But the captain saw me, I was standing right near.

Platonia beside me, his nose in my hand,
The cap knew my horse was the best in the land.
He said, "If there's any one soul can get through
And outrun the redskins, my boy, it is you."
Proudly I looked at my pony, I know
Platonia and I are both ready to go.
They all shook my hand, as I leaped he dashed forth,
We swung down the trail, I headed him north.

The black strikes a trot and he keeps it all night.
And just as the horizon's beginning to light,
Not very far back there arose up a wail,
I knew that the Indians were hot on our trail.

I stroked his black neck and I called him by name,
He answered my call by shaking his mane.
His dark body lengthened as faster we sped,
And my rifle kept popping as onward we fled.

The Indians surround us, I swung his head west.
The arrows keep falling, a blow to my chest.
I speak to my pony, the best on the range,
"Steady, Platonia, the pride of the plains."
Bloody the froth flowing down o'er his bit,
The arrows all marking where he has been hit.
Platonia, poor feller, I knew he was hurt,
But he dashes right onward and up to the fort.

I give them the message, there's a dull haze around.
My cow pony stumbles and then he goes down.
Though wounded and weak, I'm feeling right bad
For the best pony comrade that man ever had.
But before very long we are both pulling through.
Of his death years later I'll not tell to you.
Oh, many good horses I've handled the reins,
But none like Platonia, the pride of the plains.

24

Walking John

It would probably be hard to find a working cowboy who wouldn't remember a horse like Walking John. John is well broke and gentle but has to have his fun in the morning when he starts out. A lot of ranch horses are this way. They buck and clown around when first mounted but "settle right down like an eight-day clock" when they are satisfied. While wrangling dudes for Al Gamble in Tucson in '44, we got a kick out of this song that Powder River Jack Lee came over and sang for us. Larkin's book gives a much longer version, with a part to the story I have never heard sung. Over the years I have known the three verses given here, but I also wish I'd known the verse that has the great words "He'd bust through those murderous cholla spikes without losing an inch of stride. / Maybe you wished you was home in bed, but brother, he'd make you ride." Al Gamble would have loved that verse, because he always razzed me about a cold-jawed white horse of his that ran off with me. We knocked down a lot of cholla cactus — in fact, we were both covered with cholla joints when the episode was over. Although I pulled with all my might and circled him, I couldn't slow the horse up one bit. Al always claimed I failed to "pull on the reins."

61

A couple months later I had the last laugh, however, when I suggested Al ride the white horse when we answered a call from a private school out on the desert to chase some stray horses from their grounds. The upshot was that when we got to running the loose horses, the white horse wouldn't stop and ran plumb off with Al. He really tore through the brush and cactus and wound up sailing off a ten-foot bank into a dry riverbed. There they stopped. When I rode up and parted the brush and looked down at them, I said, "Why didn't you pull on the reins?"

Back to "Walking John" and his habit of bucking — this is most common among horses that are used through certain seasons and then turned out several months each year. I have an old gray mare named Star that tries me out nearly every time I mount her. She is gentle and handles well and likes to look at cows but has it in her nature to hop around a bit. I use Star the year round, but it doesn't seem to make any difference.

WALKING JOHN

Walking John was a big rope horse from over Morongo way.
When you laid your twine on a raging steer old John was there to stay.
And if your rope was stout enough and your terrapin shell stayed on,
Dally welta or hard-and-fast, it was all the same to John.

Now, John was willing and stout and strong, surefooted and Spanish broke,
But I'll tell the cross-eyed universe he sure enjoyed his joke.
As soon as the morning sun come up he bogged his head right down,
Till your chaps was a-flapping like an angel's wings and your hat was a
floating crown.

Now, that was breakfast regular, and whether you fell or stuck,
At throwing a whing-ding John was there, a-teaching the world to buck.
But as soon as he got it off'n his chest and the world came back in sight
He'd settle right down like an eight-day clock with the innards piled in right.

25

Pride of the Prairie

"Pride of the Prairie" is one of the many delightful songs I got from Raymond Sanders of Mountain View, Arkansas. Raymond started taping songs for me in 1963 and years later is still remembering some real surprises. Raymond began learning songs from his mother and relatives in Kentucky some seventy years ago. As a young man in Stone County, Arkansas, he picked up more songs from friends and fellow workers in the "bolt woods," including a good many western or cowboy pieces. Before finally retiring in Arkansas, he also spent twenty years near Yakima, Washington, and he enjoyed and learned songs there as well. Raymond is interested in a wider variety of material than any other singer I know of in Stone County. Mrs. Ollie Gilbert probably knows more songs, but they are more what you would expect in this part of the country.

PRIDE OF THE PRAIRIE

On— the wild and wool-ly prai - rie,— Not so far from old Pu-eb-lo Town, Lived a lit-tle girl named Mar - y, Eyes— of blue— and tress-es of brown. O'er— the plains there came a cow-boy. He said, "Let's name our wed-ding day." She bowed her head and whis-pered,

"Now, boy," And on their bron-cos they rode a-

way, They ride a - way, one sum-mer day.

CHORUS ♩=175

Pride of the prai - rie, Mar-y, my own, Jump up be-

side me, ride to my home. My heart's been las-soed,

no_ more to roam, Pride of the prai - rie, Mar-y, my

VERSE 2 ♩.=120

own. He held her bron-co while she mount-ed, He

asked her, "May I steal a kiss?" He stole more

than she ev - er count-ed, And hand in hand she an-swered

CHORUS

this, "You stole a kiss, you stole a kiss."

On the wild and woolly prairie,
Not so far from old Pueblo town,
Lived a little girl named Mary,
Eyes of blue and tresses of brown.

O'er the plains there came a cowboy.
He said, "Let's name our wedding day."
She bowed her head and whispered, "Now, boy,"
And on their broncos they rode away,
They rode away, one summer day.

Pride of the prairie, Mary, my own,
Jump up beside me, ride to my home.
My heart's been lassoed, no more to roam,
Pride of the prairie, Mary, my own.

He held her bronco while she mounted,
He asked her, "May I steal a kiss?"
He stole more than she ever counted,
And hand in hand she answered this,
"You stole a kiss, you stole a kiss."

Chorus:

26

Charlie Quantrell, Oh

Another of Raymond Sanders's songs is this western version of "Brennan on the Moor," an Irish folksong. Raymond learned "Charlie Quantrell" from a fellow he worked with in the woods of Stone County, cutting white-oak bolts for whisky-barrel staves. Raymond says the man who sang this song seemed fascinated by Quantrell. However, the real Quantrill, the raider of Civil War fame, was not named Charlie but William Clarke Quantrill.

CHARLIE QUANTRELL, OH

Young peo-ple, lis-ten un-to me, a sto-ry I will

tell.___ His name was Char-lie Quan-trell, in Kan-sas he did

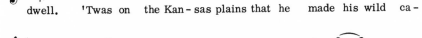
dwell. 'Twas on the Kan-sas plains that he made his wild ca-

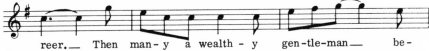
reer.___ Then man-y a wealth-y gen-tle-man___ be-

fore him stood with fear. Char-lie Quan-trell, oh.

Young people, listen unto me, a story I will tell.
His name was Charlie Quantrell, in Kansas he did dwell.
'Twas on the Kansas plains that he made his wild career.
Then many a wealthy gentleman before him stood with fear.
Charlie Quantrell, oh.

He fell in with a packman whose name was K. O. Fine.
They traveled on together till the day had nearly gone,

When the packman missed his money, likewise his watch and chain.
Then he encountered Quantrell and robbed him back again.
Charlie Quantrell, oh.

Now, Charlie found the packman just as good a man as he.
"Will you join me on the highway to be?"
The packman he consented without more delay
And proved a royal comrade until his dying day.
Charlie Quantrell, oh.

It was on the prairie at the place they call Lamar
Where Charlie and his comrades were driven to their woe.
The jury read the sentence, the judge made his reply,
"For robbing on the highway you are condemned to die."
Charlie Quantrell, oh.

Now, Charlie's wife to town did go, provisions for to buy.
When she seen poor Charlie boy, she began to weep and cry,
"I wish I had a sixpence." No more than had she spoke
When she handed him a blunderbuss from underneath her cloak.
Charlie Quantrell, oh.

Now, with this loaded blunderbuss, this story must be told,
He made them all to tremble and robbed them of their gold.
Their hundreds and their thousands they laid down by his side.
With their horses and saddles to the mountains they did ride.
Charlie Quantrell, oh.

Now, Charlie being an outlaw upon the mountain high,
Both infantry and cavalry to take him they did try.
He laid out in the bushes that grew thick in the field
And received nine wounds before that he would yield.
Charlie Quantrell, oh.

"Farewell to my old father, wherever he may be,
And to my little sister, who shed a tear for me,
And to my dear old mother, who having wrung her hands and cried,
'Would been better, Charlie Quantrell, in your cradle you had died.' "
Charlie Quantrell, oh.

27

The Sierry Petes

Gail Gardner, an old-time rancher of the Prescott, Arizona, country, wrote a poem in 1917 he called "The Sierry Petes (or, Tying the Knots in the Devil's Tail)." His title refers to the Sierra Prieta, a mountain range near Prescott. The poem was first set to music by Gail Gardner's friend Bill Simon, and it soon became known as a song or poem to cowboys everywhere. As the song spread to different parts of the West a few words were changed, as cowboys don't universally use all the Prescott area lingo. The names of the characters changed and also the location. Mrs. Ruth Fields of Mountain View, Arkansas, tells me it started out "way high up in the Tetons" when she was a girl in Idaho. I learned it as "The Sierry Peaks." George B. German of South Dakota sang it on the Yankton radio station as "Sierry Petes" and "up in the Mokiones (Mogollons)." In his book *West of Powder River,* Jack Lee started the action "way high up in the Bighorns"; however, he recorded it under the title "Tying Knots in the Devil's Tail" and sang it "Sierry Peaks." George B. German said he heard Gail Gardner recite it as a poem in the early twenties in Arizona; German published it in an early song folio, giving credit to Gardner as the author of that version. In 1935 Gail Gardner included "The Sierry Petes" in a book of his own verse entitled *Orejana Bull: For Cowboys Only.*

As "Tying Knots in the Devil's Tail," Gardner's song has a strong place in cowboy tradition. More of my cowboy friends, from old-timers to ultra-modern college rodeo team cowboys, have asked me about this song than any other. In turn, I have collected versions from South Dakota to Arkansas. I have been familiar with it myself since the thirties, when you could hear George German sing it on the radio. I also heard Powder River Jack sing it in Arizona in 1944.

The words are presented here as Gail Gardner originally wrote them. The way Sandy Bob and Buster Jig (not Jiggs) handle the Devil, roping him by the horns and feet and leaving him yoked to a tree, is exactly the way Arizona brush hands handled wild outlaw cattle. I wonder if anyone tried to lead him in the next day!

THE SIERRY PETES

A - way   up   high   in the   Sier - ry   Petes, Where the

69

yel - ler   pines grows tall,   Ole_   Sand - y Bob   an'_

Bust - er Jig,_ had a   ro - de - er   camp last   fall.   Oh, they

tak - en their hoss -es and   run - nin' irons ___ And

mab - be a   dawg or_ two,   An' they 'lowed they'd brand all the

long-yered calves, That   come with - in _   their   view.

Away up high in the Sierry Petes,
Where the yeller pines grows tall,
Ole Sandy Bob an' Buster Jig,
Had a rodeer camp last fall.

Oh, they taken their hosses and runnin' irons
And mabbe a dawg or two,
An' they 'lowed they'd brand all the long-yered calves,
That come within their view.

And any old dogie that flapped long yeres,
An' didn't bush up by day,
Got his long yeres whittled an' his old hide scortched,
In a most artistic way.

Now one fine day ole Sandy Bob,
He throwed his seago down,
"I'm sick of the smell of burnin' hair,
And I 'lows I'm a-goin' to town."

So they saddles up an' hits 'em a lope,
Fer it warn't no sight of a ride,

And them was the days when a Buckeroo
Could ile up his inside.

Oh, they starts her in at the Kaintucky Bar,
At the head of Whisky Row,
And they winds up down by the Depot House,
Some forty drinks below.

They then sets up and turns around,
And goes her the other way,
An' to tell you the Gawd-forsaken truth,
Them boys got stewed that day.

As they was a-ridin' back to camp,
A-packin' a pretty good load,
Who should they meet but the Devil himself,
A-prancin' down the road.

Sez he, "You ornery cowboy skunks,
You'd better hunt yer holes,
Fer I've come up from Hell's Rim Rock,
To gather in yer souls."

Sez Sandy Bob, "Old Devil be damned,
We boys is kinda tight,
But you ain't a-goin' to gather no cowboy souls,
'Thout you has some kind of a fight."

So Sandy Bob punched a hole in his rope,
And he swang her straight and true,
He lapped it on to the Devil's horns,
An' he taken his dallies too.

Now Buster Jig was a riata man,
With his gut-line coiled up neat,
So he shaken her out an' he built him a loop,
An' he lassed the Devil's hind feet.

Oh, they stretched him out an' they tailed him down,
While the irons was a-gettin' hot,
They cropped and swaller-forked his yeres,
Then they branded him up a lot.

They pruned him up with a de-hornin' saw,
An' they knotted his tail fer a joke,
They then rid off and left him there,
Necked to a Black-Jack oak.

71

If you're ever up high in the Sierry Petes,
An' you hear one Hell of a wail,
You'll know it's that Devil a-bellerin' around,
About them knots in his tail.

28

The Strawberry Roan

The late Curley Fletcher's "Strawberry Roan" is another cowboy song familiar throughout the United States and Canada. George B. German reports hearing both Curley Fletcher and Romaine Lowdermilk sing about the old roan outlaw in Arizona in the twenties. When German started broadcasting at Yankton, South Dakota, in 1928, this was the first song he performed. It was sung by many of my childhood friends and by an aunt and uncles on my mother's side of the family.

Curley Fletcher was himself a bronc rider and knew what he was writing about. I have Curley's booklet, *Songs of the Sage* (1931), that includes "The Strawberry Roan." It also contains photos of the curly-headed Fletcher riding bucking horses and bulls, bulldogging, and trick roping. The photos are interesting, as the clothing, saddles, and livestock are typical of the early twenties. The bull-riding pictures were taken before the advent of Brahma bulls to the rodeo arena; they show Curley decked out in the old angora fur chaps and riding a spotted bull of doubtful breeding. Cowboy artist, rodeo hand, and movie rider Walt Larue used to mention Curley Fletcher when we would discuss songs; they had worked together in western movies.

The story is always the same, but a few words are usually different, such as "hangin' round town," "layin' round town," and so on. In some versions the strawberry roan is branded with a big "44" brand or a "map of Chihuahua." In Curley Fletcher's original poem the roan is carrying a "double square" brand. The old Double Square ranch in Nevada actually was known among cowboys as having a cantankerous bunch of horses. I've seen several broncs in West Coast rodeo strings bearing this brand.

THE STRAWBERRY ROAN

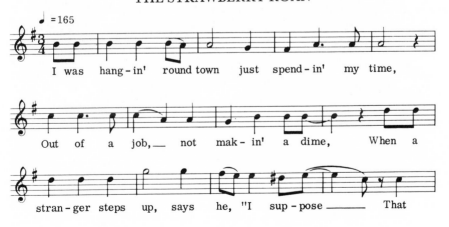

I was hang-in' round town just spend-in' my time,

Out of a job,— not mak-in' a dime, When a

stran-ger steps up, says he, "I sup-pose ——— That

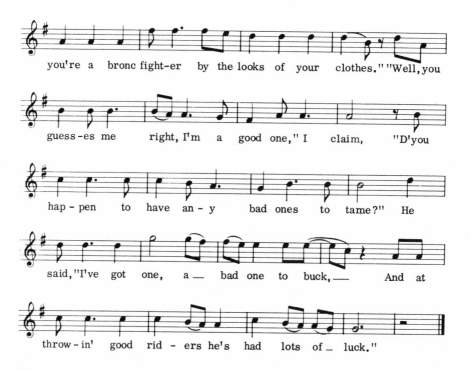

you're a bronc fight-er by the looks of your clothes." "Well, you

guess-es me right, I'm a good one," I claim, "D'you

hap-pen to have an - y bad ones to tame?" He

said, "I've got one, a — bad one to buck, — And at

throw-in' good rid - ers he's had lots of _ luck."

I was hangin' round town just spendin' my time,
Out of a job, not makin' a dime,
When a stranger steps up, says he, "I suppose
That you're a bronc fighter by the looks of your clothes."
"Well, you guesses me right, I'm a good one," I claim,
"Do you happen to have any bad ones to tame?"
He said, "I've got one, a bad one to buck,
And at throwin' good riders he's had lots of luck."

He says that this pony ain't never been rode,
The man that gets on him is bound to get throwed.
Well, I gets all excited and asks what he pays
If I ride this old cayuse a couple of days.
He offers me ten. Says I, "I'm your man,
For the bronc never lived that I couldn't fan,
For the bronc never lived or ever drew breath
That I couldn't ride till he starved plumb to death."

He says, "Get your saddle, I'll give you a chance."
We hops in the buckboard and rides to his ranch.
I stays until morning, and right after chuck
I goes out to see how this outlaw can buck.
Down in the horse corral, standing alone,
Is this caballo, a strawberry roan.

He had little pin ears that touch at the tip,
And a "double square" brand was stamped on his hip.

His legs are all spavined, he's got pigeon toes,
Little pig eyes, and a long Roman nose.
He's ewe-necked and old, with a long lower jaw,
I can see with one eye he's a regular outlaw.
I buckles on my spurs and was sure feelin' fine,
Pulls down my hat and I coils up my twine.
I throws my loop on him, and well I knew then,
If I ride this old pony I sure earn my ten.

I gets the blinds on him, it sure was a fight.
My saddle comes next and I screws her down tight.
Then I piles on him and raises the blind,
And it's get out of the way to see him unwind.
He bowed his old neck and he leaped from the ground.
Twenty circles he made before coming down.
He went up in the east and went down in the west,
To stay in his middle I'm doin' my best.

He sure was a frog walker, he heaves a big sigh.
He only lacked wings for to be on the fly.
He turned his old belly right up to the sun,
He sure is a sunfishin' son of a gun.
He was the worst bucker I seen on the range,
He can turn on a nickel and give you some change.
While he's a-buckin' he squealed like a shoat.
I tell you that pony has sure got my goat.

He hits on all fours and turned up his side,
I don't see how he keeps from losin' his hide.
I loses my stirrups and also my hat,
I starts pullin' leather as blind as a bat.
With a phenomenal jump he goes up on high
And leaves me a-settin' up there in the sky.
And then I turned over and comes back to earth,
And I lit into cussin' the day of his birth.

Then I knows there's old ponies I ain't able to ride.
There's some of them livin', they haven't all died.
But I bet all my money the man ain't alive
Can ride old Strawberry when he makes his high dive.

29

He Rode the Strawberry Roan

"The Strawberry Roan" inspired many sequels and parodies, both sentimental and bawdy. This one is about Harry Knight, former top bronc rider
and now one of the world's largest rodeo producers. My first clue to this
song came during George Williams's editorship of the *Rodeo Sports News*,
the official publication of the Rodeo Cowboys Association. In his column
and elsewhere George Williams got in a lot of rodeo history and scraps of
songs and poems. I finally got the words from D. K. Wilgus of the John
Edwards Memorial Foundation at UCLA.

This parody was written by Canadian singer Wilf Carter (better known in
the States as "Montana Slim"). Carter was at one time a dude wrangler
at Banff, in the Canadian Rockies; he tried bronc riding at the Canadian
rodeos and was a friend of many great rodeo hands through the twenties
and thirties. A Canadian friend, Jack Lauder, says that a lot of good bronc
riders came out of Banff in Harry Knight's heyday. Wrangling dudes was
their primary occupation, however.

HE RODE THE STRAWBERRY ROAN

We're all layin' round, spinnin' some yarns.
Up rides a stranger and stops at the barns.
His chaps were gold-spotted, on the leg at the right
Was a name in gold spots, 'twas Harry H. Knight.

He looked like a kid that had just left his home,
And I says, "Say, young feller, how long have you roamed?"
He says he's no phony and loosened a cinch,
Took a seat in the shade on a rickety bench.

Then up comes the boss. "Whose bronco is that?"
"That kid's over there in a ten-gallon hat."
The boss looks him over, "S'pose you wants a job?"
He said that he did, so he says, "See here, lad,

"In the mornin' we're roundin' up a bunch o' mustangs,
I think I can use you if you're a good man."
Next morning we started on the old prairie trail,
To round up them horses back to the corral.

Fin'ly we sights 'em, starts chasin' 'em back,
But the kid he's done missin' in a ten-gallon hat.

So we sees him come on a horse white with foam,
An' ahead of him, snortin', come a strawberry roan.

"Say! Here's one you missed, he sure made me ride."
We tells him no man livin' can stick to that hide.
"I'd just like to try him, doggone that ol' hide,
I've never seen a pony that I couldn't ride."

Well, right after chuck, took a good snort o' rum,
We sit on the corral bars to watch all the fun.
He uncoiled his rope like a hiss of a snake,
Ol' Strawberry ducked just a second too late.

Well, he gets his ol' saddle, screws her down tight,
Ol' Strawberry stands there a-shakin' with fright.
He woke with a snort when he felt the sharp spur
Rake down his two shoulders an' back to his rear.

Across the corral he goes like a shot,
While the kid started fannin' that ol' ten-gallon hat.
The way that horse bucked no man can describe,
His tail's all that saved him from losin' his hide.

We kept a-yellin' with all our might,
"Ride him, cowboy, you're winnin' the fight!"
He lay down an' rolled, squealed like a rat,
But the kid kep' a-fannin' that ten-gallon hat.

He turned an' looked back, just seemed to say,
"It's all right, ol' feller, you've won out today.
You're the first guy that's ever been known
To stay on my back, I'm ol' Strawberry Roan."

Poor ol' Strawberry Roan,
All the guys tried to board him got thrown.
But a kid came from Banff, an' he took a big chance,
But he rode the ol' strawberry roan.

77

30

The Fate of Old Strawberry Roan

In this song by Wilf Carter the old bronc cashes in. There have been other "Strawberry Roan" sequels out of Canada, including "The Son of Strawberry Roan." Curley Fletcher, author of the original "Strawberry Roan," was a Californian and a typical West Coast–style buckaroo. The language in his original poem plus his bawdy "Castration of the Strawberry Roan" has a saltier flavor than the Canadian sequels I have been able to find.

THE FATE OF OLD STRAWBERRY ROAN

A bunch of us boys sittin' on the corral,
Talkin' 'bout old Strawberry, a real cowboy pal,
Of throwin' most cowboys time after time,
Turning in circles as small as a dime.

From the west rides a stranger, the ranch Lazy J.
"Just wonderin', boys, if you seen any strays?"
An old .45 hung low on his hip,
A cigaret butt burnin' close to his lip.

"What's all the attraction in that there corral?"
"Why, just an old roan, a real cowboy pal.
Harry Knight's only guy ever rode that old roan.
Go ahead, stranger, ride him, but I think you'll get thrown."

"I'll just call your bluff on that little red roan.
Here's one cowboy left he never has thrown.
Stick on that saddle, I ain't got much time,
I've heard how that cayuse could really unwind."

He swung to the saddle with the greatest of ease.
Old Strawberry seemed just to float in the breeze,
And under his belly we saw the blue sky.
We yelled at the stranger a parting good-bye.

Then we saw a sight that surely read fate
As Strawberry went over the old corral gate.
A flash of a hand and out come a gun,
While on the corral the pair of them hung.

We rushed to the rider, his right foot held tight.
Old Strawberry lay there, a pitiful sight.

"Say, fellers, no hurry, I stopped him with lead."
One look at that roan and we knew he was dead.

Soon all the ranch hands were gathered around,
It seems all were shocked as we gazed at the ground.
"I'm really sorry, boys," said a voice very low,
"Was me or that cayuse, and one had to go."

We uncinched the saddle and called it a day,
Old Strawberry Roan has gone on his way.
That evening at sunset we laid him to rest
At the head of his grave we all signed this request:

"Poor old Strawberry Roan,
All the names signed below he has thrown.
His saddle hangs here, please leave it alone.
This marks the fate of old Strawberry Roan."

31

Pete Knight

Who was the greatest saddle bronc rider? There are some strong differences of opinion on this point, and I have heard arguments for several great riders of the past. Some say Burel Mulkey of Idaho, champion saddle bronc rider in 1937 and '38. Some state emphatically it was Howard Tegland of Montana during the twenties and early thirties. Many agree that Tegland was the wildest-spurring bronc rider of them all. He always went for broke and kept both feet going full stroke from the chute gate to the whistle. Bob Askins of Ismay, Montana, is often mentioned by old-timers. From what I've heard, Fritz Truan must have been as tough to unload as anyone of any time. I personally think that many champions and near-champions, past and present, have had their days when it couldn't be done any better. One of the greatest bronc riders I knew personally was the 1946 champion, Jerry Ambler. Jerry would hold forth on the art of bronc riding from time to time and say it was all "balance, timing, and science." He had the balance and timing, and apparently the science figured out, for I saw him ride different types of horses easily (some guys get along fine with one type of bucking horse but have hell with others). Jerry could make a mediocre horse look better by his own motion and artistry and spur in different styles to suit different judges. In other words, he could showcase the horse and himself to the best advantage. Jerry admitted he could ride, but he claimed there was "only one Pete Knight."

Though Pete Knight, the champion bronc rider in 1932, '33, '35, and '36, was born in Philadelphia, he spent his boyhood years on his father's ranch in Alberta, Canada. Big tough broncs, about half Shire, Percheron, or Clydesdale, were plentiful up there; the farmers worked them, the ranchers rode them, and they all got together on Sundays for ranch rodeos with the same type of horse for buckers. Jerry Ambler grew up in the same country and was a kid when Pete was already a champion. Pete Knight was Jerry's hero, and Jerry Ambler became a champion himself. From Jerry's description of Pete Knight's riding and also what I have heard from others who were around then, such as Bill Callahan and Mitch Owens, it seems Pete Knight had a good claim to being the greatest. He rode as tough a horse as anyone and had a style and showmanship that set him apart. He hooked them with dull bronc spurs from high on the neck to the cantle (back) of the saddle every jump. At the Hayward, California, rodeo at Harry Rowell's ranch in Dublin Canyon, in May, 1937, Pete Knight drew Duster, Rowell's top bucking horse. Pete had ridden Duster before, but this time

PETE KNIGHT

something went wrong. Pete wound up on the ground in front of the horse and was stepped on. A rib punctured a lung, but he got up and walked toward the chutes. He collapsed and died on the way to the hospital. Pete Knight is now among the honorees in the Cowboy Hall of Fame in Oklahoma City.

A California cowboy, the late Mitch Owens (I made a few rodeos with him in the Midwest in 1950), had ridden Duster. He had also made the whistle on the famous Five Minutes to Midnight. Mitch thought Duster was the tougher horse. I have heard the same from the late Jackie Cooper, bronc rider from California. More top bronc riders of that era were in Five's camp, though. Oddly enough, in Canada, where Pete Knight is an idol to this day, in songs and write-ups they call the horse that killed him Sundown or Slow Down (Slo-Down), as in Wilf Carter's song "Pete Knight's Last Ride" (no. 33). But it *was* Duster.

This fragment of a Pete Knight song I learned from an old cowboy buddy I ran with as a kid. Red Wilson was a buckaroo on the UC ranch near Elko, Nevada, when he was about sixteen. Later, in California, he was a wild bareback rider for a while, but brittle bones slowed him up by 1947. Red learned this song fragment in Elko County, Nevada, and passed what he knew on to me. I haven't seen Red Wilson for twenty years now. Red was also a Jimmie Rodgers fan, having spent several months in a line camp on a Nevada ranch that had a Victrola and a stack of Jimmie Rodgers records. I never gave a thought to documenting songs in those days (I'd still rather just find the song), but I remember Red learned what he knew of this Pete Knight song from a UC ranch rough-string rider named Slim.

PETE KNIGHT

Pete Knight was a rid - er_ of hors- es, The
best that I ev- er ___ did _ see. But
of - ten a life _ in _ the sad - dle _____ Is
not what it's cracked up _ to be.
Ten thou - sand fans _ saw him car - ried A -
way from the field _____ and _ the horse.

82

Pete Knight was a rider of horses,
The best that I ever did see.
But often a life in the saddle
Is not what it's cracked up to be.

Ten thousand fans saw him carried
Away from the field and the horse.

. . . .

32

Pete Knight, the King of the Cowboys

Canada's Wilf Carter wrote the words and music to this piece. Since he had been a rider and knew plenty of other riders, I think his rodeo songs, like this one about a fellow Canadian, have a place in a collection of real cowboy songs. Carter knew what it was all about. He is now a member of the Rodeo Historical Society, which is based at the Cowboy Hall of Fame.

PETE KNIGHT, THE KING OF THE COWBOYS

List a while to my story
'Bout a lad from the wide open plain
Who has won a great name the world over,
Pete Knight of rodeo fame.

He was raised at Crossfield, Alberta,
Just a little cow town in the West.
Unless he was out 'mongst the broncos
It seemed he was never at rest.

He took a real love for the saddle,
Like most of us boys in the West.
He'd watch the cowboys a-ridin',
On Sundays, it seems, was the best.

That day he made it a practice,
Each day a bronco to tame.
And now he's a king of the cowboys
That ever set foot on the range.

He'll come out of the chute just a-kicking,
Both feet high up in the mane,
While bronc does his best to unseat him,
But the horse never lived he can't tame.

He's ridden in all the stampedes,
North, south, east, and west,
At the World's Fair held in Chicago
Won the world's bronc-riding contest.

But Pete, like all other cowboys,
A girl came into his life.
He took her hand at the altar
And made her his loving wife.

33

Pete Knight's Last Ride

Another song by Wilf Carter, this one is about Pete Knight's death. I found the words to this song and "Pete Knight, the King of the Cowboys," in the large collection of cowboy and hillbilly song folios at the John Edwards Memorial Foundation at UCLA.

PETE KNIGHT'S LAST RIDE

It seems my whole life's full of heartaches and sighs,
Always something to make me feel blue.
For I've just lost a pal, like a brother to me,
Seems I can't believe that it's true.
We were old pals on the prairie so gay,
Many times we have rode side by side,
Never dreaming a bronco would throw him
And Pete Knight would take his last ride.

He was riding a bronco called Slo-Down,
Many times he had spurred his old hide.
But when he left the chute, Fate played its hand.
That's when Pete took his last ride.
He'll still remain king of the cowboys,
Many times he has won worldwide fame.
And millions of people who knew him,
They all idolize Pete Knight's name.

It was only last fall that we parted, so gay,
His handshake I'll always recall,
When he said, "So long, pal, good luck to you,
I'll see you the next coming fall."
But now I stand, head bowed in silence,
While a teardrop it falls unashamed.
We'll miss him a lot since he left us,
But old memories will always remain.

    Oh, some day there'll be a great roundup on high.
    When the ranch boss starts combing the plains
    May our names all be squared on the tally,
    May we meet on that heavenly range.

34

Paddy Ryan

One of the very first famous bronc riders I can remember hearing anything about was the colorful Paddy Ryan (also called Pat Ryan). Paddy was born in 1896 in Minnesota, but the Ryans moved to a dry-land farm near Ismay, Montana, in 1910. Though homesteaders were thick in eastern Montana, there were still plenty of cow and horse outfits, and Pat was soon riding for the ranches south of Miles City, along the Powder River. Cowboys in that country had to take them as they came and ride what was handed to them to keep a riding job. Naturally, a lot of good bronc riders developed in this area. Paddy Ryan was entering and winning some of the rodeos by 1916, but it was after World War I and all through the twenties that he was a big money winner and famous all over the United States and Canada. It is said that New York Irishmen cheered and chanted his name when he rode at early Madison Square Garden rodeos. Ryan is also credited with the introduction of the short-shanked bronc-riding spur with a dull five-point rowel. Nearly all saddlery catalogs to the present time carry the Paddy Ryan bronc spur made by Crockett.

Chip Morris, one of my early rodeo friends from my first year on the road (1943), traveled with Pat Ryan and Bob Askins in 1926 and '27. That was Chip's first fling at rodeoing, and he says he was bucked off everything they put him on the first year. Chip was formerly from Baker, Montana, not far from Ismay, Ryan's and Askin's home; he now operates the End of the Trail Ranch, a riding stable at Little Rock, Arkansas. He says wherever you went in Wyoming and Montana and durn near anywhere else, everyone knew Paddy and he was right at home. At a rodeo in Tallahassee, Florida, in the fall of '49, trick roper Buddy Mefford showed some home movies of rodeo and other older rodeo movies to the rest of us. I remember all the older guys talking animatedly when a shot of Paddy Ryan or Bob Askins came on. In rodeo, those names call a whole era to mind. Askins, at this writing, is still in Montana, and Ryan is handling Quarterhorse colts in Arizona.

In June, 1968, while my wife, Kay, and I were collecting cowboy songs around Buffalo and Camp Crook, South Dakota, we got this fragment of a Pat Ryan song. Since I practically grew up on Ryan stories, I naturally perked up when rancher Dick Smith of Buffalo sang it for us. Smith said he learned what little he knew of the song from Johnny Wright. Dick Smith and Johnny Wright had ridden together on the range around Buffalo, South Dakota. Wright has since moved to Idaho.

Later that summer, while I was announcing chuck-wagon races, Jack

Lauder, a cowboy and chuck-wagon driver from Calgary and Innisfail, Alberta, said he had heard the song "Pat Ryan" in Canada. Jack has at one time competed in all events at the Calgary Stampede. His first time at Calgary as a contestant was in 1928. That was a big year at Calgary for Paddy Ryan, and Jack said, "Why, I can see Paddy Ryan as if he were standing right here!" I wish I had the rest of the song! Ryan, by the way, was not from Calgary Falls, as the last line of this song fragment suggests.

PADDY RYAN

Way up in old Calgary over the line
There came an old cowboy, his name was Pat Ryan.
He looked at the cowboys a-workin' the chutes,
"Boys, watch these spurs on the heels of my boots."

Old Thief River Duncan looks up and he squalls,
"Watch this bowlegged cowboy from Calgary Falls."

· · · ·

87

35

Fritz Truan, a Great Cowboy

When you consider the list of all the very toughest bucking horses that Fritz Truan rode during his career, he had to be what cowboys call "a real tough bronc rider," meaning he could ride the rankest horses. They say as far as style went, he was really smooth, too, and made it look easy. Fritz Truan was world champion saddle bronc rider for the years 1939 and 1940 and also the all-around champ in 1940. This fine poem by Larry Finley, which appeared in the old rodeo magazine *Hoofs and Horns,* mentions Five Minutes (Five Minutes to Midnight, owned by Verne Elliot of Colorado), Angel (Hell's Angel, of the Coburn string), and Brew (Home Brew, also of the Coburn string). Fritz rode all these truly great horses several times when they were dumping the vast majority of top bronc riders. Many consider Hell's Angel the toughest bucking horse of all time. Fritz also conquered Starlight, a horse of Harry Rowell's that bucked them off coming and going in the late thirties and early forties.

Fritz Truan was from Long Beach, California, and got his early experience with horses working around the Los Angeles area. There were weekly jackpot rodeos in the area and also a good many regular rodeos at times. Plenty of top riders resided in the area, and a young fellow had the opportunity to see how it should be done. Fritz rode saddle and bareback broncs and bulls; he also bulldogged. Early in his career the fine bronc rider Johnny Slater took Fritz in hand and showed him all he knew about saddle bronc riding. Fritz was a natural pupil; he was in fine physical condition and lived and breathed rodeo. He could be considered a prime example of the modern rodeo athlete. Like Pete Knight before him, he inspired a lot of boys to take to rodeoing and try to emulate his style. Fritz had great influence on the late Bud Linderman, 1945 bareback champion and hell on wheels any way you took him; Wag Blessing, 1947 champion bull rider, as colorful a cowboy as ever came down the road; and Larry Finley, 1948 bareback champ, who wrote "Fritz Truan, a Great Cowboy."

Early in World War II, Fritz Truan joined the Marines. He saw a lot of combat in the Pacific and took part in a servicemen's rodeo in Honolulu. In July or August of 1944 he was home on furlough, recuperating from wounds, and showed up at the Los Angeles Coliseum rodeo. It was back to the Pacific, however, and he lost his life during the Marines' assault on Iwo Jima, February, 1945. The whole rodeo world mourned his passing.

This poem by Larry Finley tells it about as well as anything could. I think it shows the cowboy's values better than nearly anything else I have found:

FRITZ TRUAN

to be a good fellow and a good sport, to do your very best at anything you
try. In a world that judges a man on what he is and what he can do, Fritz
was tops to everyone. However, the world keeps rolling along despite loss.
In 1949, at Jerry Ambler's bar in the Riverbottom of Burbank, California,
I noticed a long face on a friend, Bill Callahan. Bill was an ex–bronc rider
and a contemporary of Truan. He said he had just been to the funeral and
re-burial of Fritz Truan. They had brought him back from the Pacific. Bill

89

Callahan said there were two cowboys present, himself and Bob Burrows, another bronc rider. Fritz Truan is not forgotten, though. His saddle and trophies and other memorabilia are on display in the Cowboy Hall of Fame and Western Heritage Center in Oklahoma City.

Every now and then mention of Truan crops up in *Rodeo Sports News,* the Rodeo Cowboys Association paper from Denver, and in the new *Hoofs and Horns,* published by Gene Lamb, also in Denver. Under the editorship of the late Ma Hopkins (d. November 3, 1969) of Tucson, Arizona, *Hoofs and Horns* was the first rodeo magazine that was read by cowboys everywhere. With her piloting from 1933 to 1954, *Hoofs and Horns* became a clearinghouse of rodeo news, dates, and results. It had regional correspondents and published letters sent in by the readers, including hundreds of letters from cowboys in the service during World War II. The cowboys' artistic and poetic efforts, like this poem about Fritz Truan, also appeared.

FRITZ TRUAN, A GREAT COWBOY

Over the divide a great cowboy did go,
To ride broncs in Heaven at the big rodeo.
I've watched him ride since I was fifteen,
Up till the day he became a Marine.

The greatest bronc rider that I ever knew,
He rode Angel eight times, Five Minutes, and Brew.
He was a good friend and always played square.
I hope he draws Angel at the big show up there.

He'll ride him and spur him and I know he will win
And show the folks up there his big handsome grin.
He was one in a million, I'll tell you for true,
A fighting Marine and a wild buckaroo.

A champ to the last, you can be mighty sure
He didn't throw in when the drawing was poor.
He was a good sport but was fighting to win,
I'll bet Fritz got a hundred before they got him.

36

Heelin' Bill

"Heelin' Bill" is another example of cowboy poetry inspired by the passing of a well-liked cowboy. Bill Nix died in December, 1950, at San Angelo, Texas. This piece first appeared in the *San Angelo Standard Times*. Ma Hopkins ran it in the February, 1951, issue of *Hoofs and Horns*. All the cowboys named in the poem were famous riders and ropers who preceded Bill Nix in death. Nix must have been a good *heeler* (in team roping, the man who ropes the hind feet of a steer after the *header* catches the horns). I was familiar with his name but I can't remember if I ever saw him (most of my friends were bronc and bull riders).

This poem by an unknown author names other famous cowboys who passed on before Bill Nix. In the second verse we find Wild Horse Bob, who was Bob Crosby of Roswell, New Mexico, and Tom and Pete Knight, who were both bronc riders but no kin to each other. The Pete Knight story has already been treated (nos. 31-33). Tom Knight was a Wyoming bronc rider who was killed in a car wreck along with Mickey McCrory, who is probably the McCrory of the third verse. Clyde Burk and Clay McGonigal were famous ropers. Fritz and Doff, in the fourth verse, would be Fritz Truan and Doff Aber, both champion bronc riders.

HEELIN' BILL

Contestants galore and fans by the score
Set roostin' the gates of St. Pete,
Awaitin' the show which was scheduled to go
When the entries was all complete.

Right there for the job was Wild Horse Bob
And the Knight boys, Tom and Pete.
And there for the work was little Clyde Burk,
A-pacin' the golden street,

Clay McGonigal and Shorty Hill
And McCrory for doggin' steers,
And Jake McClure with loop so sure,
And little Jasbo for cheers,

And Fritz and Doff and just a few more
Out of rodeo's hall of fame.

Why then do they wait — this rodeo great —
The scrawl of a single name?

"Ah'll tell you why," said a blocky guy,
Pete Knight, the great bronc peeler,
"Ol' Wild Horse Bob and the ropin' mob
Are a-waitin' on their heeler."

The wait stretched on and into the dawn,
Then the yells burst high and shrill,
For amongst them all, on old Fireball,
There set ol' Heelin' Bill.

37

Kenny Madland

Kenny Madland was fatally injured in the bull riding at Apple Valley, California, in April of 1950, when Andy Jauregui's bull Gentleman Jim turned over in the air and fell on him. Kenny's best effort was riding saddle broncs, while bareback horse and bull riding were his extra events. He first burst into prominence in rodeo in 1948. His address was Portland, Oregon, but he was originally from North Dakota. I met him at the Fort Worth, Texas, stock show rodeo early in 1949. Buck Boyce introduced us and later said, "Boy, watch this kid ride broncs!" Kenny had a sensational lick on bucking horses; he always hooked high in a bronc's neck with his toes turned out straight. I never saw anyone with a better front-end lick on a horse. In early 1949 I made one trip from Kinsley's ranch at Amado, Arizona, to Phoenix in the company of Kenny Madland, Don Boag, and Bill Pierce. I was traveling mainly with Bill Pierce at the time. Kenny often lent Bill a hand saddling a bronc and helping him out of the chute. That spring in Arizona and California Kenny really did well in the riding. I never saw him after that, as I went rodeoing in South Dakota, Nebraska, Kansas, and Minnesota that summer and in Louisiana and Florida that fall. I was back in South Dakota when I heard of Kenny's accident.

This poem by Lois Green appeared in the June, 1950, issue of the *Buckboard,* which for several years before the appearance of *Rodeo Sports News* was the official publication of the Rodeo Cowboys Association.

KENNY MADLAND

The great Master has called
From Heaven above
To take Kenny Madland,
A cowboy we all loved.

His fun-loving ways,
His quick little smile
Will not be forgotten
For a long, long while.

But up there in Heaven,
When the big shows begin,
There's many a bronc riding
Young Kenny will win.

May his new life ahead
Never know sorrow or pain.
The loss we have suffered
Is Heaven's own gain.

38

Powder River Jack

After the old-time cowboy singer Powder River Jack Lee was killed in a car wreck in 1946, this poem by "Colorado Bill" appeared in Ma Hopkins's magazine *Hoofs and Horns*. Jack Lee was traveling by himself between Tucson and Phoenix when he swerved to avoid a horse that stepped into the road. The car went out of control and left the road. His wife, Kitty Lee, was in Phoenix, and it was really sad, as she was nearly blind at the time. It wasn't many years till Kitty Lee joined Jack in death. I've heard a lot of cowboys sing a lot of songs, but this collection would have a big hole in it if I hadn't heard Powder River Jack Lee.

POWDER RIVER JACK LEE

POWDER RIVER JACK

Powder River Jack and Kitty Lee,
Who rode the trails so wild and free,
On Powder River away they'd ride,
Broncs a-gallopin' side by side.

Jack Lee is gone, we miss him —
Just a cowboy troubadour,
With his songs and witty stories
And his wealth of western lore.

Wouldn't think he had no trouble,
That he always played in luck,
When he and Kitty shouted,
"Powder River, let 'er buck!"

Jack Lee was not a boozer
And he never cared for cards,
But he never was a killjoy
When he mingled with his pards.

Jack loved his pretty Kitty
And the broncs he used to ride.
Couldn't ever hurt a cayuse,
And he proved it when he died.

Seemed the old Sky Boss was needin'
One more top hand over there,
So he sent for Powder River,
With the silver in his hair.

May be singin' to the cowboys
Far across the great divide
With his old guitar a-throbbin'
And a memory by his side.

For he can't forget his Kitty,
And the two will never part.
Though a short time separates them,
They are always one in heart.

Now, some day he will be sendin'
Down a mystic telegram,
And you'll hear sweet Kitty answer,
"Powder River, here I am."

39

Riding Boy from Powder River

Late in the summer of 1943 I'd been working out of Kingman, Arizona, at Mullin's and Dozier's Rabbit Ears and got to pining for some greenery. So I headed north for Montana. I went first to the Antlers, a ranch at Wyola, Montana, where Bill Greenough was foreman, then to Charlie Miller's big outfit at Parkman, Wyoming. Both these large outfits hired lots of ranch hands and cowboys and ran a chuck wagon spring and fall. In the bunkhouse at Miller's Birdhead ranch I heard one of the hands sing this verse. Have kept my ears open ever since for the rest of the song, if there is more to it, for it reminds me of some interesting associations. Jerry Armstrong, in his column "Rodeo Arena" in *Western Horseman* (a magazine universally read by cowboys), has mentioned every now and then someone riding broncs with "the old Powder River lick." The mention of Powder River, which heads up in Wyoming and runs northeast to the Yellowstone River in Montana, makes most anyone think of broncs and bronc riders. During World War I there was an army division of westerners whose battle cry was "Powder River, let 'er buck!" There have been a good many bucking horses in various strings named Powder River. The late Shorty Farber of Mountain View, Arkansas, had lived and worked on a sheep outfit on the banks of the Powder River near Kay Cee, Wyoming. When asked about the Powder River lick in bronc riding, he said in his neighborhood they called it the "Yellowstone lick" when a rider was really wolfing one. Nevertheless, Powder River is synonymous with all that makes up cowboy and range life. Shorty was not a herder but packed supplies into summer range in the mountains for other herders. As for Charlie Miller of the Birdhead ranch, where I heard this verse, he sold out around 1946 to the Gill brothers of Exeter, California, and bought a ranch in Old Mexico. This verse is mildly bawdy, and I bet there is a lot more to the song — if I can ever find it.

RIDING BOY FROM POWDER RIVER

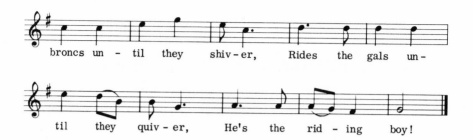

broncs un - til they shiv - er, Rides the gals un -

til they quiv - er, He's the rid - ing boy!

Riding boy from Powder River
Rides the broncs until they shiver,
Rides the gals until they quiver,
He's the riding boy!

40

Powder River, Let 'er Buck

The old World War I cry of the cowboys fighting in France became the title of one of Powder River Jack Lee's best songs. Since Jack Lee wrote and sang this song, it is natural they would be thought of together. This is a difficult piece to remember, as it doesn't have a story that unfolds but just mentions all the elements of a big roundup in Wyoming or Montana. I heard him sing this in Arizona but couldn't remember how it went. Years later, when I got to doing college concerts of cowboy songs, a discophile and folklorist, Harlan Daniel of Chicago, gave me a tape of Powder River Jack's old recording of this song. It was a real pleasure to hear it again after some twenty-one years, and a lot of it seemed familiar. Harlan also gave me a copy of Powder River Jack's book *West of Powder River,* which contains this poem. Elements of the poem and the "hollers" between verses have entered tradition by themselves. For instance, former rodeo announcer Chip Morris would say of a bucking horse, "This horse is from Powder River; Powder River is a mile wide, an inch deep, too dusty to swim, and too muddy to plow!" Maybe Jack Lee made the song partly of traditional sayings. Anyway, it's a good description of a big roundup in the northern cow country.

POWDER RIVER, LET 'ER BUCK

Pow-der Riv-er,— let 'er buck, a surg-in' mass of cat-tle,

Round-up wag-ons full of chuck, horns and hoofs a - rat- tle.

Steers an' do-gies, beefs an' broncs, heav-in' flanks a-quiv-er,—

Hear the wrang-lers yip, "Whoop-ee, hoo-ray fer Pow-der Riv - er."

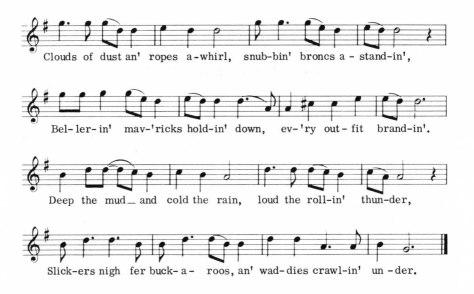

Clouds of dust an' ropes a-whirl, snub-bin' broncs a-stand-in',

Bel-ler-in' mav-'ricks hold-in' down, ev-'ry out-fit brand-in'.

Deep the mud— and cold the rain, loud the roll-in' thun-der,

Slick-ers nigh fer buck-a- roos, an' wad-dies crawl-in' un-der.

Powder River, let 'er buck, a surgin' mass of cattle,
Roundup wagons full of chuck, horns and hoofs a-rattle.
Steers an' dogies, beefs an' broncs, heavin' flanks a-quiver,
Hear the wranglers yip, "Whoopee, hooray fer Powder River."
Clouds of dust an' ropes awhirl, snubbin' broncs a-standin',
Bellerin' mavericks holdin' down, every outfit brandin'.
Deep the mud and cold the rain, loud the rollin' thunder,
Slickers nigh fer buckaroos, an' waddies crawlin' under.

Powder River, let 'er buck!

Loud the steers and heifers bawlin', dogies all a-roamin',
Strays set out fer stompin' grounds and headin' fer Wyomin'.
Bridles off fer feedin' grounds, horns and hoofs a-rattle,
One eye open, half asleep, a-herdin' ornery cattle.
Old Red Smith, the wagon cook, bacon, beans, and liver,
They're wild and they don't keer a cuss, the boys from Powder River.
"Cookie" yells from pots an' pans, "Come on, yuh ornery guzzards,
Come an' git 'er out she goes, I'll feed 'er tuh the buzzards."

Herders left an' herders right, broncs and cuttin' horses,
Sougans under starry skies, wagons fer the bosses.
Old chinook a-changin' west, angry bulls a-boomin',
Stark above the feedin' grounds the Rocky Mountains loomin'.
Floppin' hats an' shaggy chaps, dogies all a-shiver,
Top screws shoutin', "Spool yore beds, an' home fer Powder River."
Circlin' riders singin' low, a-zoomin' o'er the prairies,
Pens a-bulgin', hear them shout, "We're goin' tuh see our Marys."

Powder River, full of dust and flat fish, cross 'er anywhere!

Thunderin' hoofs across the range, sunburnt hides and faces,
Twisters spinnin' east and west, and cowboys runnin' races.
"Scratch your broncs, yuh ridin' fools," a big whoopee they give 'er,
"We're wild an' woolly, full of fleas, and bound fer Powder River."

Powder River, a mile wide and an inch deep and she rolls uphill
from Texas!

41

A Tale of the Trail

My uncle Helmer Eraker of Harwood, North Dakota, gave me a January, 1958, copy of *Bar North,* the official magazine of the North Dakota Stockmen's Association, that contained this poem. It was used as an ending to an article about the late John Goodall, a great old range foreman and later a rancher at Sanish, North Dakota, till his death in 1931. "A Tale of the Trail" is also quoted in a book put out by the Fifty Years in the Saddle Club at Watford City, North Dakota.

The copy of *Bar North* my uncle gave me also contained the North Dakota brand laws and mentioned that there were 15,196 brands registered in the state in 1957 (which adds up to a lot of ranching).

A TALE OF THE TRAIL

It ain't so far from right to wrong,
The trail ain't hard to lose.
There's times I'd almost give my horse
To know which one to choose.
There ain't no signs or guideboards up
To keep you on the track.
Wrong's sometimes white as driven snow
And right looks awful black.
I don't set up to be no judge
Of right and wrong in men.
I've lost the trail sometimes myself —
I may get lost again.
So when I see a man who looks
As though he'd lost the way,
I want to shove my hand in his
And help him find the way.

42

Sam's "Waiting for a Train"

While it is not a cowboy song, I have known plenty of cowboys who sang the late Jimmie Rodgers's famous "Waiting for a Train." When Jimmie Rodgers died in 1933, and for a long time after, railroad and hobo songs were popular with folks everywhere in the United States. Among my own buddies who sang "Waiting for a Train" were Red Sink of Malta, Montana, whom I served with in Japan in 1946, Red Wilson and Denny Krache of California and Nevada, Singing Jack Smith of "everywhere," Jack McCullar of California, Arizona, and Old Mexico, and Bill Callahan of California. At the weekly musical held in Mountain View, Arkansas, since 1963, more individuals have had this song in their repertoire than any other.

My friend and neighbor Sam Hess of Mountain View sang this older version of "Waiting for a Train" for me about 1962. Sam ran cattle in the

Sam Hess at his old pump organ. Photo by Page Stephens.

same area south of my place from his boyhood till 1968. When he sold out all but one pet cow in July, 1968, he was eighty-seven years old. I have collected a good many songs from Sam Hess over the years and have listened to him play the banjo and the old pump organ. Many a city folksong enthusiast visiting our area whom I have taken to hear Sam came away feeling he had really been to the "source." In fact, one young fellow who helped arrange college folk festivals and concerts told me he realized how shallow his exposure to folk music had been when he heard Sam Hess. Sam's voice is about gone now and his hands are twisted by arthritis and hard work, but he still makes a stab at his old music occasionally.

SAM'S "WAITING FOR A TRAIN"

cold and hun - gry I lay down, __ my heart was filled with

pain. I'm think - ing of _____ those good old days, I __

wish they'd come a - gain, __ A thou - sand miles a -

way from home, trying to catch an old __ freight train.

I was born and raised in Texas, a state that you all know.
I got on that Katy train, so cold I could hardly go.
I rode down to Memphis, and I got off to warm,
Looked out for that Katy train, but the Katy train was gone.

    They left me standing on a platform, a-waiting for a train,
    So cold and hungry I lay down, my heart was filled with pain.
    I'm thinking of those good old days, I wish they'd come again,
    A thousand miles away from home, trying to catch an old freight train.

I went up to a lady and I asked for something to eat,
A little piece of bread and a little piece of meat.
A little piece of punkin pie would soothe my appetite.
I aim to ride that old freight train a thousand miles tonight.

Well, I went up to Kansas, I didn't go to stay.
I fell in love with some Kansas girls and I had to run away.
Good-bye to all you Kansas folks, I'll bid you all adieu,
And when that old freight train runs out I'll see no more of you.

    Chorus:

43

Paddy on the Turnpike

When I contested at a lot of Paul Long's rodeos in Kansas and Nebraska in 1947, '49, and '50, Paul's regular rodeo clown was Jerry Hedricks, Sr., of Nickerson, Kansas. Often at night after a rodeo performance a few of us would gather around a bottle of peppermint schnapps in Jerry's house trailer or by a campfire on the rodeo grounds. We would sing some old cowboy songs, also "In the Pines" and a few Jimmie Rodgers items like "Waiting for a Train." Jerry often sang a song he credited to Jimmie Rodgers that had nearly the same verses as Sam Hess's "Paddy on the Turnpike." The tune was different, though, and there was no chorus that mentioned Paddy. A few rollicky recitations cropped up once in a while, too, like "Let Old Nellie Stay" (no. 44) and one about a drunken mouse who challenged cats to fight. At several shows in Nebraska an Irish couple showed up who were friends of Jerry Hedricks. This lady was always impatient with

Glenn Ohrlin on a Walt Plugge bronc at Bartlett, Nebraska, 1950. Photo by Swopes Studio, Ord, Nebraska.

the songs of others till she could sing the Irish "Galway Bay." The summer of 1950 I was up to here in Irish songs while rodeoing with announcer and bull rider Joe Cavanaugh of Chambers, Nebraska. Among other things, Joe is famous for having ridden a horse dyed green through the streets of O'Neill, Nebraska, on St. Patrick's Day. If he had known the "Paddy" part of this song, I'm sure he would have sung it.

Verses three and four of "Paddy on the Turnpike" I learned from Jerry Hedricks; the rest of the song and the chorus are from Sam Hess, of Mountain View, Arkansas. There is a fiddle tune by the same title that has nothing in common with this song.

(*Rodeo Sports News,* May 1, 1973, reports that Jerry Hedricks passed away April 15, 1973, at the age of sixty-one.)

PADDY ON THE TURNPIKE

I've been around this world a bit, I've been from coast to coast,
Had every kind of food you can mention, from an egg to quail on toast.

I'm just Paddy on the turnpike, I'll just be on my way.
I'll just paddle on down the turnpike to pass the time away.

There ain't many places that I ain't left my mark.
Sometimes I sleep in a fine hotel, sometimes on a bench in the park.

Chorus:

Now Portland, Maine, is just the same as sunny Tennessee.
Any old place I hang my hat is home sweet home to me.

Chorus:

I never had a loving wife to share my misery,
So when I die I'm very sure there'll be no tears for me.

Chorus:

I'm getting old and feeble now, can scarcely find my way.
I'll just paddle on down the turnpike to pass the time away.

Chorus:

44

Let Old Nellie Stay

This is a recitation Joe Cavanaugh often gave while we were rodeoing and whooping it up in 1950. Joe managed to get a bull rider into the story. One night Joe and I sang and told jokes and recited a number of things like this while seated in a Nebraska tavern. (I got a lot of mileage out of "The Face on the Floor" in those days.) The next morning a lady who had been present said it was the most fun she had ever had — an impressive statement, as the lady had been married thirteen times!

LET OLD NELLIE STAY

It was late in the evening,
The guests were all leaving,
O'Malley was closing the bar.
He turned and he said
To the old lady in red,
"Get up! You can't stay where you are."

She shed a big tear
In her bucket of beer,
Tears flowed from her eyes so red.
When a bull rider dapper
Stepped out of the crapper,
And these are the words that he said:

"Her mother never told her
The things a young girl should know,
About these traveling bull riders
And the way they come and go.
So do not treat her harshly
Because she went too far,
But be a little kindhearted
And let old Nellie sleep under the bar."

45

Put Your Little Foot

"Put Your Little Foot," or "Varsouviana," has been one of my favorite pieces of music since I first heard it in Pinal County, Arizona, in December of 1943. It was at a cow-country dance in a one-room schoolhouse somewhere on the east side of the Superstition Mountains, north of Florence Junction. I was working on a ranch belonging to the Clemens outfit of Florence, Arizona. I went to the dance with the ranch manager, his wife, and his son and daughter-in-law. Also along was a Texas boy who arrived there with me in early December of 1943. We had been inquiring about riding jobs at Porter's Saddlery in Phoenix, and a manager of one of the Clemens ranches hauled us out to this particular ranch. This was in rough, cactus-covered country where the cows were wild and the cholla was thick. They used a string of pack mules to haul their grub and beds on the roundup, too rough for wagons. I think the local cowboys who could ride like hell over the mountains, rocks, and cholla, and pop a loop on a wild cow were the best cowboys I ever saw.

At this dance I started telling about, all the crowd was made up of ranchers and cowboys and their families. When they danced "Put Your Little Foot," and one of the musicians sang the verses, I thought it was really nice. This is the only tune I remember from the occasion. Later that night some miners, probably from Globe, showed up, and after the dance there was a great fight. I remember standing near the porch after the dance and seeing my boss's son knock one of the miners plumb off the porch. All the non-fighters enjoyed it a lot and no serious damage was done. Later that month they sent me and this Texan to another of their ranches, at Chandler, Arizona. We got to dances at Carl Dossey's tavern in Chandler, and there, as well as at all the other ranch dances in Arizona, they always played "Put Your Little Foot" at least once. I always took note and listened and I still love to hear it or play it.

Kinsley's ranch at Amado, Arizona, had monthly rodeos and some fine dances after the rodeo. Once at Kinsley's in 1949 I was traveling with X Brands and Johnny Quijada. Johnny took great delight in dancing the varsouviana. He was a Mexican cowboy from California who contested in the bull riding. Johnny was full of surprises. He could sing Mexican songs till you thought you were around a campfire in Sonora or Chihuahua. Then he'd turn around and sing hillbilly songs and sound a whole lot like Roy Acuff. X Brands was a good bareback rider and cowboy but became an actor in movies and later television.

Every time I hear this tune I think of 1943, my first year on the road. I'd cowboyed in Nevada, Arizona, Wyoming, and back to Arizona, and also made a little start at rodeoing. It was a great time!

PUT YOUR LITTLE FOOT

Put your little foot, put your little foot,
Your little foot right there.
Put your little foot, put your little foot,
Your little foot right there.
Take a step to the right, take a step to the left,
Take a step to the rear, but forever stay near.

Put your arm around, put your arm around,
Your arm around my waist.
Hold your arm around, hold your arm around,
Your arm around my waist.

111

While the moon's shining bright, and the music's just right,
And you're holding me tight, we will dance through the night.

Put your little foot, put your little foot,
Your little foot with mine.
With your little foot, with your little foot,
Your little foot keep time.
Charming tender melody, in my heart and memory
It is there you'll always be, varsouviana's part of me.

46

Jake and Roanie

I became acquainted with "Jake and Roanie" a few years ago when it appeared as a poem in *Western Horseman*. Then Page Stephens of the University of Illinois spent the summer of '67 at my place in Stone County, Arkansas, to do an anthropological study of Stone County. Page is an old-time music enthusiast and he has a lot of dope on cowboy songs. He gave me a tape of Romaine Lowdermilk, an Arizona singer, and Lowdermilk's version of "Jake and Roanie" has been a favorite with me since. When Page got tired of digging up information, he would help me work cattle. We had some interesting roping incidents, but nothing like Jake and Roanie's! Ours generally involved a big rank cow I'd rope to doctor. While I'd sit on my horse and hold my dallies on the saddle horn, Page would bring the medicine and squirt it on where it was needed. The cow always got mad at Page, and he nearly got flattened a time or two. But it was fun, and Page said it was a big change from social anthropology.

In the second verse Jake builds him a *blocker*. That is, he prepares to make a throw of the rope called a "Johnny Blocker" after the old-time trail driver of the same name. The blocker is thrown diagonally from left to right over the animal's back, curls up in front of the target, and catches both front feet. Real tricky!

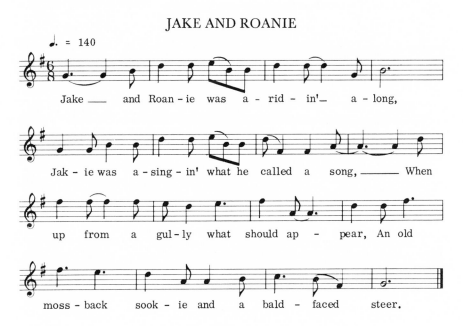

JAKE AND ROANIE

113

Jake and Roanie was a-ridin' along,
Jakie was a-singin' what he called a song,
When up from a gully what should appear,
An old mossback sookie and a baldfaced steer.

Jake took after with his hat pulled down,
He built him a blocker that would stop a town.
The steer he headed for the settin' sun,
And believe me, neighbor, he could hump it and run.

Roanie followed up his partner's deal,
Just two old waddies that could head and heel,
Both of them a-workin' for the Chicken Coop
With a red-hot iron and a hungry loop.

The sun was a-shinin' in old Jake's eyes,
He wasn't lookin' for no big surprise,
When the steer give a wiggle like his shirt was tight,
And he busted through the junipers and dropped out of sight.

Jakie's horse done a figger eight,
Jake done his addin' just a mite too late.
He went out of the saddle a-seeing red,
And he landed in the gravels of a dry river bed.

Roanie's horse was a good horse, too,
He couldn't quite figger out why Jake flew.
So he dumped old Roanie where the ground was hard,
And they both lit out a-runnin' for the home cavyyard.

Jake set a-holdin' of a swellin' thumb.
Says he, "Well, I reckon we was going some."
But Roanie hollered, "Get away from here,
We're both going to tangle with that baldfaced steer."

Roanie clumb astraddle of a juniper tree,
"There's no more room up here," said he.
Jakie, thinkin' himself to save,
He crawls in the opening of a cutbank cave.

The steer he charged with his head way down,
Rollin' of his eyes and a-pawin' the ground,
Hookin' and a-snuffin' and a-turning about,
And every few seconds old Jake'd pop out.

Roanie said, "You old fool, stay back out of sight!
You act like you hanker for to make him fight."
But Jake he hollered so the world could hear,
"Stay back nothin', there's a bear in here."

47

Lee's Ferry

I also learned "Lee's Ferry" from Page Stephens's tape of Romaine Lowdermilk. At one time the only place a person could cross the Colorado River in northern Arizona was at Lee's Ferry. Since the ferry is at the eastern end of the Arizona Strip (the corner of Arizona north of the Colorado), the rest of the Strip was really isolated as far as the state of Arizona was concerned. Since I am somewhat acquainted with the Strip and I enjoyed the song "Lee's Ferry," I wrote Romaine Lowdermilk for information about it. The following is part of his reply (April 14, 1969):

> I'm glad to hear from an ex-Arizona cowhand. You pretty well covered most of the cow-country while you were here. Now if you'd just served a term on the Mogollons and down into Gila County you'd have covered the country....
>
> As for "Lee's Ferry," you've got to think of the vast Houserock Valley, with the Vermilion Cliffs lying all along the north side. Remember the wind that sweeps through there. Try to picture old Buffalo Jones with his board cabin, immense pole corral at the foot of the great Kaibab plateau on the west. That big ever-wind-blown country of the Arizona Strip. Pahria Crick. Wolf Hole, Fredona, Kanab, St. George. Years ago the first big cattle spreads were all Mormon owned and they hired lots of cowboys, as the only market was at Salt Lake City. Wild horses, deer and wolves — coyotes, too, were abundant. And wind!
>
> I wrote "Lee's Ferry" and put a tune to it trying to bring up the picture of cowhands from the East — New Mexico, Texas, Kansas, and, yes, from Fort Smith, Arkansas, and the Indian Territory — working on the Strip and getting older every year. But what I wanted was really a tune that could make you think of wind and dust and lonely land. I've been in Arizona since 1908 and have crossed on the ferry, and driven and rode up the "dugway" and can only imagine the hardships of the pioneers who came into Arizona from Utah that way with their wagons, cattle, horses and families to settle in Arizona and pioneer from St. Johns and Springerville to Mesa and the whole Salt River Valley.

Romaine Lowdermilk went on to say that he had written "Lee's Ferry" about 1931 and that it barely hints at the story. It was fortunate I inquired about this song when I did, for Lowdermilk passed away the next year.

The ferry was named after Mormon pioneer John D. Lee, who was executed in 1877 by the government for his part in the 1857 Mountain Meadows massacre. Lee's Ferry was also a link of the old Outlaw Trail from the Little Rockies in Montana to Hole in the Wall in Wyoming, to Brown's Hole in Colorado. Next on the trail was Robber's Roost in Utah, then Lee's Ferry;

from there the route crossed Arizona to southwestern New Mexico and finally into Mexico.

LEE'S FERRY

Come all you roving cowboys, bound on these western plains, Come all you roving cowboys, we'll go back home again. We'll see old friends and neighbors and those we love so dear, We'll cross over Lee's Ferry, oh, and go back home this year.

Come all you roving cowboys, bound on these western plains,
Come all you roving cowboys, we'll go back home again.
We'll see old friends and neighbors and those we love so dear,
We'll cross over Lee's Ferry, oh, and go back home this year.

"We will, we will," they all did say, "when the fall roundup is o'er.
We'll visit scenes of olden days and see old friends once more.
We'll see old friends and neighbors and those we love so dear,
We'll cross over Lee's Ferry, oh, and go back home this year."

It's easy for to make a vow, it's easy to forget.
Those boys are old and graying now, and they're cowpunching yet,
Never saw their friends and neighbors or those they loved so dear.
We never crossed Lee's Ferry, oh, to go back home that year.

116

48

Short Creek Raid

The Arizona Strip is fascinating to me as well as to Romaine Lowdermilk. About a year before I moved to Arkansas there was an event at Short Creek, Arizona, that inspired me to start writing a song a few years later, to the tune of "When the Work's All Done This Fall." However, I did not finish the song till 1967. There were some details that were needed to fill out the last two verses. In Stone County, Arkansas, I have two friends who know the area involved in the song. One is Woodrow Rose of Fox, Arkansas, who worked on ranches in the Strip and southwestern Utah. At one time he worked for the descendants of John D. Lee, for whom Lee's Ferry is named. The other, New Mexico cowboy Jim McElroy, now ranching at Fox, Arkansas, has been all over that country. As Jim said of the folks in the Strip, "You know those people up there, being kinda cut off from the rest of Arizona, were left to shuffle for themselves, and they really got to shuffling!"

SHORT CREEK RAID

In the good old town of Short Creek, in the year of '53,
A group of peaceful families as happy as could be
By the practice of polygamy they served their Master's call,
Way out in Arizona they bothered no one at all.

117

The Colorado River made their refuge and retreat
And cut them off from Kingman, which was their county seat.
They lived in isolation their patriarchal lives,
Each elder with his cattle, his horses, and his wives.

They tended their own business just like the saints of old,
Not dreaming that the whole world their secret would be told.
One day there came a stranger who thought that they were fools,
She was the superintendent of Mojave County schools.

When she returned to Kingman, this message she brought back:
"All eighth grade girls are married to a man named Uncle Jack.
I found this out while up there inspecting of the schools.
The people up in Short Creek are breaking all our rules.

"Each man has many families, I'm sorry to relate.
Some have six or seven, and some of them have eight.
I must tell you," she babbled, "of all the things I saw.
We cannot let this happen, we must call in the law."

Oh, how the news did travel, oh, how the news did fly.
They notified the sheriff, state police, and FBI.
They notified reporters when all their plans were laid,
Said, "Boys, we're going to Short Creek and make a mighty raid."

But they couldn't get to Short Creek across Grand Canyon's gorge.
They went around through Utah, they traveled through St. George.
They headed south from Hurricane till Short Creek they did spy,
Nestled where Vermilion Cliffs are reaching to the sky.

The posse soon was gathered just a little ways from town.
Someone gave the signal, they all came swooping down.
They drove right into Short Creek, according to the plan,
Rounded up the wives and children and arrested every man.

Without a moment's warning they landed up in jail.
They had to contact lawyers, they had to raise their bail.
The papers grabbed the story about the Short Creek band,
And details of their troubles were broadcast o'er the land.

Next came legal battles and dickerings, we know.
The upshot of the story, they had to let them go.
Some left the state forever and started out to roam,
While others said that Short Creek would always be their home.

The years have passed and Short Creek no longer bears that name.
The new one I won't tell you, if it is just the same.
And now my story's ended, I've nothing left to say,
So many thanks for listening, and now I'm on my way.

SHORT CREEK - ARIZ. STRIP

49

High Chin Bob

It's nice to have friends with filing cabinets in their heads. A few years ago I asked Harlan Daniel of Chicago (formerly of Fox, Arkansas) if he knew from what piece a verse I remembered sung in Arizona twenty years ago came. As I recalled (incorrectly apparently), the verse had the words "When on the picture who should ride with sure and hungry loop, / But me and my old pony, Blue, a-tripping down the slope." Harlan said it sounded like Badger Clark's "Glory Trail," or "High Chin Bob." It turned out it was the Badger Clark poem. Harlan sent me the words and I stuck a tune to it. You may wonder after reading "High Chin Bob" if anyone would really rope a lion. Cowboys have been known to lay their twine on lions, wolves, coyotes, wild turkey, deer, elk, wild hogs, bear, and just about anything else that comes in range. In old California, roping grizzly bears was a common sport. It takes two ropers or more and horses that handle awfully good.

HIGH CHIN BOB

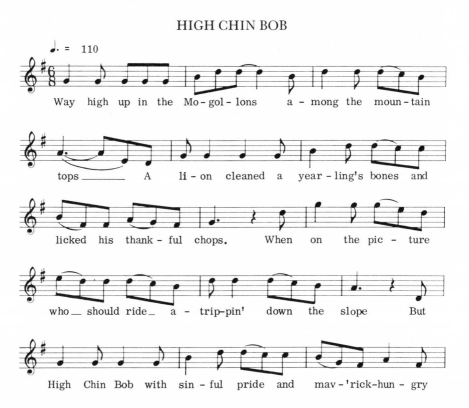

Way high up in the Mo-gol-lons a - mong the moun-tain
tops ____ A li-on cleaned a year-ling's bones and
licked his thank-ful chops. When on the pic - ture
who __ should ride __ a - trip-pin' down the slope But
High Chin Bob with sin - ful pride and mav - 'rick-hun - gry

120

rope. "Oh, glo - ry be — to me," said he, "and
fame's un - fad- ing flowers.—— All med- dlin' hands are
far a - way, I — ride my good top horse to- day, I'm
top rope of the La - zy J, Hi, — kit - ty cat, you're ours!"

Way high up in the Mogollons among the mountain tops
A lion cleaned a yearling's bones and licked his thankful chops.
When on the picture who should ride a-trippin' down the slope
But High Chin Bob with sinful pride and maverick-hungry rope.
"Oh, glory be to me," said he, "and fame's unfading flowers.
All meddlin' hands are far away, I ride my good top horse today,
I'm top rope of the Lazy J. Hi, kitty cat, you're ours!"

The lion licked his paws so brown and dreamed soft dreams of veal,
And then the circling loop swung down and roped him round his meal.
He yowled quick fury to the world and all the hills yelled back.
The top horse gave a snort and whirled, and Bob caught up the slack.
"Oh, glory be to me," said he, "we've struck the glory trail.
No human man, as I have read, dare rope a raging lion's head,
And never horse could drag one dead until we told the tale."

Way high up in the Mogollons that top horse done his best,
Through whippin' brush and rattlin' stones from canyon's floor to crest.
But ever when Bob turned and hoped a limp remains to find,
A red-eyed lion, belly-roped but healthy, loped behind.
"Oh, glory be to me," said he, "this glory trail is rough,
But even till the judgment morn, I'll keep this dally around the horn,
'Cause never any hero born could stoop to holler, 'Enough!' "

Three suns had rode their circle home beyond the desert's rim
And turned their star herds loose to roam the ranges high and dim.

But up and down and round and 'cross Bob pounded weak and wan,
For pride still glued him to his hoss and glory drove him on.
"Oh, glory be to me," said he, "he can't be drug to death.
And I know beyond a doubt those heroes I have read about
Was only fools that stuck it out to end of mortal breath."

Way high up in the Mogollons a prospect man did swear
That moonbeams melted down his bones and hoisted up his hair.
A ribby cow hoss thundered by, a lion trailed along,
A rider, gant but chin on high, yelled out a crazy song.
"Oh, glory be to me," said he, "and to my noble noose.
Go tell my partners down below I took a rampin' dream in tow,
And if I never lay him low, I'll never turn him loose."

50

Ranger's Prayer

This song-poem was passed along to me by Ruth Miller, formerly of the Happy Holler country in Stone County, Arkansas. The ranger in this home-made bit of sentiment is a forest ranger. Forest rangers are familiar figures to ranchers and cowboys near national forests in most western states. The Forest Service controls all livestock grazing in such forests, which are usually in high country and grazed only in the summer. Under this arrangement, these ranges are seldom, if ever, overgrazed. This is good for the land involved and also good for the cattle or sheep that are permitted.

RANGER'S PRAYER

Up in the mountains,
Mountains so high,
They laid a forest ranger
In a log cabin to die.

A cold north wind shook the cabin
As they laid him on the bed.
He opened his weak lips to speak,
These are the words he said:

"I have an old-fashioned sweetheart
Down there in Arkansas state.
She will never see me again,
For now it is too late.

"I love my old-fashioned sweetheart,
In spring we were to wed.
Give my love to Mary, boys,
And tell her I am dead.

"Put me in my coffin,
Lay me there to rest.
Get Mary's pictures and love letters
And put them on my breast."

A cold north wind blew through the window,
It whizzed by the ranger's bed.
One more look at the ranger,
And the ranger boy was dead.

They made a grave by the cabin,
And they laid him there to rest.
They put his sweetheart's pictures
And love letters on his breast.

A cold wind moaned so pitifully,
It moaned so pitifully and cold
When the men left the ranger
In his bed of new-fallen snow.

51

The Cowman's Prayer

"The Cowman's Prayer" was another old, scarcely remembered song that folklorist Harlan Daniel reminded me of when he gave me a tape of old recordings of cowboy songs. Carl "Doc" Sprague of Texas was singing this one on the tape. I made one change in Sprague's version. The next-to-the-last verse had the cowman praying that beef would bring "at least five cents a pound." If beef on the hoof was a nickel a pound nowdays, all us folks with cattle would have to quit, so I sing the same line "at least forty cents a pound." I'm not about to pray for nickel beef!

THE COWMAN'S PRAYER

O Lord, please lend to me thine ear,
The prayer of a cattleman to hear.
No doubt the prayers may seem so strange,
But I want you to bless our cattle range.

And bless the roundups year by year,
And don't forget the growing steer.
And water the land with brooks and rills
For the cattle that roam on a thousand hills.

The prairie fire won't you please stop,
The thunder's roll and the lightning shock.
It frightens me to see the smoke.
Unless it stops I'll go dead broke.

And view, O Lord, my happy home,
The mortgage takes a sack of gold.
I think at least forty cents a pound
Should be the price the whole year round.

Just one thing more and then I'm through,
Instead of one calf give my cows two.
I may pray different from other men,
But I've had my say, and now, amen.

Glenn Ohrlin on a colt at his home corral in Mountain View, Arkansas, December, 1965.

52

The Dying Ranger

At the University of Chicago Folk Festival in January of 1965 I was milling around Ida Noyes Hall one night before the concerts. There were groups of college kids here and there playing guitars and banjos. I noticed a group gathered around a man in his late thirties or early forties who was getting squared away to play the Irish bagpipes. These are the small bagpipes with a bellows the player pumps with his elbow so he can pipe and sing at the same time. I like bagpipes, so I oozed over there and listened. They were asking the man to play what to me were obscure Irish pieces, and he obliged. All at once the fellow — Kevin Henry — looks right at me and says, "And do you know 'The Doying Ranger'?" I says, "Sure, do you?" So he lit into it with the pipes and also sang it. Of all the music at the festival I remember that guy best.

THE DYING RANGER

The sun was sink-ing in the west and fell with lin-g'ring ray Through the branch-es of the for-est where a wound-ed rang-er lay. In the shade of a pal-met-to and the sun-set's sil-v'ry sky Far from his home in Tex-as they laid him down to die.

The sun was sinking in the west and fell with lingering ray
Through the branches of the forest where a wounded ranger lay.
In the shade of a palmetto and the sunset's silvery sky
Far from his home in Texas they laid him down to die.

His comrades gathered round him, companions in a fight.
A tear flowed down each manly cheek as he bade his last good-night.
One tried and trusted comrade was kneeling by his side
To stop the lifeblood flowing, but alas, in vain he tried.

"Draw closer to me, comrades, and listen while I say,
I'm going to tell the story while the spirit fades away.
Way out in northwest Texas, that good old Lone Star State,
There's one who for my coming with a weary heart shall wait.

"A fair young girl, my sister, my only joy and pride,
I brought her up from childhood, I never left her side.
Her father now lies sleeping beneath the churchyard sod,
And her mother too is resting in the bosom of her God.

"It's true I love my country, for it I've given all.
If it were not for my sister, I'd be content to fall.
I know I am a-dying, I'll never see her more.
In vain she'll wait my coming at the little cottage door.

"I am dying, comrades, dying, I must leave her all alone.
Who will be to her a brother who will take her to his home?"
Up stepped the noble rangers, they answered one and all,
"We will be to her a brother till the last one of us fall."

One glad sweet smile of pleasure o'er his pain-wracked face was spread,
One dark convulsive shadow and the ranger boy was dead.
Far from his home in Texas they laid him down to rest,
With his saddle for a pillow and his gun across his breast.

53

The Texas Rangers

In his story "Longrope's Last Guard," Charlie Russell has Longrope, while on night guard, amuse himself and let the cattle know where he is by singing "Texas Rangers." The narrator explains that "The Rangers" is a long song and few cowboys know all the verses. Although the time setting of the story was in the trail-driving days, "Texas Rangers" was probably already an old song. I have also read that it was the favorite song of the Wild Bunch outlaw Butch Cassidy.

The song is still in tradition in our section of the Arkansas Ozarks, being sung by Mrs. Ollie Gilbert, Raymond Sanders, myself, and others. We still have some free range in our county, and many of the very oldest cowboy songs are well known here. Many families have a recollection of a grandfather or great-uncle who punched cows in Texas and returned with a fine raft of songs. With several southwestern and Canadian cowboys living and ranching here in recent years, we have cowboy songs of many areas and eras.

"Texas Rangers" has cropped up in many collections of western and southern folksongs and also appeared in several song folios of singing cowboys during the thirties. I have an old Ken Maynard folio with a fine version of this song. An early recording of it was made by the Cartwright brothers of Texas. The story is the same in all versions I have heard, with a few small differences in words, notably in the last verse or two. The usual tune is in a minor key, but I have also heard it sung to the tune of "California Joe," which is in a major key.

Here is my favorite version of one of the old, old cowboy classics.

THE TEXAS RANGERS

Come all ye Texas Rangers wherever you may be,
I'll tell you of some troubles that happened unto me.
My name is nothin' extry and that I will not tell,
So here's to all you rangers, I'm sure I wish you well.

Was at the age of seventeen I joined the jolly band.
We marched from San Antonio down to the Rio Grande.
The captain he informed us, I guess he thought it right,
Before we reach the station we'll surely have to fight.

And when the bugles sounded, our captain gave command.
"To arms, to arms," he shouted, "and by your horses stand."
I saw the smoke ascending, it seemed to reach the sky,
And then the thought it struck me, my time had come to die.

I saw the Indians coming, I heard them give a yell.
My feelings at that moment no tongue can ever tell.
I saw their glittering lances, the arrows round me flew,
And all my strength it left me, and all my courage, too.

We fought for nine hours fully before the strife was o'er.
The like of dead and wounded I never saw before.
And when the smoke had risen and the Indians they had fled
We loaded up our rifles and counted up our dead.

And all of us were wounded, the noble captain slain.
The sun was shining sadly across the bloody plain.
Sixteen as brave a rangers as ever roamed the West
Were buried by their comrades with arrows in their breast.

I've tried the trails a-rambling, and rambling I know well.
I've crossed the Rocky Mountains, where many a brave boy fell.
I've been in the great Southwest where the wild Apaches roam.
I'll advise you by experience, you had better stay at home.

And now my song is ended, I guess I sung enough.
The life of any ranger, you see, is very tough.
So here's to all you ladies, I'm sure I wish you well.
I'm bound to go a-rangin', so ladies, fare you well.

<h1 style="text-align:center">54</h1>

<h1 style="text-align:center">Bull Riders in the Sky</h1>

In the summer of '49 or '50 it seemed every time you'd go in a cafe or bar you'd hear the jukebox playing "Ghost Riders in the Sky." The whole thing became familiar whether you tried to learn it or not. The song was sort of a natural for parodies, and "Bull Riders in the Sky" is a parody of "Ghost Riders" I made up that summer of 1950. I was traveling with rodeo announcer and bull rider Joe Cavanaugh of Chambers, Nebraska. I started the song to poke fun at Joe, because bull riders get awfully nervous at times. Bull riding is dangerous, and some of those old Brahmas will "eat you up," as they say. Nevertheless, Joe helped with the first verse and the chorus. Since I was riding broncs the bulls were no trouble to me. About seven years later at the Newport, Arkansas, rodeo, a young bull rider named Duke Clark sang me the first verse and asked if I'd ever heard it. So I sung him the second verse. Duke says, "Well, where did you learn it?" I says, "I made it up," and he says, "Well, I'll be damned!" In 1963, when I sang this for folklorist Archie Green and told about Joe and Duke, Archie said it was really something to make up a song in your work and have it come back to you via oral tradition.

Some of the words here are minced from the way Joe and I sang it. Also, it took me a while to get it all together again, as I'd forgotten some of it over the years.

<h3 style="text-align:center">BULL RIDERS IN THE SKY</h3>

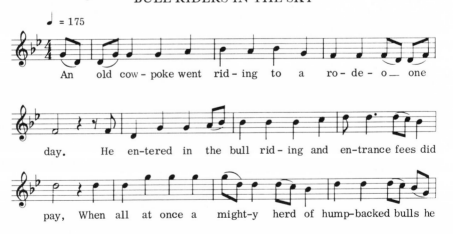

An old cow-poke went rid-ing to a ro-de-o one day. He en-tered in the bull rid-ing and en-trance fees did pay, When all at once a might-y herd of hump-backed bulls he

132

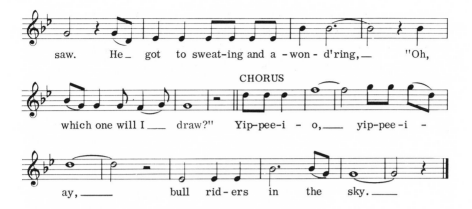

saw. He got to sweat-ing and a -won- d'ring, — "Oh, which one will I draw?" Yip-pee-i - o, — yip-pee-i - ay, — bull rid-ers in the sky. —

An old cowpoke went riding to a rodeo one day.
He entered in the bull riding and entrance fees did pay,
When all at once a mighty herd of humpbacked bulls he saw.
He got to sweating and a-wondering, "Oh, which one will I draw?"

   Yippee-i-o, yippee-i-ay, bull riders in the sky.

A bolt of fear went through him as they thundered in the chutes.
He knew that any moment he'd be on them burly brutes.
Their horns was black and shiny and just as slick as glass.
He knew that any moment they might gore him in the back.

   Chorus:

He asked another cowboy if the bull he drawed could pitch.
The cowboy answered firmly, "He's a terrible son of a gun.
But if you chance to ride him I'm sure that you can win,
But I don't think you will ride him when he goes into his spin."

   Chorus:

His face was drawn, his mouth was dry, his knees began to shake.
Someone said, "Lad, don't feel so bad, you'd better be awake."
He put his bull rope on the bull and rosined up his glove.
He done a dozen deep knee bends and prayed to Heaven above.

   Chorus:

He didn't feel much better when it came his time to ride.
He bravely climbed aboard him and he weakly said, "Outside."
He made a mighty effort to stay behind that hump,
But just the same the poor boy only lasted half a jump.

   Chorus:

133

He hit the ground, he scrambled up, he ran right up the gate.
He said, "I'm gonna quit these bulls before it is too late.
But just the same I have to think of the money I'd have won.
I'm sure that I will ride him before my race is run."

Chorus:

55

Backward, Turn Backward

At the La Belle, Missouri, rodeo in 1954 I ran into Joe Cavanaugh again after seeing him only once (at the Spooner, Wisconsin, rodeo that same year) since 1950. Joe was announcing and riding bulls. He hadn't been on a bull for a year or two since an arena mishap at Omaha. When he turned the mike over to someone and climbed down to get his bull ready to ride, I caught him singing and making up this little parody to the old familiar song right on the spot. A tender sentiment, indeed, from the Irish bull rider!

BACKWARD, TURN BACKWARD

Back-ward, turn back-ward, O Time, in your flight,
Bring back my a-bil-i-ty— if just for to-night.
Bring back that rid-ing— a-bil-i-ty— of — mine,
Don't let the bull buck my ass off this time!

Backward, turn backward, O Time, in your flight,
Bring back my ability if just for tonight.
Bring back that riding ability of mine,
Don't let the bull buck my ass off this time!

135

56

Make Me a Cowboy Again

"Backward, Turn Backward, O Time, in Your Flight" has been a familiar sentimental song since before the turn of the century. While I heard Joe Cavanaugh in the process of making his parody in 1954, there is an older cowboy version of the same song. George B. German of South Dakota credits this version to Joe and Zack Miller of the old 101 ranch Wild West show. I have the old Peg Moreland record of it on tape. I also collected it in manuscript form from Jim McElroy of Fox, Arkansas, who thinks a lot of this song because "it sure gets a bunch of good stuff in there." I agree, Jim!

MAKE ME A COWBOY AGAIN

Back-ward, turn back-ward, — O Time, with your wheels,

Aer - o - planes, wag - ons, and au - to - mo - biles.

Dress me once more in — som - bre - ro — that flaps,

Spurs and a flan - nel shirt, slick - er — and chaps.

Put a six - shoot - er — or two in — my — hand.

Show me the year - lin' to rope and to brand.

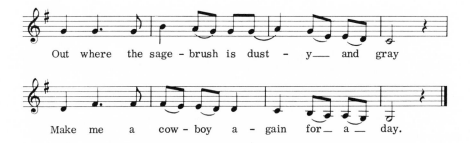

Out where the sage - brush is dust - y—— and gray

Make me a cow - boy a - gain for— a— day.

Backward, turn backward, O Time, with your wheels,
Aeroplanes, wagons, and automobiles.
Dress me once more in sombrero that flaps,
Spurs and a flannel shirt, slicker and chaps.
Put a six-shooter or two in my hand.
Show me the yearlin' to rope and to brand.
Out where the sagebrush is dusty and gray
Make me a cowboy again for a day.

Give me a bronco that knows how to dance,
Buckskin of color and wicked of glance,
New to the feel of bridle and bits.
Give me a quirt that will sting when it hits.
Strap on a poncho behind in a roll.
Give me a lariat dear to my soul.
Over the trail let me gallop away.
Make me a cowboy again for a day.

Galloping over the ranges so wide,
Sizzle of iron and smoking of hide,
Beller of maverick and snort of cayuse,
Longhorns from Texas as wild as the deuce.
Midnight stampede and the millin' of herds,
Shouts of the cowboys too angry for words.
Right in the midst of it all I would say,
"Make me a cowboy again for a day."

Under a star-studded canopy vast,
Campfire and comfort and coffee at last.
Bacon that sizzles and crisps in a pan
After a roundup tastes good to a man.
Stories of ranchers and rustlers retold
Over the pipes as the embers grow cold —
These are the tunes that old memories play.
Make me a cowboy again for a day.

137

57

Sporting Cowboy

"Sporting Cowboy" is one version of the song known also as "Moundsville Prisoner," "Dallas County Jail," and various other place names. Sam Hess of Mountain View, Arkansas, calls it both "The Old Jail Song" and "Johnny Merle." I like the name "Sporting Cowboy" the best. I have put verses together from several sources. The tune is about the same in all cases. Here is one of my versions, with thanks to Sam Hess and an old record by Weaver and Wiggins.

SPORTING COWBOY

When I was a cowboy I learned to throw the line.
I used to pocket money, boys, and used to dress so fine.
I used to pocket money, boys, and make the gamblers squeal,
And when I made a big haul how happy I did feel.

I used to wear a white hat, drive a horse and buggy fine.
When I spied a pretty girl you bet I called her mine.
I courted her for beauty, her beauty was so great,
And when I'd go to see her she'd meet me at the gate.

At working I'm not able, and begging is too low.
Stealing is so dreadful, to jail I must go.
I woke up brokenhearted in Dallas County jail,
No one here to love me, no one to go my bail.

Along come my true love, ten dollars in her hand,
Said, "Give it to the cowboy, 'tis all that I command.
Give it to the cowboy, for days of auld lang syne,
So he won't forget his darling, the one he left behind."

Along came my true love, exactly ten o'clock,
Saying, "Oh, my darling, what sentence have you got?
Oh, may the Lord go with you wherever you may go.
The Devil hang the jury for sending you below."

Down came the jailer, exactly eleven o'clock,
The keys all in his hand, the door to unlock.
"Wake up, wake up, my prisoner," I heard the jailer say,
"You are bound for Huntsville for many long years to stay."

Come all you sporting gentlemen, wherever you may be,
Don't you go to stealing, and let that gambling be.
The jury will find you guilty, the judge says you must go
Way down to Huntsville, away down below.

58

Come All Ye Western Cowboys

This antique-sounding song with its minor melody is one rare old cowboy song that has survived in Stone County, Arkansas. The first time I heard it was while visiting with the great old ballad singer Ollie Gilbert of Mountain View, Arkansas. Mrs. Gilbert has the titles of all the songs she knows closely written on a strip of grocery-bill paper that must be twenty-five feet long. She can recall and sing, instantly, any song you pick from the list. She also has a similar list of jokes she tells.

Vance Randolph includes "Come All Ye Lonesome Cowboys" in Volume 2 of *Ozark Folksongs*. I find it reminiscent of "The Texas Rangers."

COME ALL YE WESTERN COWBOYS

Come all ye western cowboys, bound on this sober land,
I'll tell you of some troubles, I'll now before you stand.
I left my home and country on the wild and windy plain,
And now I'm going to leave you to ne'er return again.

My mother's hand did tremble, said, "Son, oh, son, I fear
Some accident may happen, I'll never see you here.

Oh, may the Lord go with you wherever you may roam
And send this wandering cowboy back to his native home."

A girl so sweet and lovely drew closer to my side
And promised me so faithfully she would be my bride.
I kissed away the flowing tear that filled her deep blue eyes.
I'll ne'er forget the girl I love until the day I die.

I've tried the trails of rambling, and rambling I know well.
I've crossed the Rocky Mountains, where many a brave boy fell.
I've been in the great Southwest with Apaches fierce and wild.
I ne'er forgot the girl I love or seen a sweeter smile.

59

Cole Younger

In October, 1965, while visiting my grandmother, the late Dina Eraker, and my uncle Clarence Eraker and his family at Winger, Minnesota, I sang a few of the songs I'd learned in the Ozarks over the years. Among those I sang one night was the outlaw ballad "Cole Younger," which I first heard from Ollie Gilbert. Their nearest neighbor, Otto Roste, was present, and it turned out Otto spent his boyhood years near Northfield, Minnesota, where Cole Younger was captured during the James brothers' and Younger's raid on the Northfield bank. Otto, who was raised on stories of the famous holdup attempt, said the song was very accurate and that the words "Three of the brave companions made it home alive, / Three of the brave companions sleep beneath Minnesota skies," were just the way he'd heard it told. This song also appears in the Vance Randolph collection.

COLE YOUNGER

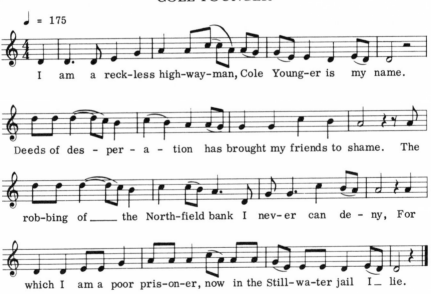

I am a reckless highwayman, Cole Younger is my name.
Deeds of desperation has brought my friends to shame.
The robbing of the Northfield bank I never can deny,
For which I am a poor prisoner, now in the Stillwater jail I lie.

Of all my bold robberies a story I will tell
Of a California miner, upon him I fell.
I robbed him of his money, boys, and made my getaway,
For which I will be sorry of until my dying day.

"It's now we've got fast horses," as brother Bob did say,
"It's now we've got fast horses to make our getaway.
We'll ride to seek our father's revenge and we will win the prize.
We'll fight those anti-guerrilla boys until the day we die."

We started out for Texas, that good old Lone Star State.
On Nebraska's burning prairies the James boys we did meet.
With knives and guns and pistols we all sat down to play,
A-drinkin' of good whiskey, boys, to pass the time away.

We saddled up our horses and northward we did go
To the godforsaken country called Minneso-ti-o.
We went to rob the Northfield bank and brother Bob did say,
"Cole, if we undertake this job we'll always rue the day."

We stationed out our pickets and into town did go.
There upon the counter we struck our fatal blow.
"It's hand us o'er your money, boys, and that without delay.
We are the notorious Youngers and we have no time to play."

We got on our horses and we rode out of town.
The lawmen pursued us and Jim was shot down.
Three of the brave companions made it home alive,
Three of the brave companions sleep beneath Minnesota skies.

60

The Cowboy's Christmas Ball

This poem by Larry Chittenden has appeared in print many times. In recent years the Colorado Springs magazine *Western Horseman* ran it. I learned this tune as a kid and as many words as given here (the original is longer) somewhere along the back trail.

THE COWBOY'S CHRISTMAS BALL

Way out in west-ern Tex- as,— where the Clear Fork's wa-ters flow, Where the cat-tle are a-brows-in' and the Span-ish— po-nies grow, Where the north-ers come a-whis-tlin' from be-yond the Neu-tral Strip, And the prai-rie dogs are wheez-in' as though they had the grippe, Where lone-some, taw-ny prai-ries— melt in-to air-y— streams, While the Dou-ble Moun-tains slum-ber in heav-'n-ly kinds of dreams, Where the an-te-lope is graz-in' and the lone-ly plov-ers call, It was there that I at-tend-ed the cow-boy's Christ-mas ball.

Way out in western Texas, where the Clear Fork's waters flow,
Where the cattle are a-browsin' and the Spanish ponies grow,
Where the northers come a-whistlin' from beyond the Neutral Strip,
And the prairie dogs are wheezin' as though they had the grippe,
Where lonesome, tawny prairies melt into airy streams,
While the Double Mountains slumber in heav'nly kinds of dreams,
Where the antelope is grazin' and the lonely plovers call,
It was there that I attended the cowboy's Christmas ball.

The boys had left the ranches and come to town in piles.
The ladies, kinder scatterin', had gathered in for miles.
And yet the place was crowded, as I remember well.
'Twas gave on this occasion at the Morning Star Hotel.
The music was a fiddle and a lively tambourine,
And a viol came, imported by the stage from Abilene.
The room was togged out gorgeous with mistletoe and shawls,
And the candles flickered frescoes around the airy walls.

The women folks looked lovely, the boys looked kinder treed,
Till the leader commenced yellin', "Whoa, fellers, let's stampede,"
And the music started sighin' and a-wailin' through the hall
As a kind of introduction to the cowboy's Christmas ball.
The leader was a feller that came from Swenson's ranch,
They called him Windy Billy from Little Deadman's Branch.
His rig was kinder keerless, big spurs and high-heeled boots.
He had the reputation that comes when fellers shoots.

His voice was like a bugle upon the mountain height.
His feet were animated and a mighty movin' sight,
When he commenced to holler, "Now, fellers, stake your pen.
Lock horns ter all them heifers and rustle them like men,
Salute yer lovely critters, now swing and let 'em go,
Climb the grapevine round 'em, now all hands do-si-do.
You maverick, jine the roundup, jes' skip the waterfall."
Huh, hit was gettin' active, the cowboy's Christmas ball.

Don't tell me 'bout cotillions, or germans, no sir-ee!
That whirl at Anson City jes' takes the cake with me.
I'm sick of lazy shufflin's, of them I've had my fill.
Give me a frontier breakdown backed up by Windy Bill.
McAllister ain't nowhere when Windy leads the show.
I've seen 'em both in harness, and so I ought ter know.
Oh, Bill, I shan't forget yer and I oftentimes recall
That lively gaited soiree, the cowboy's Christmas ball.

61

The Stray

One of my favorite magazines was the now-defunct *Bit and Spur* published at Billings, Montana, by Bill Hagen. *Bit and Spur* ran rodeo and horse stories with lots of photos and also "cow and horse poetry" sent in by readers. This poem was run under the title "The Estrays," by Pecos the Ridgerunner, in 1948. I liked the poem and put the tune to it. In late years I find that folklorists remark how so much of cowboy song has originated as printed poems in livestock journals and similar publications. Here is my contribution to the practice. In this one it's the cow that does the talking, not the cowboy.

THE STRAY

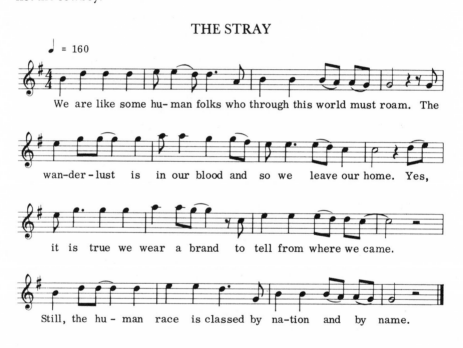

We are like some human folks who through this world must roam.
The wanderlust is in our blood and so we leave our home.
Yes, it is true we wear a brand to tell from where we came.
Still, the human race is classed by nation and by name.

We think that just beyond the brow of yonder sloping hill
The grass is tender, rich, and sweet, the water pure and still,
That there's shelter from the storm in gulches deep and wide,
Where salt licks crop out from the ground and cowboys never ride.

146

But it always seems our lot to be caught in the drive.
We cannot dodge the cowboys' path no matter how we strive.
They seem to ride in every gulch, they know our rendezvous,
And so we pass on down the trail, there's nothing left to do.

And then we're guarded through the night and held in herd by day
Until we reach the old home range, from which we chose to stray.
But we are just like human folks who through the world must roam.
We tire of the same old hills and so we leave our home.

62

Trail to Mexico

One night before the rodeo at Andalusia, Alabama, in October, 1963, a few of us were sitting around a motel room swapping yarns, telling jokes, and so forth. The oldest cowboy present was Johnny Webb of Hamshire, Texas, who was picking up broncs at the rodeo. Johnny asked me if I knew the song "The Trail to Mexico," which he hadn't heard in thirty years. I said yes, and he asked me to sing it. When I had finished I looked over to see how he took it, and he said, "You got one word wrong in the last verse." Nevertheless, every time I ran into Johnny Webb over the next couple years he got me to sing "Trail to Mexico."

About Johnny Webb, who was raised in Old Mexico, I never saw a cowboy with more guts about roping real bad Brahma bulls. He'd sail right in and lay his twine on the worst ones of the "muss hog" variety. In his present home, the Gulf Coast of Texas, he is in demand catching cattle gone wild in the marshes. He's a cowboy of the old school, Johnny Webb.

"The Trail to Mexico" is one of my favorite cowboy songs and one of my earliest. My own source could have been a book, folio, record, or person. I don't remember. Over the years, however, I have heard it many times and in many versions. Where I live now, in Stone County, Arkansas, it has a strong tradition and is sung variously as "Trail to Mexico" or "Year of Eighty-three." Here are two versions, my own longest version and that of Raymond Sanders. Raymond's is unusual with its "hooray-hoo" at the end of some verses.

One phenomenon that a trail-driving song such as this brings to my mind is how so many writers wrote finis to cowboying when the great trail-driving days ended. I suspect that people can grasp the idea of a long-distance trail drive but fail to understand day-to-day cow and horse work such as still goes on. Granted there are vast changes, but a lot is the same. I know personally of cow outfits in Arizona, Nevada, Wyoming, and Montana that still run a chuck wagon on roundup, spring and fall. With the passage of time since the range cattle business started, many areas now have enough roads and permanent cow camps so that even big outfits can do all their work from camps. The permanent camp would have corrals, water, holding pasture, cook shack, and possibly a bunkhouse. Magazines and TV often show some outfit with an oil well for every cow, sporting an airplane or helicopter, but it still takes the cowboy on the ground to doctor a cow for pinkeye, or pull a calf, or dozens of other common chores. Very long rides are no longer necessary where roads permit a pickup truck to haul the cow horse near the scene of work. On the other hand, in Arizona particularly, there are ranches that must send a pack mule string instead of a chuck wagon into extremely rough country for working cattle. There are a lot of wire fences in the country, too, but if you are riding a fifty- or one-hundred-section pasture (a section is 640 acres), it doesn't make such an awful difference if there is a fence around it. Some states, such as Nevada, have more open range than fenced to this day.

While the thousand-mile trail drives are over forever, drives of fifty to one hundred miles from winter range to summer pastures high on western mountain ranges still go on year after year. Often these mountain pastures are part of a forest preserve and all livestock are under permit. Also the public domain is now mostly under the Bureau of Land Management and requires a permit which carefully controls the number of livestock in a given area. My Canadian friends Cliff Claggett and Jack Lauder tell me that in remote areas of British Columbia trail drives to the railroad shipping point of two hundred to three hundred miles are still necessary. The search for grass, water, and room to build and expand has sent American ranchers to remote areas of Canada, Brazil, Australia, and to parts of the United States that are not traditional ranching areas but where farming is dying out, leaving empty acres.

There was another type of overland trail drive, and I remember the tail end of that era. Herds of western or bronco horses were driven from Montana and the Dakotas to farming states to the east. These horses were sold to farmers to break for work; some wound up as saddle horses. Also a good many were shipped by rail. This continued up till the late 1930s. Going back in time, my mother remembers these horse-trading drovers when she was a child in northwestern Minnesota before World War I. Mother knew some local boys who went to Montana and trailed horses back. Best remembered were the Lokken boys of happy-go-lucky Viking spirit. At home they were in demand as fiddlers at country dances. They ended every dance fighting each other, just for fun! My own memory, still vivid from the time I was a little boy, includes the horses themselves. Of the men who drove them, I remember only the name Diamond.

Maybe this is far afield from "The Trail to Mexico," but it shows that some elements of trail drives are not such ancient history.

TRAIL TO MEXICO
(my own version)

♩ =' 155

It was in _ the mer - ry _ month of _ May   I left my

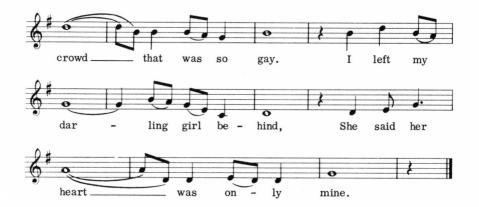

crowd _____ that was so gay. I left my

dar - ling girl be - hind, She said her

heart _____ was on - ly mine.

It was in the merry month of May
I left my crowd that was so gay.
I left my darling girl behind,
She said her heart was only mine.

It was in the year of '83
When A. J. Stimpson hired me.
He said, "Young fellow, I want you to go
And drive this herd to Mexico."

Oh, it was a long and a lonesome go
Along the trail to Mexico.
With laughter light and a cowboy song
To Mexico we rode along.

When I arrived in Mexico
Want to see my girl but I couldn't go.
So I wrote a letter to my dear,
But not a word did I ever hear.

When I arrived in my once-loved home
Went to see the girl that I called my own.
But she had married a richer life.
They said, "Wild cowboy, seek another wife."

Oh, it's curse your gold and your silver, too.
God pity a girl that won't prove true.
I'll go out west where the bullets fly,
Stay on the trail till the day I die.

"Oh, buddy, buddy, please stay at home,
Don't be forever on the roam.
Don't go out west where the bullets fly.
You'll find another, far better than I."

I cursed my love and her sister, too,
And all pretty girls that won't prove true.
Away I'll go to the Rio Grande
And get me a job with a cowboy band.

TRAIL TO MEXICO
(Raymond Sanders's version)

It was way back in sev-en-ty-three When an old
Mex - i-can hired me. He said, "Young
man, you suit my mind, To me your
things looks ver-y fine." And a hoo-ray-
hoo and a hoo - ray - hoo.

It was way back in '73
When an old Mexican hired me.
He said, "Young man, you suit my mind,
To me your things looks very fine."
And a hooray-hoo and a hooray-hoo.

Oh, early, early in the year
We started out fer to drive those steers.
It was a long and lonesome go,
The herd rolled on for Mexico.

Oh, when I got to Old Mexico
I wanted to see my love and I could not go.

151

I wrote a letter to my dearest dear,
And not one word did I ever hear.
And a hooray-hoo and a hooray-hoo.

When I returned from the Mexican land
I found she's married another man.
Away I'll go to the Mexican land,
And I'll pop my whip in the wild cow band.

My sister said, "Oh, brother, don't go.
Why don't you quit your rambling so?
Oh, get you a wife and settle down
And never go back to the wild cow band."
And a hooray-hoo and a hooray-hoo.

I cursed my love and her sister, too,
And all pretty girls that was not true.
Away I'll go to the Mexican land,
And I'll pop my whip in the wild cow band.

63

Utah Carol

Often known as "Utah Carl," this song has a strong place in tradition. In fact, there are so many little variations of tune and words that I have never sung it without being corrected in both. In our area of Arkansas a good many of the older ballad singers include it in their repertoires. Ollie Gilbert of Mountain View has a long, interesting version. A neighbor, Mrs. Hub Willis, also sings "Utah Carol" (or "Carl") and sings it "right." Over the years I have noted a brisk exchange of song ballets of "Utah Carol" among my neighbors. I have written it off on request myself and had it given to me in turn.

As in this song about Utah Carol, death on the trail was common in the older cowboy songs. In modern times, with today's rodeo cowboys traveling incessantly by car and by air to cover fantastic travel schedules, the automobile and to a much lesser extent the airplane account for a lot of cowboy deaths. However, I haven't found any songs or poems on the subject. Death in the arena from broncs and bulls has cropped up in song, though the highway gets many times more victims.

UTAH CAROL

Kind friends, you may ask what makes me sad and still
And why my brow is darkened like clouds upon a hill.

Rein in your pony closer and listen while I tell
Of Utah Carol, my partner, and his last ride on the trail.

Mid the cactus and the thistle of Mexico's fair land,
Where the cattle range by the thousands of many a mark and brand,

153

In a grave without a headstone, without a date or a name,
Quietly sleeps my partner, in the land from which he came.

Long, long we rode together, had ridden side by side.
I loved him as a brother, and I wept when Utah died.

Long, long we rode together, we threw ropes and burnt the brand.
In dark and stormy weather we gained night herder's stand.

On rounding up one morning, our work was almost done,
The cattle quickly started on a wild and maddened run.

The boss's little daughter, while herding on that side
Rushed in to turn the stampede — it was there that Utah died.

Lenore upon her pony tried to turn the cattle right.
Her blanket slipped beneath her, and she caught and held on tight.

And when we saw the blanket each cowboy held his breath,
For should her pony fail her, none could save the girl from death.

Lenore soon saw her danger and turned her pony's face
And bending in the saddle tried the blanket to replace.

Just then she lost her balance in front of that wild tide.
"Lie still, lie still, I say," 'twas Utah Carol that cried.

Then close up beside her came Utah riding fast.
But little did the boy think that ride would be his last.

He swung low from out his saddle to raise her in his arms.
He thought he had succeeded to save the girl from harm.

But such strain upon his saddle had never been before.
The cinch it broke beneath him, and he fell beside Lenore.

When Lenore fell from her pony she dragged the blanket down.
It lay there close beside her where she fell upon the ground.

Utah picked up that blanket and waved it o'er his head
And started across the prairie. "Lie still," again he said.

He turned the maddened cattle from Lenore, his little friend.
As the mighty herd rushed upon him, he paused to meet his end.

As the mighty herd rushed upon him, his pistol he quickly drew
To fight to his last minute, as all brave cowboys do.

The weapon flashed like lightning, it sounded loud and clear.
As the mighty herd rushed upon him, he dropped the foremost steer.

When I broke in the circle where poor Utah lay,
From a dozen wounds and bruises his lifeblood ebbed away.

I knelt beside him, I knew it was all o'er
As I heard him whisper, "Good-bye, good-bye, Lenore."

On Sunday morning I heard the preacher say,
"I don't think our young cowboy was lost on that great day.

"He was a much-loved cowboy and not afraid to die.
I hope you all will meet him in the home beyond the sky."

64

The Cowboy #1

A Campus Folksong Club member at the University of Illinois pointed out to me in 1964 the words from Shakespeare's *As You Like It* in the third verse of this song. He thought it strange they should wind up in a cowboy song. It's not surprising, though, especially in an older song, since the range cattle business attracted a good many well-educated young men from the eastern United States and the British Isles. Many a younger son was packed off to Wyoming and Colorado as well as other states to learn the business and get a start in life.

I sing two versions of this old song, which I have known since I was a kid. Here is the longer of the two and my favorite.

THE COWBOY #1

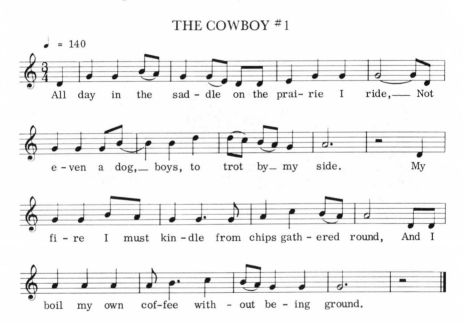

All day in the saddle on the prairie I ride,
Not even a dog, boys, to trot by my side.
My fire I must kindle from chips gathered round,
And I boil my own coffee without being ground.

For want of a stove I cook bread in a pot.
I sleep on the ground for the want of a cot.

I wash in the creek, I dry on a sack,
And I carry my wardrobe all on my back.

My books are the brooks and my sermons the stones.
My parson's the wolf on his pulpit of bones.
My roof is the sky, my floor is the grass,
My music's the lowing of herds as they pass.

And then if my cooking's not very complete,
You can't blame me for wanting to eat.
But show me the man who sleeps more profound
Than the big puncher boy who's stretched out on the ground.

But society brands me so savage and dodge
The Masons would bar me out of their lodge.
If I had hair on my chin I might pass for the goat
Who bore all the sins in the ages remote.

And why it is so I cannot understand,
For each of the patriarchs owned a big brand.
Abraham immigrated in search of a range.
Because of a drought he was seeking a change.

Isaac run cattle in charge of Esau,
And Jacob punched cows for his father-in-law.
David went from night-herding to using a sling,
And winning the battle, became a great king.

My friends gently hint I am coming to grief,
But men must make money and women have beef.
And Cupid is always a friend to the bold,
And all of his arrows are pointed with gold.

65

The Cowboy #2

This song entitled "The Cowboy" has nothing in common with the preceding one. In the late thirties it was known as given here. There were also bawdy versions, which I have forgotten.

THE COWBOY #2

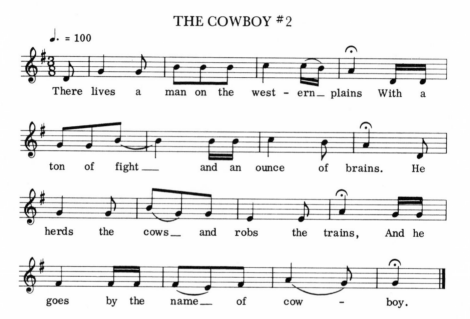

There lives a man on the western plains
With a ton of fight and an ounce of brains.
He herds the cows and robs the trains,
And he goes by the name of cowboy.

He sets up drinks when he hasn't a cent.
He'll fight like hell with any young gent.
When he makes love he goes it hell-bent.
Oh, that's the way of the cowboy.

He shoots out lights in a dancing hall.
He gets shot up in a drunken brawl,
And a coroner's jury ends it all.
And that's the last of the cowboy.

66

Franklin Slaughter Ranch

This song must have had a wide following from Texas, where the Slaughter ranch is, to Oregon, for some versions have it on French ranch, which was once a grazing empire in southern Oregon. It is also reported as "The Cowboy's Home Sweet Home" and in Vance Randolph's *Ozark Folksongs* as "The Wandering Cowboy."

Bill Tharp of Mountain View, Arkansas, sang me this version in 1965. Bill learned the song while working on the famed Miller brothers' 101 ranch in Oklahoma in 1931. This was near the end of the 101 ranch, when it was upon hard times. Bill learned the song from a cowboy named "Jap" Looney. The 101 ranch worked both cowboys and farmhands and had produced a topflight, world-traveling Wild West show. The 101 hands also took time off to contest at major competitive rodeos. The cowboys usually preferred the contesting, particularly where the prize money was large. But there were not enough rodeos to keep them busy all year, with the result that the 101, in its heyday, had numerous top hands on its Wild West show.

The words *prepelled* and *crimonly* in this text are Bill Tharp's own coinage, apparently.

FRANKLIN SLAUGHTER RANCH

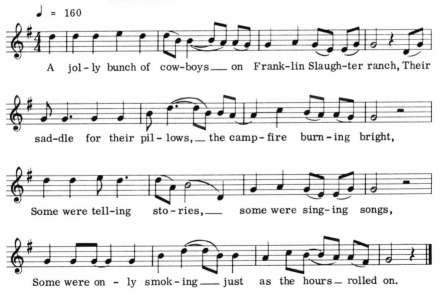

A jol-ly bunch of cow-boys— on Frank-lin Slaugh-ter ranch, Their

sad-dle for their pil-lows,— the camp-fire burn-ing bright,

Some were tell-ing sto-ries,— some were sing-ing songs,

Some were on-ly smok-ing— just as the hours— rolled on.

159

A jolly bunch of cowboys on Franklin Slaughter ranch,
Their saddle for their pillows, the campfire burning bright,
Some were telling stories, some were singing songs,
Some were only smoking just as the hours rolled on.

Some begin to talk of home and the ones they loved so dear,
When a boy raised from his saddle and brushed away a tear,
Said, "To be at Messenger cottage, although I'm prepelled to roam,
I'd give my pony and saddle to be back home sweet home."

They asked him why he left his home, if it was so dear to him.
The boy gazed round a moment, his dark blue eyes grew dim.
"I fell in love with a neighbor's girl whose cheeks was snowy white,
And another fellow loved her, too, so it ended up with a fight.

"And in my dreams I can hear Tom's voice as he sunk upon the ground.
Said he to me, 'I'm dying, go gather my people around.'
I then knelt down beside him and tried to stop the blood,
But still from his wounded side life flowed like a crimonly flood.

"And now you know the reason that I am prepelled to roam,
I'm a murderer of the deepest stain and far from home sweet home."

67

My Harding County Home

"My Harding County Home" is Tex Fletcher's song about the great ranching county in the northwest corner of South Dakota. Tex Fletcher landed in Buffalo, South Dakota, in the hungry thirties and remained to work on local ranches. He began a career as a movie cowboy and entertainer before World War II, based on his experiences in Harding County. During the war Tex was wounded in Italy and wrote this song while convalescing in a hospital there.

Harding County went through the era of huge cattle outfits on the free range, such as the E6, the Turkey Track, the Mill Iron, the CY, and others. When the big outfits began breaking up and cowboys started their own small outfits, it wasn't long till the homesteaders, or "Honyockers," came in droves. The trend was reversed in the early thirties; the farming is about over, and the entire county is mainly taken by family ranches. Some of the ranches go back to the earliest settlers, such as the Catron ranch at the little cow town of Camp Crook.

We got this song about Harding County from Dean Tarter, a young rancher from the Camp Crook area. We met Dean at a dance at Mill Iron, Montana, in June, 1968, and taped him the next day at his ranch home. There were ranch people from thirty miles in all directions at the Mill Iron dance. While Dean Tarter's ranch was in South Dakota, his summer range was just over the line in the Long Pine Hills of Montana. This whole area is unspoiled by tourist junk, and it is, in my estimation, as beautiful a country

as you'd find. It is a rolling prairie country broken by numerous coulees and streams and badlands' breaks. The "buttes that rise like mountains to the sky" are another feature of the country. The main river in Harding County is the Grand, which eventually runs to the Missouri River just above Mobridge, South Dakota. The county seat of Harding County is Buffalo.

MY HARDING COUNTY HOME

Not so many years ago I left old Buffalo,
The place that I have always loved the best.
Where the antelope they play, I'm yearning today
For my Harding County home out in the West.

   I can see the mustang band grazing by the river Grand.
   I see the range where white-faced cattle roam.
   And the lights in Buffalo will guide me home, I know,
   Guide me to my Harding County home.

As I wander down Broadway, my memory does stray
To the buttes that rise like mountains to the sky.
I can hear a coyote wail as he roams along the trail,
"Come back to your prairie home" is his cry.

   Chorus:

68

Tipperary

There is probably no one in northwestern South Dakota that doesn't know about Harding County's famous old bucking horse, Tipperary. Interest in the great bucker of the World War I era and the twenties is still strong nearly forty years after his death in a blizzard in 1932. Tex Fletcher wrote this song about the horse years after his passing, and many years later, citizens of Buffalo, South Dakota, erected a monument to Tipperary. Probably a person not acquainted with an area so steeped in range and rodeo tradition would fail to understand the sentiment and pride that western people have for their greatest bucking horses. It is like the interest in famous racehorses or athletes in other parts of the country.

At one time there were thousands of range horses over the entire area of western Dakota and Montana and Wyoming. Miles City, in eastern Montana, was the largest horse-shipping center in the world. During World War I thousands of range horses were bought by France and other allied nations and shipped across the Atlantic for use as cavalry horses. Old-timers tell of the marathon bronc ridings that took place as American bronc riders rode these horses one after another for foreign buyers' inspection. If the horse could be ridden past the inspector's stand, he passed. Ranchers unloaded a lot of real snaky individuals on these buyers. It took a first-class bronc twister to get through a rugged day riding inspection. The mind boggles at picturing the European cavalrymen, accustomed to gentle-raised horses, going to the fray on some of those broncs.

One of the horses that unloaded his riders too soor to pass was a nice-looking bronc brought out by Doc Latham of Camp Crook, South Dakota. The bucker's reputation followed him home, and Camp Crook folks figured their local number-one bronc rider, Ed Marty, could ride him. A match was arranged right in the town of Camp Crook, and Ed Marty knocked a big hole in the ground. One story has it that Marty picked himself off the ground singing, "You can't stay on Tipperary!" — and the horse was named. From that time on, at local rodeos and for years at the great annual rodeo at Belle Fourche, South Dakota, Tipperary unloaded all comers. One man is credited with making a qualified ride on his rough old back. That rider was Yakima Canutt, one of the greatest bronc riders of the twenties. Some have it that Oklahoma Curly, Sam Brownell, and Leonard Stroud managed to ride him, but from Belle Fourche to Buffalo to Camp Crook only Yakima Canutt is credited with a ride. There are supporters of the horse who claim Canutt lost a stirrup momentarily and should have

Hack Rosenthal on Tipperary, Buffalo, South Dakota, June, 1924.

been disqualified. During his rodeo career Tipperary was also owned by Art Ritchie and Charlie Wilson.

What a picture it must have been to those ranch country people who loved a good bucking horse! In his heyday during the twenties, Tipperary, who was halter-broke, was led past the grandstand at old Belle while the band played the World War I song "Tipperary." The horse was saddled in the open, while snubbed up to a saddle horse, and mounted in front of the stand. When he was released, the bucking was on. Old rodeo friend Chip Morris, who saw Tipperary buck many times, has this to say about his style of bucking: "If there ever was a sunfisher that sunned his belly it was Tipperary. Besides that, he was stout and gave it all he had and was really fast. Then he fought his head all the way, either jerking the rein as far as he could or looking you right in the face. So the rein was no help at all." Scotty Bagnell (I rodeoed with him in Florida and Louisiana in the fall of '49) also vividly remembered Tipperary from his boyhood in North Dakota. Scotty saw him buck at Belle and other places and had this to say: "He was a terrible son of a bitch!"

In the late twenties the old horse was retired and turned out to pasture. He was brought back to Belle Fourche after his retirement and led past the grandstand, for the people still wanted to see him. Of course the band played "Tipperary." The bronc pranced past the people and looked at his last crowd.

165

When my wife, Kay, and I journeyed to Buffalo, South Dakota, in June, 1968, I'd known about the song for some time and about the horse himself for twenty-five years or more. Inquiring at the *Buffalo Times Herald* office brought from editor Don Cammack the information that local rancher Dick Smith could sing Tex Fletcher's song about Tipperary, "the great outlaw bronc." It was raining the day we looked for Dick Smith, and the ranch roads were "about 100 percent apt to stick you." Luckily, Smith was in town and graciously agreed to tape the song for us. When we finished, Dick Smith had sung some thirty songs for us, including two others in this book, "Paddy Ryan" (no. 34) and "Little Joe the Wrangler's Sister Nell" (no. 69). Smith ran cattle, sheep, and horses on his ranch twenty miles from Buffalo. He had spent a lifetime on the range in Harding County, had ridden with old-timers who had come up the long trail from Texas. He had also seen Tipperary buck many times and had respect and sentiment for the great old horse. According to Dick Smith, his neighbor Harold Ekberg made a ride on Tipperary in the Buffalo arena.

Though Tex Fletcher was a professional entertainer, one would suppose that he wrote the song mainly for his old South Dakota neighbors. Tipperary was gone when Fletcher arrived in Harding County, but the story of the horse was so strong that Tex apparently had a feeling for the horse, too. Personally, I think this is one of the most significant songs in this collection.

About Ed Marty, who gave Tipperary his name, we met his nephew Bill Marty at the 1968 St. Onge, South Dakota, rodeo. Bill said Ed was then living in Sturgis, South Dakota. Another Marty tends bar at a club in Ekalaka, Montana. They have a bucking horse tryout in the arena behind the bar each spring. They try out lots of colts of the famous Tooke ranch broncs. The Tookes have a strain of bucking horses that trace back to an unmanageable Shire stallion that weighed close to eighteen hundred pounds. Nearly all the horses of this strain are rank bucking horses; the more they try to handle them, the worse they get. So great broncs are still coming out of the northern ranges.

TIPPERARY

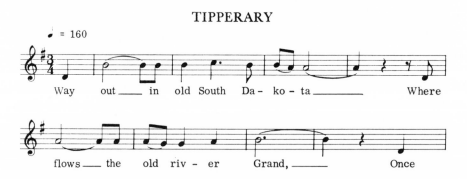

roamed the great-est of out - laws, Who was known all o-ver the land. CHORUS His name was old Tip-pe-rar-y, Tip-pe-rar-y of ro-de-o fame. The great-est of all the bronc rid-ers Will nev-er for-get that great name.

Way out in old South Dakota
Where flows the old river Grand,
Once roamed the greatest of outlaws,
Who was known all over the land.

His name was old Tipperary,
Tipperary of rodeo fame.
The greatest of all the bronc riders
Will never forget that great name.

The grandstand in Belle Fourche was crowded,
'Twas on the Fourth of July.
Tipperary, the king of the outlaws,
Came out of the chutes on the fly.

Chorus:

He went to frog-walkin' and bucking
And then did an old Spanish dance,
With a bebop thrown in for good measure
And a quadrille imported from France.

167

Chorus:

His rider was neatly unloaded,
That buster was sure badly shook.
And when he came back down from heaven
Tipperary was back in Camp Crook.

Chorus:

He was known all over this nation,
From Buffalo, on the banks of the Grand,
To Nome and the big eastern cities
And the Bighorns way up in Montan'.

Chorus:

69

Little Joe the Wrangler's Sister Nell

Next morning after sunup we found where Rocket fell,
Way down in a washout twenty feet below.
And beneath his horse, smashed to a pulp, his spurs had rung their knell,
Was our little Texas stray, poor wrangler Joe.

So ends the better-known song "Little Joe the Wrangler." It's the story of
a kid horse wrangler who got up to help turn a stampede at night. The
sequel, "Little Joe the Wrangler's Sister Nell," which I hadn't heard for
many years and had failed to learn, also comes from Dick Smith of Buffalo,
South Dakota.

LITTLE JOE THE WRANGLER'S SISTER NELL

Oh, she rode up to the wag-on, the sun was sink-ing low,
A slen-der lit-tle fig-ure dressed in gray.
We told her to get down, of course, and pull up to the
fire, And red-hot chuck would soon be on its way. An
old slouch hat with a hole in the top was perched up-on her
head, A pair of bull-hide chaps well-greased and worn, An

169

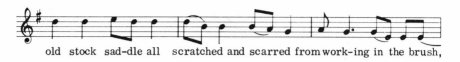

old stock sad-dle all scratched and scarred from work-ing in the brush,

___ And a mag-uey___ rope tied to her sad-dle horn.

Oh, she rode up to the wagon, the sun was sinking low,
A slender little figure dressed in gray.
We told her to get down, of course, and pull up to the fire,
And red-hot chuck would soon be on its way.
An old slouch hat with a hole in the top was perched upon her head,
A pair of bull-hide chaps well greased and worn,
An old stock saddle all scratched and scarred from working in the brush,
And a maguey rope tied to her saddle horn.

She said she'd rode from Llano, four hundred miles away,
And her pony was so tired he couldn't go.
She asked if she could stop a day or two and kinda rest him up,
And maybe she could find her brother Joe.
We asked where Joe was workin', if she knew the outfit's brand.
She said his letter said it was the "circle bar."
It was mailed at Amarillo about three months ago
From a trail herd headed north to Cinnabar.

I looked at Jim, he looked at Tom and then looked back at me,
There was something in our hearts we couldn't speak.
She said she got so worried when she never heard no more,
And things at home grew tougher every week.
I gave the kid my bedroll, while I rolled in with Jim.
We talked and planned and schemed the whole night through
As to which of us would tell her the way that Joe got killed
And to break the news as gently as we knew.

"I'll wrangle in the morning, boys," she said as she turned in,
"I'll have the horses at the wagon before the day."
And the morning star was rising as I saw the kid roll out,
Saddle up the gray night horse, and ride away.
Soon we heard the horses coming, a-heading into camp.
It wasn't light, but we plainly heard the bell
And then someone a-cryin', a-coming on behind,
It was little Joe the wrangler's sister Nell.

170

We couldn't quite console her, she'd seen the horses' brand
As she drove them from the riverbank below.
From the looks upon our faces she seemed to realize
That she never again would see poor wrangler Joe.

70

Windy Bill's Famous Ride

George B. German of Yankton, South Dakota, says he wrote "Windy Bill's Famous Ride" more as a recitation than as a song. German's model for the Windy Bill of the poem was an old cowboy pal of his years in Arizona, Shorty Harris. In the early twenties George B. German was working on Arizona cattle and sheep ranches for his health's sake. One day while sacking wool on a sheep outfit near Wickenburg, Arizona, he decided to ride over to Romaine Lowdermilk's nearby dude ranch. When he rode up to Lowdermilk's, he found Romaine playing his guitar and singing "The Strawberry Roan." German says he fell in love with the old cowboy songs that day. He soon was working for Lowdermilk wrangling dudes. His work took him on long rides to the Weaver Mountains and other points of interest. They also attended all the local rodeos and picnics, where he heard other cowboy singers, such as Powder River Jack and Kitty Lee, Jules Verne Allen, and Curley Fletcher. He also heard Gail Gardner recite his "Sierry Petes (or, Tying the Knots in the Devil's Tail)" (no. 27). In an interview in the summer of '68, German told us that Romaine Lowdermilk's singing had the most influence on his own and that Romaine was a well-liked "Will Rogers sort of a personality" in Arizona.

German's favorite song was Curley Fletcher's "Strawberry Roan." On a visit to Yankton, South Dakota, in 1928 a friend talked German into singing it on the Yankton radio station, WNAX. The song caused so much comment that he was given his own program. Over the years George B. German's program put many southwestern cowboy songs into circulation over a wide area of farming and ranching country, from eastern Montana through North and South Dakota, Nebraska, western Minnesota, and Iowa. Over the air he also sold thousands of folios containing the old cowboy songs. His later folios contained songs made popular by singers of the late thirties and early forties, such as Gene Autry. My own earliest interest in cowboy songs was probably directly sparked by one of his folios, which had a bucking horse photo in it, and my aunt Irene's bag of cowboy and hillbilly songs, which she learned from both the folio and the radio program. With the songbook was an autographed photo of German on a roan horse. I still have the picture after thirty-odd years. The photo shown with this song was taken in South Dakota on the banks of the Missouri River.

Although I contested in the bronc riding at Yankton rodeos in 1949 and 1950, I didn't know at the time that German was in Yankton. I had a vague idea that he was from North Dakota. So we never met till the summer of

George B. German on Ole Paint, South Dakota, early thirties.

1968. I was announcing and Kay was timing at a series of chuck-wagon races in surrounding states, and we arranged to tape an interview with German. We found him a very interested and articulate man, eager to help with our work of collecting cowboy songs and digging up background on them. At the present time he is a roving farm and ranch reporter for WNAX, taping interviews with farmers and ranchers all over that broadcast area. He says he often is told at ranches how his program was their main entertainment in the dirty thirties. His work brings out some "real down-to-earth talk" with the people visited. German also announced and sang at rodeos in South Dakota and knew many people I know, though our paths never crossed when I was contesting there and in neighboring states some twenty years ago.

WINDY BILL'S FAMOUS RIDE

Windy Bill was loafin' round town one sunny day,
He was nigh out of terbacker an' not drawin' any pay.
When a feller steps up gently, and he says, "Well, how-de-do,
You look like one rough-ridin', bronc-bustin' buckaroo."

Then Windy, he looks up with that curt, satirical grin,
And he says, "Well, holy moses, who in blazes left you in?
And speaking of my ridin', now say, what do you mean?
I'm the roughest ridin' buckaroo that you have ever seen.

"I've rode the Spanish ponies, and I've rode the wild mustang,
And I've rode these western broncos till their nerve just went kerbang.
I've rode elephants and camels, and I've rode all kinds of fish,
And when it comes to bears and lions, why shucks, they're just my dish.

"I can ride those alligators that swim around the lakes,
And way down south in Africa I've rode them cobra snakes.
I can ride these bucking mules that old Barnum raves about,
And once I rode a boxcar when my pocketbook got out."

While Windy's gettin' breath the feller says, "Well, I don't know,
This outlaw that I've got to ride, I'm telling you, ain't slow."
"Oh ho!" says Windy Bill, "git them thoughts out of your head,
For I'll surely ride the critter till he's either broke or dead."

So the feller says, "All right, step up into this machine,
It's a big twelve-cylinder giant high-powered limousine."
Windy takes a chaw of terbacker, then he gits up in the seat,
And the feller starts the motor and they're headed down the street.

Next they're goin' 'cross the prairie making more than a mile a minute,
And Windy begins to cuss himself for ever gettin' in it.
Then they're a-runnin' into chuckholes and they hit a million bumps,
And once they go through water, and Windy nearly jumps.

Then they're headed round toward town again, and Windy wonders why:
"Lord, the feller must be crazy, and here's where I must die."
Then they pull up where they started from, and the driver he gets out,
And Windy starts to roarin', asking what it's all about.

"Where is that horse, you crazy loon, that I'm supposed to ride?
Come clean, you ugly sinner, or I'll tan your measly hide!"
But the feller he just grins as a guy hands him some bills.
Then he turns and speaks to Windy, who's a-boilin' to the gills:

"Take this money, my dear Windy, and tuck it in your vest.
We just won five thousand dollars in a car endurance test!"

71

I Learned about Horses from Him

This song, which is modeled on Kipling's "The Ladies," was written by George B. German for his old cowboy buddy Shorty Harris. According to German, Shorty Harris was a real character who rode broncs for years at rodeos and in ranch rough strings.

I LEARNED ABOUT HORSES FROM HIM

'Twas on the Horse Shoe in old Ar - i - zo - na
That I rode my first buck - ing out - law.
He could throw an - y man on the ranch - o, And
how that ca - bal - lo could paw. Well, I lays down my
Span - ish gui - tar - o, It was mon - ey I need - ed, by
jim. I hoists my - self in - to the sad - dle,
And I learned a - bout hors - es from him.

'Twas on the Horse Shoe in old Arizona
That I rode my first bucking outlaw.
He could throw any man on the rancho,
And how that caballo could paw.

Well, I lays down my Spanish guitaro,
It was money I needed, by jim.
I hoists myself into the saddle,
And I learned about horses from him.

Then I trails to a ranch in the rimrock,
Where broncos are thicker than men.
There was one needed tamin' right badly.
I needed a job there and then.

So I curls up my maguey so neatly,
And I hangs my old pack on a limb.
Then I slips through the bars quite discreetly,
And I learned about horses from him.

Next I wanders down into Sonora,
Where horses are horses, you bet.
There was good ones, bad ones, and tough ones,
And some of them darned hard to get.

A senorita wanted one for a plaything,
A black filled with hell to the brim.
She begs me with a sweet little smile-o,
And I learned about horses from him.

Then I drifts on up into Texas,
Where horses are wild, rough, and game,
And I says to the pinto I'm ridin',
"I'll get me a good one to tame."

So I takes to the hills and the canyons,
And I waits till I'm haggard and grim.
Then my loop settles down on a picture,
And I learned about horses from him.

Well, I rides up into Wyoming,
For I'd heard of a bad one called Bear,
And I heard they were offering money
To the guy that got on and stayed there.

Well, I found him, a bleary-eyed loco,
With ears that were pointed and thin.
And from the time I stepped in his middle
I learned about horses from him.

Then I stopped in Cheyenne for the rodeo.
To win me some money I tried.
A horse you all know, name was Steamboat,
That's the bugger I drew for to ride.

Now, something says, "Mister, you're crazy!"
But my bankroll says, "Don't you give in!"
Three jumps from the time the gates opened
I'd learned about horses from him.

Now, I've heard a lot about horses,
And I've rode 'em both large and small.
Sometimes I got on and I stayed there,
Sometimes what a hell of a fall!

But they's one horse I never have ridden,
It's Conscience they call it, by grim.
But I reckon when we have the last roundup
I'll learn about that horse from Him.

72

Button Willow Tree

This is a cowboy version of an old English sailor song. I learned it from Roy Mack at Leslie, Arkansas, in 1965. Roy had lived in Arizona through parts of the twenties, thirties, forties, and fifties, before moving to Arkansas. He has since moved to Oklahoma. Roy is best known in these parts for his playing of the Scottish bagpipes. He also plays the four-string and five-string banjo, fiddle, guitar, and some brass. During the depression he conducted a Mexican orchestra in Arizona. It turned out we knew many people and places in common in that state. When asked how he knew so many cowboys, he replied he had served as a bartender all over Arizona. Roy Mack was well acquainted with Romaine Lowdermilk, Powder River Jack, and Jules Verne Allen, all cowboy singers. He said there was one fellow who sang a hundred songs, all to the tune of "Strawberry Roan." "Button Willow Tree" Roy learned from the late Bob Fedder, an old-time Arizona cow puncher. Fedder, in turn, had learned it from an Australian puncher working in Arizona.

The mention of Gallup saddles in the last verse is interesting. George Gallup was a famous saddle maker at Pueblo, Colorado, prior to World War II. Another firm, R. T. Frazier, also manufactured a large line of saddles at Pueblo. I had a Frazier catalog as a boy but only have one page left from it, in a scrapbook. Frazier's had salesmen and dealers, and their saddles had a wide distribution. Many old-timers and some not so old here in Stone County, Arkansas, rode Frazier saddles. The Gallup saddle, Frazier's rival, I have never seen but have heard a lot about it since childhood.

BUTTON WILLOW TREE

The punch-er be-ing cold,— he went up to bed. He

asked for a can-dle to light his way to bed. She

showed him up to bed like a good girl__ should. He__

CHORUS

said, "Young la - dy, will you go__ to bed, too?" It's

home to your home,__ wher - ev - er you may be, It's

home to your home,__ to your own coun - try, Where the

oak and the ash and the but - ton wil - low tree And the

lark sings gai - ly in his own__ coun - try.

The puncher being cold, he went up to bed.
He asked for a candle to light his way to bed.
She showed him up to bed like a good girl should.
He said, "Young lady, will you go to bed, too?"

It's home to your home, wherever you may be,
It's home to your home, to your own country,
Where the oak and the ash and the button willow tree
And the lark sings gaily in his own country.

Early in the morning the puncher arose.
He filled her apron with silver and with gold.
"With silver in your pocket and gold in your purse,
If you get into trouble you can hire you a nurse."

Chorus:

"Oh, if it's a girl, pat her curly head
And remember the night when with me you went to bed.

Oh, if it's a girl, bounce her on your knee
And tell her of her daddy who is far across the sea.

"If it's a boy, call him Willie Lee,
And when he's twenty-one you can send him o'er to me.
With his boots and his chaps and his Gallup saddle new
I'll make him punch cows like his daddy used to do."

   Chorus:

73

Down in the Tules

This was written by Jim McElroy of Fox, Arkansas. Earlier, Jim ranched in New Mexico and punched cows in Texas, New Mexico, and Arizona. In Arkansas, Jim has been busy establishing his ranch, training cutting horses for the public, and calf and team roping at local rodeos. He is raising some fine cowboys of his own, his sons Shane and Lacey.

Many may be surprised to learn of the numerous western ranchers who have moved to the Ozarks. The local amateur rodeos all over Arkansas have plenty of Arkansas contestants who can ride and rope like nobody's business. The state championship high school rodeo at Conway draws some four hundred contestants annually. The economics of cost per acre, number of acres to run a cow, taxes, grass, water, climate, and many other considerations are behind this growth in ranching and its allied sports. Moreover, much of the Ozarks has some free range today. Going north a thousand miles, there is a trend toward ranching in northwestern Minnesota, my mother's old home and my early stomping grounds. Usually in that area ranching takes the form of grazing steers in summer for a gain on the lush grass. Some of these operators take in as much as forty sections (640 acres a section), and trainloads of steers come from as far as Colorado.

Getting back to Jim McElroy's song "Down in the Tules," it was the first mention of tules I'd heard since moving to Arkansas. *Tules* are the reed grasses that grow around bodies of water and along rivers in the West. The term is also used like *boondocks*. While the song "Windy Bill" (no. 5) advises to dally your rope (take a turn) according to the "California law," you will note that Jim disdains the dally style of roping and says, "We tie hard and fast, no dallies to throw, / Just pitch the slack and let 'er go!" Personally, I like the dally style for ranch work. You have more alternatives if there is a wreck, or you can take the rope off the saddle horn quickly and snub a cow to a tree without carrying a yoke rope. Also, you can give slack and not get jerked around so much.

Anyway, Jim McElroy is a cowboy's cowboy, and he's drunk enough coffee from a chuck wagon to float a pretty good ship.

DOWN IN THE TULES

Oh,— down in the tu - les,— a-wrang - lin' a -

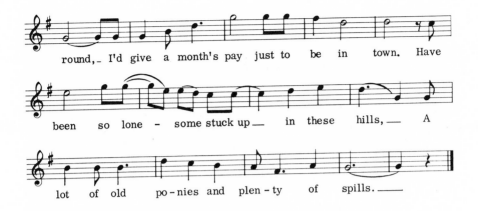

round,— I'd give a month's pay just to be in town. Have
been so lone - some stuck up — in these hills, — A
lot of old po - nies and plen - ty of spills. ——

Oh, down in the tules, a-wranglin' around,
I'd give a month's pay just to be in town.
Have been so lonesome stuck up in these hills,
A lot of old ponies and plenty of spills.

Riding brush by day and the draws by night,
Gathering those mavericks that stay out of sight,
Rope-burned hands and scratches on my face,
Always hoping that my rope won't break.

We tie hard and fast, no dallies to throw,
Just pitch the slack and let 'er go!
Sometimes there's a wreck, but through the dust ya see
You still have the brute wrapped up pretty neat.

Payday or not, I'm through for a spell.
I'm going to town to raise some hell.
Saturday night's over, it's back to the hills.
I've had enough drinkin' and fightin' for a spell.

Things will be better up there alone,
Back in the tules, the place I call home!

74

Tell Your Horse's Age

From young Shane McElroy comes this recitation of how to tell a horse's age by his teeth. Shane learned the poem from a 4-H Club instructor. This also appeared in the Billings, Montana, magazine *Bit and Spur* in 1948.

TELL YOUR HORSE'S AGE

To tell the age of any horse
Inspect the lower jaw, of course.
Two middle nippers you'll behold
Before the colt is two weeks old.

Before six weeks two more will come.
Twelve months, the corners cut the gum.
At two the middle nippers drop.
At three the second pair can't stop.

At four years old the side pair shows.
At five a full new mouth he grows.
Black spots will pass from view
At six from the middle two.

The side two, at seven years.
At eight we find the corners clear.
The middle nipper upper jaw,
At nine the black spots will withdraw.

At ten years old the side pairs are light.
At eleven, find the corners white.
As time goes on, the horseman knows,
The oval teeth three-sided grow.

They longer get, project before,
Till twenty, when we know no more.

75

Outlaw Dunny

Jim McElroy wrote "Outlaw Dunny" while breaking Quarter horses in New Mexico for a few months in 1969. While Jim was working in New Mexico, his wife, Johnnie, and his boys, Shane and Lacey, and a cousin did the cowpunching on their spread at Fox. When Jim returned to Arkansas, he brought this set of words he'd written for Shane's birthday.

OUTLAW DUNNY

I jingle the horses before daybreak,
And the cookie's a-hollering, "Hurry up, you're late."

So I jerk down my rope right hard on their tails,
Make a long swing toward the rope corrals.

But the cook he's a-rattling his pots and his pan.
Ole Dunny he hears him and leaves this fair land.

The rest are following, and they go out of sight.
I'm cussing the cook — can't he do anything right?

We go hard and fast on up through the draw,
But I'm gaining a little on the ole outlaw.

So I get 'em turned and headed in,
But the chuck is all cold and the biscuits are thin.

No more beans and a handful of rice,
A tin cup of coffee, but I thought it all right.

The boys were all saddled and ready to go,
And the boss he's saying, "Don't be so damn slow.

"Go catch ole Dunny, we're making a drive."
I knew I was in trouble, 'cause ole Dunny don't ride.

The rawhide snakes out and I missed the first throw,
But the next one I catch him just so so —

He paws the ground and rolls his glass eye.
I knew he was mean, that sure ain't no lie.

I got him all saddled, he stands real still.
The boss says, "Get on him," then I had a cold chill.

But I step up on him to let him explode.
Then he dives to the left and I get a spurhold.

I'm hanging on, sitting pretty tight,
But he throws a duck and turns to the right.

We goes up high, but I make one more round —
The next thing I knew I'd hit the ground.

I was bruised and skint from head to toe.
My shirt was all rags, and I felt mighty low.

The cook come running with needle and thread,
Took seventeen stitches to sew up my head.

My eye was black, my jaw all torn.
I didn't think I could stand much more.

"You can have this job," I says to the boss,
"I didn't hire out to ride no outlaw hoss.

"So give me my time, and I'll be on my way.
I won't need ole Dunny no more today."

76

The Fair at Batesland

In August of 1968 we visited sandhills rancher and former rodeo producer Walt Plugge of Bartlett, Nebraska. We discussed our project of collecting cowboy songs and poetry with Walt, and he promised to round up some old-time ranch music makers when we came through again in a couple of weeks. Since we were headed for South Dakota, Walt suggested we look up Jake Herman of Pine Ridge, South Dakota. Jake had been one of the earliest rodeo clowns and rode broncs for a long time. He was a full-blooded Sioux Indian in his eighties. Jake, in turn, recommended we see another Sioux cowboy, Raymond Runnels of Batesland, some thirty miles east of Pine Ridge.

This first original poem by Runnels, "The Fair at Batesland," brings into focus the days of spontaneous bucking contests and impromptu rodeos that were held all over the West. In the Southwest this often took the form of roping contests, while in the northern range states bronc riding seemed to be the favorite. Bronc ridings were held in connection with picnics, ball games, and other doings. Though surrounded by ranch country on all sides, the area right around Batesland is now mostly farmed. Runnels grew sad as he remembered the old open-range days. He said when he was a young

man there were lots of horses, more horses than cattle. Most of his friends wanted to be and had the opportunity to become bronc riders. Raymond Runnels passed on a month after we visited him, and old Jake Herman passed away in December of '68. Raymond's own comments on his area and this poem are worth reporting verbatim (from our tape made in August of 1968):

After the First World War, in our bleak country, they weren't too much for entertainment, so they had what they called victory celebrations. That's when our so-called sodbusters first moved in. We had all kinds of nationalities. We had Russians, Bohunks, and Germans moved in here and tore our grass country up and scattered our wild horses and shot our coyotes and took over. They had a post office and store at what they call Batesland now. That's what you might call our first civilization. Anyway, we gathered here all nationalities, and there were only a few of us Sioux. Me and a hostile friend of mine came here for the picnic. Well, there wasn't much for entertainment, so this crazy friend of mine and I suggested we'd ride a team of mules belonging to this German Lutheran preacher. Well, the preacher was a good sport, so he let us try his mules. One of these mules was a little sharp-eared mule, and the other was an old lop-eared mule that didn't look like much. So they had us draw straws to see who got which mule. We had to draw straws since we didn't have any coins to match. My partner drew the little sorrel mule, the spirited one, so he saddled her up and got on her and gouged her with his spurs, but she wouldn't buck a jump, just turned around and wrung her tail. So that spoiled that exhibition. So I was next on this old lop-earned mule, and I put my saddle on her and mounted, sorta grumbling. Didn't think I'd get any response either. Anyway, this is my version of it.

THE FAIR AT BATESLAND

I hit the town of Batesland, it was on the afternoon of the fair.
I entered in the bucking contest more for fun than on the square.
I stuck around about an hour with nothing else to do,
And every time I'd feel my nerve a-slippin' I'd go and drink a few.

Then finally I heard the band a-playin', out toward the track.
I went and threw my saddle on my old nag's back.
We rode out to the fairgrounds, a happy bunch of boys.
We seen a couple races and we heard a lot of noise.

Then finally the old judge hollered, "You riders come and line up for
    the draw."
I drawed an old brown mule 'bout as handsome as a squaw.
But when I stepped upon her, the crowd was mighty still.
A bunch of cowboys sat around and grinned as if they knew I'd spill.

But I pulled off my hat and hollered, and I hit her in the flank,
And I hooked her in the shoulder with a silver-mounted shank.
She left this world a-bawlin', she made one jump plumb grand.
I reached down for old safety and I grabbed a claw of sand.

Then the crowd they hollered, "Rotten, your riding's mighty cheap."
So I drifted to the mountains and got a job a-herdin' sheep.

77

The Cowboy's Prayer

This is another poem Raymond Runnels recited for us at his home in Batesland, South Dakota, the summer of 1968. About the poem Raymond says, "Our honorable Frank L. O'Rourke organized what they called 'Old-Time Cowboys Association.' At our first meeting they asked for any talents of any kind, so I offered 'The Cowboy's Prayer.' It was at our first breakfast. They hold a breakfast each year at Gordon, Nebraska, which is at the heart of the cattle industry. So this is my version."

THE COWBOY'S PRAYER

Guard me, Lord, while I'm a-riding 'cross the dusty range out there
From those dangers that are hiding on the trail so bleak and bare,
When around the herd I'm bogging in the darkness of the night,
Or across the mesa jogging with no known view in sight.

Won't You ride, Lord, there beside me when I see the danger sign.
Through storm and stampede guide me with Your hand a-holding mine.
Let that rope of sin ne'er trip me when to town for fun I go.
Let the Devil's herders skip me on their roundup here below.

May my trail be decked with beauty, with their blossoms ever love.
May I see a new wide duty ere I ride that range above.
Let me treat my foes with kindness, let my hand from blood be free,
And never through sheer blindness put that brand of Cain on me.

On that range of glory feed me, guide me over draw and swale,
And at last to Heaven lead me, up in the home corral.

78

Wild Horse Charlie

Raymond Runnels picked this poem up in his travels; he didn't know the author.

WILD HORSE CHARLIE

We were riding after dogies on the Crossbar Lazy B,
Where the foreman, Wild Horse Charlie, lit his pipe and said to me,
"I don't say as women may not be the proper dope,
But me, I'm more contented with my bronco and my rope."

He said, "I ain't a-knowin', partner, of this species none, you see,
But one damned dad-blamed adventure was a-plenty do for me."
He said, "She taught the school at Dobie, and I must state in comment wide
A better-lookin' critter never crossed the Great Divide."

He said, "I was losing all my senses, I went trailing her until
I finally asked the question, and she answered and said, 'I will.'
We had it all considered, we were to meet in Santa Fe
At the courthouse and be married on the twenty-third of May.

"I was at that wedding right on schedule, and I'll say
There's never been so many punchers seen in Santa Fe.
They were hanging round the courthouse, so I figured they were wise
To our nuptials and aimed to give us a surprise.

"So I kept a-waiting, waiting to claim my blushing bride,
When the sheriff he waved a message and he called us all inside.
'Twas just a little message from a town in Illinois
Reading 'On my way to Boston, say good-bye to all the boys.'

"And then the plot developed that this scheming little bait
Was engaged to all the punchers she could locate in the state.
They all had paid her money, each a hundred bucks a school,
Just to learn a woman's tricky and a puncher is just a fool!

"And then I ambled home in sadness, and I'm a-saying plain to you
That I'm all cut up on women, which is meaning I am through."
"Ha! The most of them are noble, good, and true," I weakly said,
But the foreman, Wild Horse Charlie, never spoke or turned his head.

191

79

When Uncle Sam's Doughboy Roped
a Wild Irish Rose

This song, to which we have no tune, was written by the late Rusty Holman of Marmarth, North Dakota. It was given to me by a young rancher, Dean Tarter of Camp Crook, South Dakota. Other songs by Rusty Holman, which unfortunately we were not able to find, include "That Is My Mother in Ireland," "I Want to Go Back to Montana," "Down Where the Colt Sucks," and "Just a Cowboy's Dream."

WHEN UNCLE SAM'S DOUGHBOY ROPED
A WILD IRISH ROSE

An Uncle Sam's doughboy roped a wild Irish rose,
Way over in Ireland where the sweet roses grow.
He could tell she was wild, as he could not get near.
She ran through the trees like a wild mountain deer.

Now, this wild Irish rose gets tamer each day,
Comes out in the evening and sings and she plays.
She wants to go away far out in the West,
Where the coyotes howl and the sage hens nest.
She wants to ride around those wild broomtails.
There they'll raise little doughboys where your friends never fail.

This Uncle Sam's doughboy was raised out in the West,
Where they rope and they ride 'em and top out the best.
Then this wild Irish rose then came galloping by,
So he roped and eloped, then made his fast tie.

Chorus:

80

Midnight

One of the most famous bucking horses of the twenties was the mighty Midnight, owned during the height of his bucking career by McCarty and Elliot of Chugwater, Wyoming, and Platteville, Colorado. Midnight was raised by Jim McNab of Macleod, Alberta, Canada, and was brought to the Calgary Stampede in 1924. Midnight unloaded all who drew him. He went into the bucking string of Peter Welsh of Calgary for a series of rodeos in Canada. Welsh went broke, and the horse wound up in Colonel Jim Eskew's Wild West show. Midnight and the smaller Five Minutes to Midnight, who also went to Eskew, proved too rank for the Eskew show of that time (in later years the Eskew show became a first-class Rodeo Cowboys Association–approved competitive rodeo). McCarty and Elliot bought the pair and used them at such great contests as Cheyenne and Fort Worth.

Midnight was a powerful, honest bucker that got tougher the further he went. Any straightaway horse that can unload the top riders year after year has got to be bucking really hard. This is the type of horse bronc riders like and respect. Five Minutes to Midnight also bucked them off coming and going, but he was fast, tricky, and smart. Midnight was retired to pasture in 1933, and Five was retired in 1946. Both these great broncs have been reburied at the Cowboy Hall of Fame in Oklahoma City. When Midnight died in 1936 the following poem, signed "a cowboy," was inscribed on his monument:

MIDNIGHT

Under this sod lies a great bucking hoss.
There never lived a cowboy he couldn't toss.
His name was Midnight, his coat black as coal.
If there's a hoss heaven, please, God, rest his soul.

81

Starlight

Starlight was a great bucker in the Harry Rowell string from Hayward, California, in the late thirties and first half of the forties. Starlight was a terrific bucking horse, and in 1940 only Fritz Truan was able to make the whistle on him. Starlight was foaled in Nevada, a sorrel with light mane and tail. My old buddy, the late Mitch Owens, rode Starlight at Livermore, California, in 1944 or '45. As sometimes happens on a truly great horse, Mitch didn't know how he got the job done, but the whistle finally blew and he was still up there. The author of this poem, Noah Henry, was a fine early-day rodeo contestant in all events. I never met Noah but knew his son, Carol Henry, who was a bulldogger and rodeo judge in the forties and a movie stunt man. I have often wondered if cowboy Noah Henry chose the name Carol for his son from the old song "Utah Carol."

"Starlight" appeared in the May, 1958, issue of *Hoofs and Horns* magazine.

STARLIGHT

It was the last day of the rodeo,
And in one of the stout corrals
There stood a big sorrel outlaw horse
A-lookin' at me and my pals.

He went by the name of Starlight,
A bronc as tough as gristle.
Few boys had ever rode that nag
Up to the judges' whistle.

He looked at us and seemed to say,
"I've got my aces backed!
And any that want to call my hand
Can feel me come untracked!"

The boy that drew Starlight that day
Was kinda pale and shaky,
For he knew before this day was o'er
He'd be bruised and hurt and achy.

They chuted Star up, they cinched him down,
And the sun shown low and round;

194

The cowboys stood in silent groups
And hunkered on the ground.

Whoever had named him Starlight
Had named the horse all wrong;
The way he jumped and sunned his sides
Made you think of a bad cyclone.

The old horse bawled his challenge;
The cowboy raked his flanks.
The old horse pawed the dusty air;
Then the cowboy gave his thanks.

For quicker than a lead balloon,
The cowboy landed — splat!
"I've had enough of him," he groaned,
"He sure don't travel flat."

82

The Bronco Buster

The words to "The Bronco Buster" come from Walter Plugge, Sr., of Bartlett, Nebraska. In 1950 I tried out a lot of bucking horses for Walter Plugge.
Also in 1954, '55, and '56 I got a lot of Plugge's horses at the Billy Veach
rodeos in Missouri and Arkansas.

Plugge himself is a long-time rancher in the Nebraska sandhills and has
been through several eras of the rodeo game in his lifetime. At his rodeos
in the late forties Plugge had buffalo riding as a regular contest event. Walt
bought a lot of horses from the Sioux in South Dakota and trailed several
bunches two hundred miles or more. In August of '68 Plugge had old-time
ranch-dance fiddler Stub Bently to his home to tape his music for us. It is
notable that Stub Bently lived in his father's original sod house till 1950.
While Walt Plugge, Sr., now gives his time to ranching, his sons, Walter,
Jr., and Jack, still take part in Nebraska rodeos as bull riders.

THE BRONCO BUSTER

I once knew a guy that thought he was swell,
He drifted out west where the cowpunchers dwell.

He wore a loud hat with a brim that was wide,
And a .45 gun hung down by his side.

His cayuse and saddle were branded the best,
His chaps and his bridle and all of the rest.

He blowed in at a place that was called Camp Custer
And let it be known that he was a bold bronco buster.

He tooted and spouted and gave it out fair
He could ride any critter that ever wore hair.

Now, the boys at the ranch soon heard of this gent,
And down to Camp Custer a bunch of them went.

They brought along Sue, a flea-bitten roan,
The worst bucking bronco that ever was known.

Not a man from the west, the north, or the east
Could stay on the back of the old buckin' beast.

They soon found this duffer that said that he could ride,
Took him out to the corral where old Susan was tied.

They strapped on a saddle and told him to mount,
And if he pulled leather it sure wouldn't count.

When old Sue humped her back the boys gave a yell,
And that guy left the saddle like a bat out of hell.

He made seven turns in the air, it was said,
And lit on the ground on the back of his head.

One more bold buster who said that he could —
But evidence shows that he didn't make good.

83

My Stetson Hat

This poem has circulated over the years in the old *Hoofs and Horns* magazine, when it was published by Ma Hopkins in Tucson, Arizona, and more recently in *Western Horseman*. I have been singing it to the tune of "Soldier's Joy" for a good many years.

MY STETSON HAT

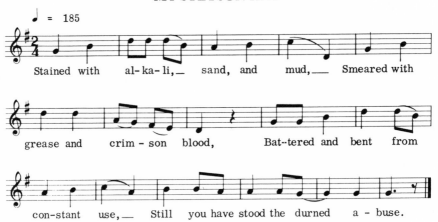

Stained with alkali, sand, and mud,
Smeared with grease and crimson blood,
Battered and bent from constant use,
Still you have stood the durned abuse.

A true companion through all these years,
Fanning broncs and longhorn steers,
I dedicate this to the old gray lid
For the useful things the old hat did.

Coaxing a smoldering fire in the cold,
Panning dust in search of gold,
Pushed up big and knocked down flat
Has been the lot of my Stetson hat.

Carrying oats to a spooky bronc,
Security for drinks at a honky-tonk,
Mistreated, abused on a roundup spree,
Walked-on, tromped-on old J.B.

Fighting fire in a clapboard shack,
Stopping wind in an open crack,
Been everywhere that a hat can go,
Forty-eight states and Mexico.

I've grown old as we trailed along,
While you, old hat, are going strong.
You've been a good pal through all of that,
You dirty old gray Stetson hat.

84

The Girl I Left in Missouri

Raymond Sanders gave me this song about the Missouri man who goes to Colorado and whose girl at home marries someone else. Other versions of the same song have the man leaving Tennessee and going to Missouri, or leaving Ireland and coming to America. Romaine Lowdermilk, the Arizona cowboy singer, sings it as "The Girl I Left in Texas."

THE GIRL I LEFT IN MISSOURI

My parents treated me kindly, having no one but me.
My mind was bent on rambling, with them I couldn't agree.
My mind was bent on rambling, which vexed my heart most sore,
To leave my aged parents, to see them nevermore.

200

There lived a wealthy old farmer in the country mild or nigh.
He had a lovely daughter, on her I cast an eye.
I asked her if it made any difference if I sailed o'er the plain.
She said it made no difference, if I'd return again.

We kissed, shook hands, and we parted, and I left that gal behind.
I landed in Denver city, boys, it's Pikes Peak I was bound.
Money and work was plentiful, lots of pretty girls I could find,
But the girl I left in Missouri was an object on my mind.

As I went out a-walking down on the public square
I heard the mail hack rattling, the mailman met me there.
He handed to me a letter which gave me to understand
The girl I left in Missouri had married another man.

I read a few lines further, and I found these words were true.
Then turning myself around and around, I didn't know what to do.
I'll spend the rest of my life in rambling, card playing I'll cast o'er.
For the girl I left in Missouri it makes my heart most sore.

85

'Longside of the Santa Fe Trail

The first person I heard sing this song was Powder River Jack Lee. This was in Arizona in 1944. Another Arizona cowboy who sang it was Jules Verne Allen, whose book of songs, *Cowboy Lore,* was listed in the catalogs of several saddle makers in the thirties and forties. For example, Hamley and Company of Pendleton, Oregon, listed this book in their 1941 catalog (they also advertised *Songs of the Open Range,* a collection by Ina Sires, and *Cowboy Songs,* edited by John A. and Alan Lomax). George B. German remembers Romaine Lowdermilk's rendition from the twenties, when he worked for Lowdermilk in Wickenburg, Arizona. My friend Roy Mack, the bagpiper who spent so many years in Arizona and heard all those singers, once asked me to sing "'Longside of the Santa Fe Trail" for him and then reminisced about Verne Allen's performance of it (the version given below comes from the Allen recording). That walking archive of folksong, Raymond Sanders, also remembers parts of "The Santa Fe Trail" but has a more elaborate "yo ho" after the verses than do the rest.

Jules Verne Allen was one of the original singing cowboys on records and radio. Roy Mack, who knew Allen in Arizona in the twenties and thirties, says he was a "cowboy sure enough." Jules Verne Allen probably got a lot of good old cowboy songs into circulation by his singing. From what I can gather, Allen, Powder River Jack, Romaine Lowdermilk, and George B. German shared a lot of songs in common in Arizona in the twenties. Early radio singer John White was also learning from Romaine Lowdermilk at the same time, before taking to the airwaves.

Some of the words in the third verse got changed a little. There are versions that mention "fruffles and sweetin'," also "fruffles and beadin'." In the last line of that verse they have, variously, "stampeding," "Sam sweetin's," and "Sam beatin' " (the last is an old term for whiskey). It's a nice old song that I enjoy and get sort of a kick out of.

'LONGSIDE OF THE SANTA FE TRAIL

Say, pard, have you sight-ed a schoon-er Way

out on — the San-ta Fe Trail?—— It may get here·
Mon–day or— soon-er———— With a wa-ter— keg
tied to its tail.——— There's Pap- py and Ma—
— on— the mule— seat——— And some-where a-
long by— the— way——— A lit-tle tow-head-ed
gal— on— a— pin - to———— Jest a-gan-glin'— for
old— San - ta— Fe,——— Yo ho,———
——— jest a-gan - glin'— for old San- ta— Fe.———

Say, pard, have you sighted a schooner
Way out on the Santa Fe Trail?
It may get here Monday or sooner
With a water keg tied to its tail.
There's Pappy and Ma on the mule seat
And somewhere along by the way
A little tow-headed gal on a pinto
Jest a-ganglin' for old Santa Fe,
Yo ho, jest a-ganglin' for old Santa Fe.

203

I saw her ride down the arroyo
Way back on the Arkansas sand,
With a smile like an acre of sunflowers
And a little brown quirt in her hand.
She mounted her pinto so airy
And rode like she carried the mail.
Her eyes nigh set fire to the prairie
Way out on the Santa Fe Trail,
Yo ho, way out on the Santa Fe Trail.

Well, I know a gal down by the border
I'd ride to El Paso to sight.
I'm acquainted with the high-flying order
And I sometimes kiss some girls good night.
But law, they're all fruffles and beadin'
And afternoon tea by the pail
Compared to the sort of Sam sweetin'
That I got on the Santa Fe Trail,
Yo ho, that I got on the Santa Fe Trail.

Well, I don't know her name on the prairie,
When you're huntin' one girl it's unwise.
And it's shorter from Hell to Hilary
Than it is on the Santa Fe line.
I'll maybe reach Plummer by sundown,
Where a camp may be made in the swale,
And I'll come on a gal with a pinto
Camped 'longside the Santa Fe Trail,
Yo ho, camped 'longside the Santa Fe Trail.

86

The Sweeter the Breeze #1

From Chip Morris comes this cross between a verse and a saying that has been used in whole or in part by numerous rodeo announcers over the years. I have been around Chip off and on since 1943 and have heard him recite this countless times, just before a bronc came out of the chutes. Chip Morris started in the rodeo game in 1926 as a bareback bronc rider. He later took up saddle bronc riding and bulldogging and finally broke out with announcing and a trained horse act. His great trick and "drama" horse, Fox, was known all over the rodeo world. Old black Fox died in Mountain View, Arkansas, about 1953.

Chip's younger brother, Pee Wee Morris, was the Rodeo Cowboys Association world's champion bull rider in 1946. They both rodeoed in the unorganized (for the cowboys) days of rodeo, the late twenties and the thirties, and they spent a lot of time working Wild West (exhibition) shows as well as contests. Pee Wee suffered a badly broken leg in Fort Worth, Texas, in 1948, when a bull stepped on him. Many bone grafts and operations and two or three years later he managed to get back into competition. At New York's Madison Square Garden a bull broke his leg again in the chute, and Pee Wee finally quit. He turned to bartending.

When I moved to Stone County, Arkansas, in 1954, Chip had been here about a year and was running a bunch of steers on the free range in the Sunnyland area. We got to some of the same rodeos the next several years, till he left Stone County and went on the road with his horse acts as part of a circus. At the present time he operates a riding, training, and boarding stable, the End of the Trail Ranch, on West Baseline Road in Little Rock, Arkansas. Chip still breaks horses, and the last time I saw him he had a couple of snuffy ones to ride.

THE SWEETER THE BREEZE #1

Take a deep seat and a faraway look,
Keep him between your knees.
The higher he goes, the sweeter the breeze.
Keep your mind in the middle and let both ends flop!

87

The Sweeter the Breeze $^\#2$

Some years back I made up a poem about bareback bronc riding that used Chip's great words "the higher he goes, the sweeter the breeze." This little rhyme gives a bit of advice on bareback riding style. Bareback, like saddle bronc, riding is scored by the judges according to how well the horse bucks and how well the rider spurs. The spurs must be dull and the rowels turn fast so they will not harm the horse. The idea is for a rider to compete in sticking his neck out, taking chances by keeping his feet moving. This takes a lot of skill, where just sitting there like a dummy does not, particularly. In the saddle event the rider's feet move back and forth from the horse's shoulders to the cantle of the saddle. In bareback riding the past thirty years or more the style has been to spur ahead throughout the ride. It usually works something like this: The rider marks the horse out, that is, qualifies by having his spurs over the point of the horse's shoulder the first jump. If his toes are out as the rhyme suggests, he is less apt to miss him out and garner a goose egg (zero) from the judges. When he gets the feel of the horse in a few jumps, he will jerk his knees, which rolls his spurs up the horse's neck at the hardest jerk of the horse's jump. When the horse's front feet hit the ground, the rider's feet drop into place in front of the shoulder and start another cycle. The press of competition has brought about some truly wild and spectacular styles of riding. Some can throw their feet straight up in the air in front of them and drop them back in every jump. While all this is going on, the rider keeps one handhold on a rigging that is cinched around the horse. The other hand must stay free from the chute to the whistle and not touch the horse or rigging.

The first bareback bronc I ever rode at a rodeo was at Caliente, Nevada, the Fourth of July in 1943. This must have been one of the last places they still rode bareback horses with a loose rope instead of the present-day rigging. That first one bucked like the dickens, and I rode him all right. It might have saved me twenty-three years of knocking big holes in the ground if he'd bucked me off that first time. Some of the names I remember from that rodeo are Bill, Slick, and Cordy Lamb, one of the rodeoing Fanchers, and local buckaroos Stinky and Herb. There was also a young fellow from Hurricane, Utah, whose name I forgot, who rode bareback pretty good. Cordy Lamb made a bareback ride on a tricky bucking mule that ducked and dived as he bucked. Cordy hooked him high on the neck with both feet and deliberately crossed over and spurred with both feet on one side of the mule's neck, then switched to both feet on the other side. Needless to say,

my young eyeballs popped. There was another rider in this family at the same rodeo, Bill Lamb, who was bucked off and kicked in midair by one of their wild bareback horses. He came out with a broken leg.

While many present-day contestants think they are the wildest bunch there ever was, there have long been many wild-hooking bareback riders. In the late thirties and early forties Kid Fletcher, Carl Dossey, and Dutch Martin could turn handsprings on any kind of bareback horse. I have heard that Dutch Martin jerked his knees so high on a bareback horse that he broke his nose with his knees several times. In the forties and into the fifties Jimmy "Slugger" Sloan of Phoenix made hair-raising rides, as did Sonny Tureman, Wag Blessing, Gail "Boston Blackie" Orr, Jack Spurling, and Gene Rambo. According to Duncan Brown and Tommy Cahoe, whom I heard discussing wild bareback riders in 1949, the wildest-spurring man of all was John Penick. John was known mainly in California. I saw him a few times before he quit, and he was just a shade out west. Bud Spealman, the 1946 champ, and movie cowboy Dick Farnsworth could also drag it through them. This list could go on and on, but here is my verse.

THE SWEETER THE BREEZE #2

Turn your toes out, jerk your knees.
The higher he goes, the sweeter the breeze.
The more he bucks, the more you spur.
All I want to see is flying fur!

Glenn Ohrlin on Flaxie, Nashville, Tennessee, October, 1954. Photo by Stanley E. Hime.

88

Keep Your Saddle Tight

In 1964 John Schmidt, then of the University of Illinois, sent me some tapes of early cowboy recording artist Carl "Doc" Sprague. Sprague, a Texas man who recorded "When the Work's All Done This Fall" and other real cowboy songs back between 1925 and 1929, had one song I got a kick out of. The whole tape was a pleasure to hear, and I hope Mr. Sprague, who now lives in Bryan, Texas, doesn't mind my crediting him with this.

KEEP YOUR SADDLE TIGHT

know that it's good and tight.

A bunch of foaming mustangs
Charging around the corral,
You know just how to ride one,
No need for me to tell.
So if you get the right one
And you're sure that you are right,
Don't step into that saddle
Till you know that it's good and tight.

Of all the crazy critters
You ever tried to halter,
A woman is the worst one
When she's prancing around the altar.
But if you get the right one
And you're sure that you are right,
Don't step into that saddle
Till you know that it's good and tight.

89

My Old Pinto Pal

"My Old Pinto Pal" has the words "oh, give me the life on the prairie" in the third verse, and the lady who sang it for us, Nellie Westerskow of Buffalo, South Dakota, had sure enough spent her life on the prairie. Kay and I were taping rancher Dick Smith at his winter house in Buffalo, when Mrs. Westerskow came over to listen. She wound up singing one herself. This song is probably from a record (possibly by Gene Autry) from the early forties. When Harding County residents sing of the prairie and roundups and branding corrals, they are singing about something they know well. Nellie Westerskow's own obvious enjoyment of the song made it seem real nice. We remember this episode in our collecting with affection.

MY OLD PINTO PAL

I'm head-in' once more for the prai - rie, To be
back in the sad - dle a - gain,
Throw my old rope on a cow - horn Way
out on the wide o - pen plain. Once
more to ride in the round - up,
Head - ing for the brand - ing cor - ral, A-

211

strad-dle old Pin - to, my faith - ful, Yip-pee -

i - o, my old pin - to pal.

I'm headin' once more for the prairie,
To be back in the saddle again,
Throw my old rope on a cowhorn
Way out on the wide open plain.
Once more to ride in the roundup,
Heading for the branding corral,
Astraddle old Pinto, my faithful,
Yippee-i-o, my old pinto pal.

Once more to sit around the campfire,
Gaze at the skies above,
Listening to songs of rangers,
Refrain from guitar that I love.
Oh, sing me "The Red River Valley,"
My favorite's "The Home on the Range."
You may have your delights in the city,
While I take my rough life on the plains.

Oh, give me the life on the prairie,
Out where the air is like wine,
Out where the coyotes are howling
In the good old summertime.
The fragrance so sweet from the willows,
My life's a jubilee,
A-ridin' an old cowpunch saddle
Out over the sagebrush sea.

Old pal, I know you're leg-weary,
Many years you've been on the trail.
We've shared our hardships together,
Not once have I known you to fail.
Old pal, I'm giving you freedom,
You're dearer to me than a gal.
Farewell, old boy, I'll sure miss you,
Old faithful, my old pinto pal.

90

Chuck-Wagon Races

This poem about the famous chuck-wagon races at the Canadian rodeos, or "stampedes," was given to me by Jack Lauder of Calgary and Innisfail in Alberta, Canada. Jack has wintered in Timbo, Arkansas, since 1968. We first met Jack Lauder at the chuck-wagon races staged by Cliff Claggett at South Sioux City, Nebraska, in August of 1968. I was announcing the event, and Jack was driving wagons in the pony division as well as with the big Thoroughbreds. At that time Lauder had been in the business for forty years, first as an outrider (the rider who loads the camp stove on the back of the wagon and follows through the race) and then as a driver. Through the years he contested in all other rodeo events and was one of the best at handling wild horses in the wild-horse race. He also worked at packing dudes into Canadian Rockies wilderness areas and hunting coyotes for bounty on the prairies. He was ranch-raised at Innisfail, Alberta.

The chuck-wagon races were begun at the famous Calgary Stampede in 1923. The first wagons were actual roundup wagons from Canadian ranches, pulled by their regular four-horse teams. As the purses grew and the sport became more competitive, lighter wagons were used, and the teams were Thoroughbred racehorses off the tracks. There are some hair-raising spills and wrecks from time to time. It really is a wild spectacle, three or four wagons with four horses each, plus outriders following. It looks like a whole herd running off down the track. Cliff Claggett says chuck-wagon races actually began on the Alberta and Saskatchewan prairies in the days of big pool roundups, when more than one wagon would be on the same roundup. Cliff claims they would sometimes race for the best campsite after breaking camp in the morning. Each cook would try to be first to reach the best spot for his wagon as they moved about the country working cattle.

The poem given here was written by a wagon man whose name Jack Lauder has forgotten. However, all the men mentioned in the poem are his personal friends, and all have made their mark in this wild event. Kamp, mentioned in the sixth verse, was one of Jack's best wagon horses. There is another poem about the chuck-wagon races at Swan River, Manitoba, that is sung to the tune of "Red River Valley," but we have been unable to find the words.

In Canada, the names Lauder, Dorchester, Glass, Cosgrove, and many others have appeared in chuck-wagon racing for two generations and sometimes more. All the Canadians I have met have been sportsmen who love a good contest. They also seem strong on partying, giving toasts and poems, and generally enjoying themselves. All my Canadian friends — cowboys, ranchers, wagon racers — have had a firm background of ranch and farm work, which their sports, riding, roping, and driving, grew out of. Another trait I find compatible is a liking for Charlie Russell's art, Robert Service's poems, and bagpipe music. Many Canadians are also familiar with the music of the late Jimmie Rodgers. Cliff Claggett tells of seeing Jimmie Rodgers in Canada at the height of his singing career. Rodgers was a favorite with the cowboys and ran some with Harry Knight and other top hands.

(Since the above was written, Cliff Claggett, of Cache Creek, British Columbia, Canada, was badly injured in a chariot race at Morris, Manitoba, late in July, 1971, and died of those injuries in September, 1971.)

CHUCK-WAGON RACES

Come gather round the wagon, we'll sing a little song
Of the wagon racing, it will not take us long.
There's thrills and spills and doctor bills, we take them in our stride.
Here's to the wagon racing — it is a mighty ride.

We wreck them, yes, aplenty, these wagons are not toys.
They're a little rough on horses and mighty hard on boys.
They come out just a-skidding and a-rollin' mighty fast.
Usually away up in the lead is the big guy, Ronnie Glass.

There's another outfit running with a bay team on the lead.
You can tell the way they're running they've really got some speed.
When he comes out from the barrels, he really turns the crank.
It's none other than the guy around here called old Hank.

Dorchester comes out mighty fast and rolls along the way.
He's here to have a little fun and to make it pay.
He hasn't any worries — if he has, they don't last long.
He's the kind of guy that likes his fun, we call him Playboy Tom.

Now, there's another guy around that goes on the old spree.
His home's up in the wagon, it's plain for us to see.
He really comes a-rackin', this little guy called Hal.
He'll make a rough-and-ready man for any little gal.

There's another wagon man by the name of Lauder,
And when Kamp racks the wagon home, no man could be prouder.
And when Jack wanders home, to do there's just one thing,
Take old Kamp and himself and soak in the sulphur spring.

There's a big, dark, handsome guy by the name of Bill.
Once in a while he has tough luck and takes a little spill.
Though he's back in the running, his shoulder's a little sore.
The wagon bug has hit him, and he's right back there for more.

Now, there's a guy around here with a happy smile.
He can really drive a wagon for the half a mile.
Phil H. Gooch they call him, that is his full name.
His smile and wagon driving should win for him great fame.

Another guy around here who is a friend to all,
He really comes out ready, he's never known to stall.
Now, in our estimation, in Claggett there's no flaw.
He drives a wagon outfit, and he calls it Chickasaw.

The boy that really rolls 'em, he's really out for fame,
They mistake him for Ronnie Glass, but he's really Russell Swain.
There's another guy that rolls them as well as Russ, you know.
Carruthers drives three abreast, and the one that leads ain't slow.

Now, Harry's just a cowboy, he'd make a darn good pal.
The waitresses all like him, and he calls them all his gal.
Now, Lem's a little nervous when there are girls around,
But he guarantees good service upstairs or on the ground.

Buzz he quit the horses and went to riding bikes.
He's a wild and woolly driver, especially when he's tight.
The guy they call McCullough, he sure is not a squeaker.
He's a handy guy to have along 'cause he is the head speaker.

Now, there are two fine ladies, there's Iris and there's Kay.
The best you'll get in any clan you find along the way.
Now, they have got a job to do, on wagons they keep time,
And when their husbands take to drink they never seem to mind.

Down around the trailer there's Faye and Flo to cook.
Some might call them ladies, but we just call them crooks.
But still they put up good grub, 'cause we're gaining weight.
We never have been hungry nor had a bellyache.

George he's quite a ladies' man, and Dale's a little slow.
He'll really come a-rackin' in another year or so.
The twins they never bother about the woman clan.
Just ask them and you'll hear them say, "I'm no ladies' man."

Now, there's a little lady that's oh so fine and grand.
She's always got a smile for you or lend a helping hand.

She's always very busy on the rodeos.
It's not hard to guess her name, it's Edna, we all know.

Now my song is ending, my throat is getting hoarse.
There's just three names to mention, we know them, yes, of course.
There's Deryle, Doyle, and Pancake Pete, the Bow-and-Arrow Gang.
In the crying room you'll find them almost any time.

91

The Days of the Past Are Gone

Also from Jack Lauder comes this bit of sentiment. At one time he could recite the entire poem, which was a good bit longer than what is given here. Jack learned this in Canada, where it was known by other cowboys and wagon men. I especially like his last verse and would like to find the rest of the poem.

THE DAYS OF THE PAST ARE GONE

The harness hangs in the old log barn,
The wagon rots in the shed.
And the horses are gone for fox meat,
And the days of the past are dead.

For we've caught up with the Joneses now,
With a fine new car and a truck.
It costs us lots of sweat and toil,
But some folks called it luck.

Them were the days when
We were young and able.
We rode good broncs, and we had fast dogs
And beefsteak on the table.

92

Canuck's Lament

There was no title for this poem when Jack Lauder passed it on to us, so I tacked "Canuck's Lament" on it. The author is J. K. Trout, formerly of Black Diamond, Alberta, but now living in British Columbia. The two men who are mentioned, Reg Kesler and Harry Vold, are big in Canadian rodeo and also bring their great strings of rodeo stock to the United States. At the time this poem was written, Kesler and Vold were together, but now they have their own outfits. The story seems to leave a lot unsaid.

CANUCK'S LAMENT

When you're sitting around in a dirty old shack,
You can't keep your mind from wanderin' back
To the happy old days that were sunny and bright,
When we hunted all day and gambled all night,

When horses changed hands at the flip of a card,
But nobody cared 'cause they didn't come hard.
At the roll of the dice your gun might be gone,
But spring was just handy, so it wouldn't be long

Till we round up a rough string and dummy them out
And see what we had for the cowboys so stout
And then get a contract from Kesler and Vold
And forget about days that were foggy and cold.

Then after the shows they'd pick out the best.
We'd break out a few and fox-meat the rest
And figure the profit and balance the book
And think of new suckers we maybe could rook.

Well, you had the bird, and I guess so have I.
Now life's gone rotten — who cares if we cry?
For our fair-weather friends are all over the hill,
Who missed on the chase but were in on the kill.

And though they curse and cry we were bad,
It proves in the end all the guts that they had,
For they got one thousand or more miles away
Before anything bad about us they would say.

And maybe in the end they won't think it is funny,
Bogged down in the muskeg without any money.
Now, when you think it all over, now, ain't it a curse
That we harbored such scum, but it could have been worse.

But the quarrels that we had I kinda forgot,
And I believe in the end we're the best of the lot.

93

Circuit Rider's Home

Johnny Baker, a young saddle bronc rider who also ranches at Edwards, Missouri, wrote this song, "Circuit Rider's Home," and his other rodeo songs for his cowboy friends. Twelve of his songs can be heard on an LP he produced himself, *Songs of the Rodeo*. The record can be purchased by mail from Johnny Baker, Route 2, Edwards, Missouri. Johnny has also sold his LP through *Rodeo Sports News* and other rodeo periodicals. He says some of his rodeo buddies know his songs better than he does. While his rodeoing is confined mainly to Missouri and Iowa because of his ranching activities, he has in the past spent his trick at the wheel when the highway was his home for long spells. Johnny has also done some collecting of cowboy poetry from friends and rodeo publications. Many of his buddies are from Wyoming, where Johnny cowboyed in his early working years. Mike Hubbell, a Wyoming bronc rider who is presently doing well at many rodeos, has written some rodeo rhymes that Johnny sent to me that are pretty good.

Incessant travel is the way of life for cowboys who make their living on the road contesting at rodeos. "Circuit Rider's Home" gives the feeling of the rodeo hands' life very well. The places and names in the song are familiar ones to rodeo folks. Trail's End, mentioned in one verse, was voted the best bucking horse at the 1959 National Finals Rodeo at Dallas, where the stock was the tops from twenty-six rodeo strings. While Trail's End has been ridden several times, he sure set plenty of guys afoot, too, including many champions. At his best he looks nearly impossible. When the late Oral Zumwalt owned him, Trail's End would walk over to Zumwalt to be unsaddled after unloading his rider. He was gentle in all ways, except he wouldn't stand for a rider. Sandhills was a good horse in the Beautler brothers' outfit from Elk City, Oklahoma. He was known for his spectacular first extrahigh jump out of the chute.

CIRCUIT RIDER'S HOME

220

come and then I'm gone,_ don't be-lieve in stay-in' long. The high-

VERSE 1

_ way is a cir - cuit rid-er's home. ____ I

ro-de-o__ up in_ the Rock-y Moun-tains_ And on_

_ the plains where the wind gives a mourn-ful moan, Where

sand and tum - ble-weeds keep on a - blow-in' A - cross_

_ the high-way that I call my home.

Well, you know I have no permanent address,
This rodeo cowboy's on the roam.
I come and then I'm gone, don't believe in stayin' long.
The highway is a circuit rider's home.

I rodeo up in the Rocky Mountains
And on the plains where the wind gives a mournful moan,
Where sand and tumbleweeds keep on a-blowin'
Across the highway that I call my home.

Chorus:

I rode old Trail's End in Miles City.
I still can hear that welcome whistle blow.
I thought I'd hit my lick, but what a pity
When Sandhills bucked me down in Broken Bow.

Chorus:

Now, don't forget the gay life and the ladies
Who thrill to the man that rides that old bronco.
He whispers lies and tells them, "Someday maybe,"
But then he's gone and headed down the road.

    Chorus:

Johnny Baker bronc riding in California, 1968.

94

Average Rein

In "Average Rein" Johnny Baker shows one of the big problems that beset bronc riders. When a saddle bronc rider gets a horse in the draw (all rodeo stock is drawn by number for the contestant), the first thing he tries to find out from other riders, if he doesn't know, is how much rein the horse will take. Some horses drop their heads low when they buck, which the bronc rider must allow for or be pulled forward and maybe off by the single braided-rope rein that attaches to a plain halter he is allowed to use. Other broncs, particularly high-kicking horses, might buck with their heads up and not take much rein. For most riders an average rein is grasped about six inches back of the saddle horn, though some may have a bit shorter or longer average, according to their riding style. Riders like Winston Bruce and Casey Tibbs, former world champions, didn't pull on the rein much and could ride with a long rein. Others might get the job done with more muscle and need to pull hard on the rein. A *head-fighting horse,* such as mentioned in the seventh verse of this song, might take an average rein for a ways, then suddenly root his head or throw his head back and look you in the face. This is pretty miserable for most riders, if not all. In the sixth verse Johnny says, "I'd pitch him the rein." When a rider does this, he holds the rein out in front of himself for balance but does not pull himself down with it. This makes it plain he is riding chiefly on balance rather than main strength and awkwardness, and it is real pretty.

Another term that may be unfamiliar to the reader is *committee,* which is the committee- or association-prescribed saddle for contest bronc riding. *Popped me from the swells* means he lost his leg grip on the swell of the saddle, which is difficult to regain. When the horse rears or fights in the chute, or *rattles the cage,* this is dangerous business for the rider trying to mount. Probably as many bronc riders are hurt in the chutes trying to get a seat on a chute rattler as are bunged up in arena falls. A bad chute fighter is guaranteed to make any rider a bit nervous.

AVERAGE REIN

♩ = 110

Some cow-boys once told me a-bout_ the horse I drew, The

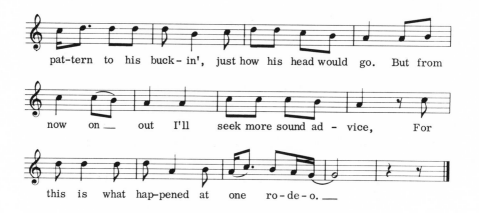

pat-tern to his buck-in', just how his head would go. But from

now on — out I'll seek more sound ad - vice, For

this is what hap-pened at one ro-de-o. —

Some cowboys once told me about the horse I drew,
The pattern to his buckin', just how his head would go.
But from now on out I'll seek more sound advice,
For this is what happened at one rodeo.

I drew a rangy and stout-lookin' bay,
They called him big Lumberjack.
My old committee I eased into place
Upon the old bronco's back.

The cowboys helpin' me down on the horse
Said, "He takes an average rein."
So I measured it off and marked the spot
With a piece of the old bronco's mane.

With the utmost of care I eased in the saddle,
For fear he might rattle the cage.
Then I swallowed my pride as I hollered, "Outside!"
And held to my average rein.

As up and out he came, he tried to pop me loose,
But I held my spurs up in his shoulders tight.
And with every high, rollin' jump that he made
He'd beller with all of his might.

He'd kick out behind, I'd pitch him the rein
And give the old bronco some slack.
Then with his next jump to the cantle I'd go.
Lord, I really rode old Lumberjack.

Well, I really got with him and spurred with the rhythm.
That's when he took to fightin' his head.

As he popped me from the swells with my head aimed toward the ground,
I recalled what my buddies had said:

"Well, John, he takes an average rein."
He put on quite a show as he bowed his head low,
And me with an average rein.

95

Ballad of Billy the Bull Rider

This song about Billy, a young bull rider, also composed by Johnny Baker, describes about the worst that can happen in the arena. While deaths in the arena are not frequent, they do happen, and bull riding has accounted for several. The phrase *taking a death wrap* in the fourth verse might be a mystery to some. When a bull rider sticks his hand into the handhold of the braided bull rope and it is pulled tight, the loose end of the rope is laid across the palm of his riding hand and one wrap made around the hand to prevent the rope from loosening. Some riders have been known to take an extra, or "death," wrap through determination not to have the rope jerked away from them. If they make the whistle, they unwrap their hand and jump off. If the bull bucks them off, however, they may be hung up in their rope. A rider hung up on a fighting-mad bull is in trouble, and even one wrap gets a rider in trouble pretty often.

BALLAD OF BILLY THE BULL RIDER

♩ = 190

Bil - ly was rid - ing at Tuc - son, He was
up — for the eve - ning show. _____ He
took his sweet-heart to watch him ride The bulls —
— at the big ro - de - o. _____

Billy was riding at Tucson,
He was up for the evening show.
He took his sweetheart to watch him ride
The bulls at the big rodeo.

He sat with her in the grandstand
Until his time came to ride.
He said, "You stay here and don't worry, dear,
I'll soon be back by your side."

As he rose up to leave her
He kissed her and whispered good-bye.
But little they knew it would be their last kiss,
Tonight poor Billy would die.

Billy's sweetheart was tremblin'
When it was announced he would ride.
Billy eased down on old Number Seven,
Took a death wrap and hollered, "Outside!"

The bull jumped high and kicked over
And swung his big horns to and fro.
He jerked poor Billy from off of his back
And straight o'er the horns Bill did go.

227

But poor Billy's hand wouldn't come loose,
And as the bull spun around
He'd swing back his head and hook with his horns,
Till Billy lay limp on the ground.

A hush now fell over the grandstand,
And a young girl started to cry.
She knew there wasn't a thing she could do
But stand there and watch the boy die.

When Billy died her life ended,
And it hurt the poor girl so.
She still wakes from dreams while watching her Billy
Ride bulls at the big rodeo.

96

Blue Bell Bull

Another song about rodeo's bucking Brahmas is Johnny Baker's tale of old Number Three, the champion bull Blue Bell. More bulls are known by number (all rodeo bulls are numbered) than by name, but many have imaginative or descriptive names — Popeye, Spillum, Dirty Gertie, Sky-High, Droopy, Squarehead, Rainbow, Little Joe, Iron Ore, Panther, Meat-head, and Big Bad John, for example. When Blue Bell overalls started making Wrangler cowboy jeans, the company advertised in all rodeo and horse periodicals and outfitted many rodeo clowns with baggy jeans with *Wranglers* in bold letters on the seat. At the same time, the name Blue Bell or Wrangler was given to more than one rodeo bull. This continued a custom, as there have been bucking horses named Levi Strauss and Lee Overalls after the other two main brands of cowboy blue jeans.

In writing this song Johnny Baker is following the tradition of Curley Fletcher's "Strawberry Roan" and "Bad Brahma Bull," Powder River Jack's "Preacher Dunn," and someone's "Zebra Dun." All of these are about tough bucking animals. The cowboy has respect and genuine affection for those four-legged adversaries that really play the game and make it interesting. If one reads the words to this song carefully, he will find an outstanding description of the sensations of being mounted on a really rank bull. The first verse gives an idea of the heady feeling of a young fellow making the pay window by winning the first go-round. (A *go-round* means that each contestant in a particular event has competed once; the money set aside for that go-round is split 40–30–20–10 percent among the first four place winners.) Then we see how a bull rider might get banged around in the chute. Once the gate is opened, the rider feels "a great eruption neath that rollin' hairy hide," which I consider great words to fit the occasion. The rider in the song seems to be making a good try, but the bull is playing around at first, then really cranks it up. This reminds me of a Hereford bull named Iron Ore that was in the late Paul Long's string of bucking bulls in Kansas in the late forties and early fifties. Iron Ore never fought or looked for anyone, but he could really buck. A bull ride lasts eight seconds, which is long enough to test anybody. Iron Ore would spin fast for about seven seconds, and many good bull riders who lasted that long on him thought they had it made. About that time, however, the old bull threw some kind of a diddy which is hard to describe — it looked like a lightning-fast ripple went down his back — and down came Mr. Bull Rider. The only cowboy I know of to ride that bull successfully was Bob Chartier of Colorado. The song goes on till the rider joins the bird gang. It ends with a fitting moral.

229

BLUE BELL BULL

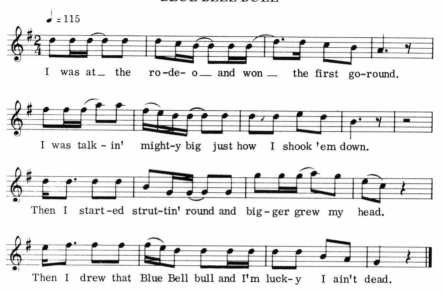

I was at the rodeo and won the first go-round.
I was talkin' mighty big just how I shook 'em down.
Then I started struttin' round and bigger grew my head.
Then I drew that Blue Bell bull and I'm lucky I ain't dead.

They put him in the chute, and he was standin' real nice.
I throwed my bull rope round him, and a feller pulled it tight.
I rosined up my glove and was workin' up a heat,
When he slammed my leg against the gate just as I took my seat.

I hollered, "Let me have him!" and they turned Blue Bell outside.
I felt a great eruption neath that rollin' hairy hide.
You bet they let me have 'im, for my riding hand was full —
Full of champion Number Three, mean old Blue Bell bull.

He jumped way up towards Heaven, and he twisted clear about.
He's actin' kinda juicy and feelin' mighty stout.
I heard a feller on the crowd yell, "You're mounted, son!"
But old Blue Bell was playin' round — the worst is yet to come.

I felt myself to weaken, and I knew I was nearly gone.
Blue Bell was gettin' ranker, and he really turned it on.
He clicked his heels and cocked his head, and as I sailed past
I had a feelin' then and there this rodeo'd be my last.

Eight long weeks in traction, I ain't never been the same.
I was goin' to be a champion and have a real big name.
So if you're at the rodeo don't brag and play the fool.
You may draw old Number Three, champion Blue Bell bull.
Mean old Blue Bell bull.

97

Trading-out Blues

Probably no other occupation calls for as much hectic travel as that of the professional rodeo contestant. The travel itself is the toughest part of rodeo-ing. A cowboy trying to make one rodeo at a time has to travel hard enough. Those who follow the practice of trading out so they can compete in two or more concurrent rodeos really have a lot of continuous driving or flying. Since many two- and three-day rodeos have so many contestants that only one go-round can be held in some or all events, positions, or the performances they are to compete in, are drawn the same as the livestock. After all positions are drawn, the cowboys arrange to trade positions with one another so as not to be up at two rodeos at once on the same day. This allows a cowboy to get to as many rodeos as possible and have a shot at much more money during his career as a contestant. All rodeos do not allow trading out, but it is to the advantage of some rodeos, as they get more top-flight cowboys entered. A rodeo secretary's job — keeping track of all this and the riding scores and the roping and bulldogging times plus figuring all the prize-money splits — is a chore guaranteed to keep a person busy.

Occasionally, concurrent rodeos will have an afternoon performance at one and a night performance at the other. While it might not be necessary to trade out to make both of them, some tall driving is called for. Many top hands who win enough to afford airplanes have taken to the air, thus getting around some of the long hours on the road. This "Trading-out Blues" by Johnny Baker has got to be the most ultra-modern cowboy song of them all, up to now. Any rodeo hand should know how the poor fellows in the car in Johnny's song feel.

TRADING-OUT BLUES

In the mid-dle of the night if you hear a scream

And there's a flame burn-in' up and down the road,

232

Don't you_ fear,_ it's just a car - load of cow - boys Trad - in' out at _ the next ro - de - o._

CHORUS

Lis – ten to the rum - ble, hear the mo - tor scream, It sounds like some-thing from a bad, bad_ dream. Cow - boy a-sleep- in', the cock just crew. Nod-din' cow - boy at the wheel is sing - in'_ the trad - in'-out blues._

In the middle of the night if you hear a scream
And there's a flame burnin' up and down the road,
Don't you fear, it's just a carload of cowboys
Tradin' out at the next rodeo.

Listen to the rumble, hear the motor scream,
It sounds like something from a bad, bad dream.
Cowboy a-sleepin', the cock just crew.
Noddin' cowboy at the wheel is singin' the tradin'-out blues.

Listen to the squeal and smell the burnin' rubber,
They're wearin' that tread down mighty thin.
But they keep on rollin', you can bet they're goin' to make it.
If they have to, they'll drive in on the rim.

Chorus:

As they hit that curve you're goin' to hear them shift down,
'Cause the brake goes a half inch from the floor.
But around that curve they leave ninety feet of rubber.
It's like nothin' that you've ever seen before.

Chorus:

Though the moon shines down you'll never see their faces,
But through the window stares a bloodshot eye.
Don't you blink, 'cause if you do you'll see nothin'.
It takes 'em just a wink to go by.

So in the middle of the night when you hear a scream
And there's a flame burnin' up and down the road,
You'll know not to worry, it's a carload of cowboys
Tradin' out at the next rodeo.

Chorus:

98

The Chuck Wagon's Stuck

From George B. German of Yankton, South Dakota, comes this song about the cowboys on a roundup crew or drive helping the cook pull his wagon out of a boggy place. The roundup wagon was usually pulled by four stout horses driven by the cook. When the wagon stuck, the boys would tie onto it with their catchropes, take a couple dallies or tie to their saddle horns, and pull with their saddle horses. This song describes such a scene.

The worst episode of this kind I ever heard about was related by John Cordova, who now runs some cattle on Sugar Hill in Stone County, Arkansas. John (Juan) was raised on the big Gallegos ranch in New Mexico. His father was caporal (cow boss), and John got in on everything from big roundups to holding down a line camp to farming and shearing sheep. One spring the Gallegos cowboys, including John, were out with the roundup wagon branding calves. This was really a big outfit, and as the saying goes, "They camped out so long they turned green." One day there came a big rain (or maybe it lasted several days), and the wagon was camped in a basin. The more they tried to get her out, the deeper she sank, as the whole basin had turned to soupy mud. Cordova says the chuck wagon was stuck for a solid month!

George German learned this song from Romaine Lowdermilk in Arizona in the twenties. German says the usual practice in Arizona at that time was for cowboys to trade songs: "You couldn't buy one, you just had to give another for the one you wanted." However, German was with Lowdermilk long enough to learn a lot of his songs and would practice singing them while guiding long trail rides.

THE CHUCK WAGON'S STUCK

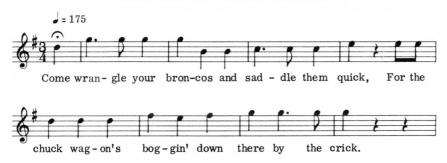

Come wran- gle your bron-cos and sad - dle them quick, For the chuck wag-on's bog-gin' down there by the crick.

Cinch up your la-ti-gos, all of you runts, And pull 'em up tight till your old bron-co grunts. For the chuck's stick-ing fast _ down there in the bog, And it's go-in' on down_ like a wa-ter-soaked log.

Come wrangle your broncos and saddle them quick,
For the chuck wagon's boggin' down there by the crick.
Cinch up your latigos, all of you runts,
And pull 'em up tight till your old bronco grunts.
For the chuck's sticking fast down there in the bog,
And it's goin' on down like a water-soaked log.

Oh, the cattle are scattering over the plain.
The punchers are yelling in language profane.
But let 'em scatter, all of you men,
For the chuck wagon's boggin' down there by the bend.
Come on with your ropes that are lengthy and stout.
The chuck's in the bog, come help pull it out.

It's in to the hub, a-goin' down slow.
The cook's standin' by, a-watching her go.
But now is the time every puncher's his friend.
The chuck wagon's bogging down there by the bend.

(Spoken) Come on, you rascals! Get 'em out o' there!

The strainin' of ropes and the gruntin' of nags,
Woe to the puncher whose lariat sags.
Kick 'em and spur 'em and make 'em lay to.
Now she's comin', now she's through.
Well, it's worth all the time and the effort required —
There's nothin' to eat when the chuck wagon's mired.

99

Billy Venero

This has long been a favorite ballad, though I do not remember where I first heard it sung. Some of this song had got away from me, but hearing "Haywire Mac" McClintock's early recording refreshed my memory, and I have enjoyed singing it again the past several years. It seems the first part of the song had more verses about the early part of Venero's ride, but they didn't add much to the telling of the story. Anyway, I like it a whole lot the way it is here.

With "Billy Venero," the last ballad in this collection, I'd like to say that my involvement in the folk music scene since my first meeting with folklorists and aficionados in 1963 has been a great experience. Besides meeting a heck of a lot of swell people and having fun at it, these same folks have helped me gain a new appreciation for much that my cowboy buddies and country friends and I had taken for granted. Also, it has been enjoyable to find missing parts to half-remembered old songs as well as turn up stuff I'd never have known about. So, many thanks to you all, and here is "Billy Venero."

BILLY VENERO

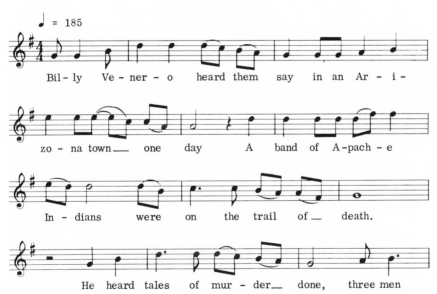

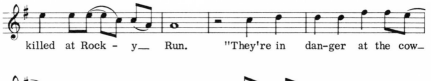

killed at Rock - y— Run.   "They're in   dan-ger at the cow—

— ranch," cried Ve - ner - o   un-der his— breath.

Billy Venero heard them say in an Arizona town one day
A band of Apache Indians were on the trail of death.
He heard tales of murder done, three men killed at Rocky Run.
"They're in danger at the cow ranch," cried Venero under his breath.

The cow ranch forty miles away, in a little place that lay
In a deep and shady valley in the mighty wilderness,
Half a score of homes were there; in one a maiden fair
Held the heart of Billy Venero, was Venero's little Bess.

Not a moment he delayed when his brave resolve was made.
"Why, man," his comrades told him when they heard his daring plan,
"You are riding straight to death," but he answered, "Save your breath,
I may never reach the cow ranch, but I'll do the best I can."

Low and lower sank the sun, he drew rein at Rocky Run.
"Here three men met death, my chapo," and he stroked his glossy mane.
"So shall those we go to warn, ere the coming of the morn.
If we fail, God help my Bessie," and he started on again.

Sharp and clear a rifle shot woke the echoes of the spot.
"I'm wounded," cried Venero as he swayed from side to side.
"While there's life there's always hope, slowly onward I shall lope,
If I never reach the cow ranch, Bessie Lee shall know I tried.

"I shall save her yet," he cried, "Bessie Lee shall know I tried,"
And for her sake he halted in the shadow of a hill.
Then with trembling hands he took from his chaps a little book,
Tore a blank leaf from its pages, said, "This shall be my will."

From a limb a twig he broke, and he dipped his pen of oak
In the warm blood that was flowing from a wound above his heart.
" 'Rouse," he wrote, "before too late, Apache warriors lie in wait.
Good-bye, God bless you, darling," and he felt the cold tears start.

Then he made the message fast, love's first message and its last,
To the saddle horn he tied it, and his lips were white with pain.

"Take this message, if not me, straight to little Bessie Lee."
He tied himself to the saddle, and they started on again.

Just at dusk a horse of brown, wet with sweat, came panting down
The little lane to the cow ranch, and he stopped at Bessie's door.
But the rider was asleep, and his slumber was so deep
Little Bess could never wake him, though she tried forevermore.

You have heard the story told by the young and by the old,
Down yonder at the cow ranch the night the Apaches came,
Of the sharp and bloody fight, how the chief fell in the night,
And the panic-stricken warriors when they heard Venero's name.

Now the heaven and earth between keeps a little flower so green
That Bessie Lee had planted ere they laid her by his side.

100

Cheers!

We sang of Windy Billy, High Chin Bob, and all the rest,
And some of their adventures was just a shade out west.
They might awake a memory and maybe a laugh or two,
So try to sing 'em all again, and boys, "Here's luck to you!"

Biblio-Discography

The popular images of the intellectual collector and the "inarticulate" folk-song composer do not match the realities of cowboy songs. The roles of collector and songwriter are often reversed. Glenn Ohrlin follows in the footsteps of Jack Thorp, Jules Verne Allen, and other working cowboys who have made collections of cowboy songs. The pieces they collected have often been the products of intellectuals. E. A. Brininstool, who wrote "The Cowboy's Prayer" (no. 77) and "The Chuck Wagon's Stuck" (no. 98), and Joseph Mills Hanson, writer of "The Railroad Corral," were noted historians. The author of " 'Longside the Santa Fe Trail" (no. 85), James Grafton Rogers, was dean of the University of Colorado Law School. Many cowboy songs have been written by novelists. Glenn's book contains "Ten Thousand Cattle" (no. 6), for which Owen Wister wrote both words and music, and two of Henry Herbert Knibbs's songs, "Walking John" (no. 24) and "Jake and Roanie" (no. 46). These writers are seldom given credit in academic collections; in most cases their work is attributed to the folklorists' deity Anonymous. They have no better luck gaining recognition for their songs than does the most inarticulate horse wrangler.

The mobility of the American West is indicated by the number of songwriters who were born in the East. Jack Thorp (no. 69) was born in New York City but moved west as a youth and became, successively, a cowboy, a livestock inspector, and a ranch owner. E. A. Brininstool (nos. 77, 98) was born in Warsaw, New York, but moved west and became a newspaperman and historian. Tex Fletcher (nos. 67, 68) came from Harrison, New York. Dane Coolidge was born in Natick, Massachusetts. Henry Herbert Knibbs (nos. 24, 46) originally came from Clifton, Ontario. Montclair, New Jersey, was the home of Larry Chittenden (no. 60). That the horse was probably a symbol of this mobility explains why the cowboy — rather than the granger, sheep herder, lumberjack, or follower of some other trade — came to represent the American West. For discussions of the symbolism associated with the cowboy and western mobility see Walter Prescott Webb's *The Great Plains* (New York: Ginn and Co., 1931) and *The Great Frontier* (Boston: Houghton Mifflin, 1952).

The books by Jules Verne Allen, Dane Coolidge, and Charles J. Finger in the list of basic references below contain important material about the process of collecting. John A. Lomax discusses collecting from the viewpoint of the folklorist in *Adventures of a Ballad Hunter* (New York: Macmillan, 1947). For the perspective of the pioneer cowboy collector, see *Pardner of the Wind* (Caldwell, Idaho: Caxton Printers, 1945), by N. Howard "Jack" Thorp and Neil McCullough Clark. Charles Wellington Furlong's *Let 'er Buck* (New York: G. P. Putnam's Sons, 1921) contains a chapter on swapping songs after a rodeo; this book also gives a very good description of the early days of rodeo. For portrayals of rodeo life in more recent times see Gene Lamb's *Rodeo back of the Chutes* (Denver: Bell Press, 1956) and *Rodeo Cowboy* (San Antonio: Naylor Co., 1959).

The biblio-discography for Ohrlin's songs is organized according to the following categories:

A. Basic references

Books which are cited often in these notes are coded by a key word. The numbers after each title refer to the songs in *The Hell-Bound Train* which each contains.

Allen	Allen, Jules Verne. *Cowboy Lore*. San Antonio: Naylor Co., 1933. 5, 14, 19, 22, 51, 52, 56, 62, 63, 64, 85.
Coolidge	Coolidge, Dane. *Texas Cowboys*. New York: Dutton, 1937. 2, 12, 16, 19, 52, 99.
Fife (1969)	Fife, Austin E., and Alta S. Fife. *Cowboy and Western Songs*. New York: Clarkson N. Potter, 1969. 5, 9, 12, 14, 15, 19, 22, 23, 27, 28, 49, 51, 56, 59, 62, 63, 64, 65, 66, 99.
Fife (1970)	Fife, Austin E., and Alta S. Fife. *Heaven on Horseback*. Logan, Utah: Utah State University Press, 1970. 7, 15, 49, 51, 64, 77.
Finger (1923)	Finger, Charles J. *Sailor Chanties and Cowboy Songs*. Girard, Kans.: Haldeman-Julius Co., 1923. 16, 18, 59, 60.
Finger (1927)	Finger, Charles J. *Frontier Ballads*. Garden City, N.Y.: Doubleday, Page and Co., 1927. 15, 52.
Larkin	Larkin, Margaret. *Singing Cowboy*. New York: Alfred A. Knopf, 1931. 5, 6, 14, 22, 23, 24, 27, 62, 63, 64, 66, 99.
Laws (1957)	Laws, G. Malcolm, Jr. *American Balladry from British Broadsides*. Philadelphia: American Folklore Society, 1957. 12, 26, 72, 84.
Laws (1964)	Laws, G. Malcolm, Jr. *Native American Balladry*, rev. ed. Philadelphia: American Folklore Society, 1964. 4, 5, 14, 16, 19, 21, 22, 23, 27, 28, 42, 52, 53, 57, 59, 62, 63, 66, 69, 99.
Lingenfelter	Lingenfelter, Richard E., Richard A. Dwyer, and David Cohen. *Songs of the American West*. Berkeley and Los Angeles: University of California Press, 1968. 5, 8, 9, 13, 14, 17, 19, 22, 23, 27, 49, 52, 53, 59, 60, 62, 63, 64, 84, 88, 99.
Lomax (1910)	Lomax, John A. *Cowboy Songs and Other Frontier Ballads*. New York: Sturgis and Walton Co., 1910. 7, 12, 14, 16, 17, 18, 19, 22, 51, 52, 53, 59, 62, 63, 64, 84, 99.
Lomax (1916)	Lomax, John A. *Cowboy Songs and Other Frontier Ballads*, rev. and enl. New York: Sturgis and Walton Co., 1916. 5, 7, 12, 14, 15, 16, 17, 18, 19, 22, 51, 52, 53, 59, 60, 62, 63, 64, 84, 99.
Lomax (1919)	Lomax, John A. *Songs of the Cattle Trail and Cow Camp*. New York: Macmillan Co., 1919. 49, 60.

Lomax (1938)   Lomax, John A., and Alan Lomax. *Cowboy Songs and Other Frontier Ballads*, rev. and enl. New York: Macmillan Co., 1938. 4, 5, 6, 7, 9, 12, 14, 15, 16, 17, 18, 19, 20, 22, 23, 26, 28, 51, 52, 53, 57, 60, 62, 63, 64, 65, 66, 84, 85, 99.

Moore   Moore, Chauncy O., and Ethel Moore. *Ballads and Folksongs of the Southwest*. Norman: University of Oklahoma Press, 1964. 12, 52, 53, 59, 62, 63, 84.

Pound   Pound, Louise. *Folk-Songs of Nebraska and the Central West: A Syllabus*. Nebraska Academy of Sciences Publications, 9, no. 3. Lincoln, 1915. 9, 19, 53, 55.

Randolph   Randolph, Vance. *Ozark Folksongs*. 4 vols. Columbia: State Historical Society of Missouri, 1946-50. 12, 14, 15, 21, 22, 23, 28, 42, 52, 53, 57, 58, 59, 63, 66, 69, 99.

Silber   Silber, Irwin, and Earl Robinson. *Songs of the Great American West*. New York: Macmillan Co., 1967. 9, 22, 27, 62, 63.

Thorp (1908)   Thorp, N. Howard. *Songs of the Cowboys*. Estancia, N.Mex.: News Print Shop, 1908. 5, 14, 17, 19, 22, 60. The recent edition of this work by Austin E. Fife and Alta S. Fife, *Songs of the Cowboys, by N. Howard ("Jack") Thorp* (New York: Clarkson N. Potter, 1966), offers substantial notes on the songs.

Thorp (1921)   Thorp, N. Howard. *Songs of the Cowboys*. Boston and New York: Houghton Mifflin Co., 1921. 5, 7, 14, 15, 16, 17, 19, 22, 49, 51, 60, 64.

B. Selected songsters and folios

What accounts for our national cognizance of cowboy songs? To answer this question, it is necessary to look beyond the songs themselves and examine how they have been spread. Songsters and song folios are among the major disseminators of cowboy music. However, like other elements of popular culture, they are sometimes overlooked by folklorists. They range in size from small books, containing words only, to tabloid sheets. Their methods of distribution are also manifold. Many are sold through music stores. Powder River Jack sold his on street corners as well as at dude ranches where he performed. George German and many other entertainers sold song folios over the radio. In the early days of radio many performers were not paid, and the only money they made came through personal appearances and from the sale of books. When John I. White was on "Death Valley Days," an NBC network radio progam, sponsors printed a book of his songs which they gave away for boxtops of their products, 20 Mule Team Borax, 20 Mule Team Borax Soap Chips, and 20 Mule Team Boric Acid.

The songsters and folios listed below are intended as a representative selection. They are also coded by a key word.

American   *American Cowboy Songs*. New York: Robbins Music Corp., 1936. 5, 6, 19, 22, 52, 62, 63, 65, 99.

Asch (1964)   Asch, Moses. *104 Folk Songs*. New York: Robbins Music Corp., 1964. 22.

Asch (1965)   Asch, Moses. *124 Folk Songs*. New York: Robbins Music Corp., 1965. 42.

Clark (1932)   Clark, Kenneth S. *The Cowboy Sings*. New York: Paull-Pioneer

	Music Corp., 1932. 4, 6, 7, 14, 19, 20, 22, 25, 52, 53, 60, 62, 63, 64, 65, 99.
Clark (1934)	Clark, Kenneth S. *The Happy Cowboy Sings and Plays Songs of Pioneer Days*. New York: Paull-Pioneer Music Corp., 1934. 5, 20, 56, 69.
Clark (1937)	Clark, Kenneth S., and Bob Miller. *Songs of the Rodeo*. New York: Paull-Pioneer Music Corp., 1937. 4, 6, 7, 14, 52, 60, 62, 64.
Clark (1940)	Clark, Kenneth S. *Buckaroo Ballads*. New York: Paull-Pioneer Music Corp., 1940. 4, 14, 60, 64.
Colby	Colby, Carleton. *Cowboy and Mountain Songs*. Chicago: Melrose Brothers Music Co., 1936. 13, 22, 85.
Davis	Davis, Joe. *Tip Top Songs of the Roaming Ranger*. New York: Joe Davis, 1935. 9, 14, 19, 20, 51, 52, 62, 65.
Eckstein	Eckstein, Maxwell. *Cowboy Time: 14 Songs of the Range*. New York: Carl Fischer, 1950. 20.
Famous	*Famous Cowboy Songs and Mountain Ballads*. New York: Padell Book Co., 1944. 53, 63.
German (1929)	German, George B. *Cowboy Campfire Ballads*. Yankton, S.D., 1929. 5, 16, 19, 22, 25, 27, 28, 63, 64, 70, 84, 98, 99.
German (1932)	German, George B. *Cowboy Campfire Ballads*. Yankton, S.D., 1932. 25, 27, 56, 64, 71, 98.
Goodwin	Goodwin, George. *88 Most Beloved, Easy to Play Cowboy and Western Songs*. New York: Song Dex, 1965. 5, 14, 19, 22, 52, 57, 62, 64, 99.
Hobo News	*Two Hundred Popular Cowboy Songs and Mountain Ballads*. New York: Hobo News, n.d. 4, 7, 13, 15, 53, 63.
Klickman	Klickman, F. Henry, and Sterling Sherwin. *Songs of the Saddle*. Cleveland: Sam Fox Publishing Co., 1933. 19.
Lair	Lair, John. *100 WLS Barn Dance Favorites*. Chicago: M. M. Cole, 1935. 4, 62.
Lee (1936a)	Lee, Jack H. *Powder River Jack and Kitty Lee's Cowboy Song Book: Cowboy Wails and Cattle Trails of the Wild West*, 1. Deer Lodge, Mont., 1936. 5, 14, 16, 17, 22, 27, 28, 60, 85.
Lee (1936b)	Lee, Jack H. *Powder River Jack and Kitty Lee Cowboy Song Book*, 2. Deer Lodge, Mont., 1936. 23, 24, 40, 52, 62, 63. These two song books by Lee (1936a, 1936b) were later combined, with consecutive pagination.
Lee (1937)	Lee, Jack H. *Powder River Jack and Kitty Lee's Songs of the Range*. Chicago: Chart Music Publishing House, 1937. 14, 16, 17, 23, 24, 27, 40, 52, 62, 85.
Maynard	*Ken Maynard's Songs of the Trails*. Chicago: M. M. Cole, 1935. 22, 53, 63, 99.
Patterson	Patterson, Patt, and Lois Dexter. *Songs of the Roundup Rangers*. New York: George T. Worth and Co., 1932. 5, 20, 22, 28, 51, 56, 63, 64.
Remick	*On the Trail: An Album of Cowboy Songs*. New York: Remick Music Corp., 1945. 25.
Robison	*Carson J. Robison's World's Greatest Collection of Mountain Ballads and Old Time Songs*. Chicago: M. M. Cole, 1930. 4, 13, 15.
Sherwin	Sherwin, Sterling, and Harry A. Powell. *Bad Man Songs of the Wild and Wooly West*. Cleveland: Sam Fox Publishing Co., 1933. 15, 59.
Sires	Sires, Ina. *Songs of the Open Range*. Boston: C. C. Birchard, 1928. 4, 5, 14, 19, 60, 63, 88.

Smith	*Smith's Collection of Mountain Ballads and Cowboy Songs.* New York: William J. Smith, 1932. 13, 19, 20.
White (1929)	White, John, and George Shackley. *The Lonesome Cowboy Songs of the Plains and Hills.* New York: George T. Worth, 1929. 19, 62, 65, 98.
White (1934)	White, John. *Cowboy Songs as Sung by John White "The Lonesome Cowboy" in Death Valley Days.* New York: Pacific Coast Borax Co., 1934. 19, 22.
Williams	Miller, Bob. *Marc Williams Collection of Favorite Cowboy Songs.* New York: Bob Miller, 1937. 4, 22, 52.

C. Additional bibliography

This section adds bibliographic references not cited in Lingenfelter, Dwyer, and Cohen's *Songs of the American West,* the best reference source for cowboy songs; in Laws's definitive works, *American Balladry from British Broadsides* and *Native American Balladry;* or in the Fifes' 1966 edition of Thorp's *Songs of the Cowboys.*

D. 78 rpm records

These entries list the performer's name, recording date (in parentheses), song title (if different from Glenn's), and label and release number. Pseudonyms are followed by the performer's real name, where known, with two exceptions. Marion Try Slaughter's popular pseudonym Vernon Dalhart is used. Francis Luther Crow is cited as Frank Luther, the name under which his book *Americans and Their Songs* was published.

Discographies are added for certain important recording artists Glenn mentions: Harry "Haywire Mac" McClintock (no. 13), Powder River Jack Lee (no. 40), the Cartwright brothers (no. 53), Jules Verne Allen (no. 85), and Carl T. Sprague (no. 88).

E. LPs

These entries list the performer's name, song title (if different from Glenn's), album title, and label and release number.

The following is a list of recommended LP albums which include at least one of the songs in this book (indicated by the numbers after each entry).

Sam Agins, *Singin' Sam's Saddlebag of Songs,* Haywire ARA 6419. 27, 28, 46.
Authentic Cowboys and Their Western Folksongs, RCA Victor LPV-522. 5, 14, 22, 27, 40, 53, 62, 63.
Johnny Baker, *Songs of the Rodeo,* Audio Arts 705. 93-97.
Bill Bender and Cisco Houston, *Traditional Songs of the Old West,* Stinson SLP 37. 5, 27, 28, 62.
Wilf Carter, *Songs of the Calgary Stampede,* (Canadian) Apex AL 1615. 29, 32.
Don Cleary, *Don Cleary Sings Traditional Cowboy Songs,* Palomino PAL 302. 4, 99.
Cowboy Songs, Arizona Friends of Folklore AFF 33-1. 22, 27, 46, 99.
Cowboy Songs, 2, Arizona Friends of Folklore AFF 33-2. 16, 19, 63.

Cowboy Songs, Ballads, and Cattle Calls from Texas, Library of Congress Archive of Folk Song AAFS L 28. 22, 52, 53.

Slim Critchlow, *The Crooked Trail to Holbrook,* Arhoolie 5007. 5, 14, 19, 20, 62.

Dave Fredrickson, *Songs of the West,* Folkways FH 5259. 66, 84.

George Gillespie, *Cow Camp Songs of the Old West,* Thorne TR 200. 24, 27, 28, 49, 85.

Harry Jackson, *The Cowboy,* Folkways FH 5723. 4, 5, 22, 27, 28, 63, 69, 84.

Merrick Jarrett, *The Old Chisholm Trail,* Riverside RLP 12-631. 4, 28, 49, 63, 64.

Peter LaFarge, *Peter LaFarge Sings of the Cowboys,* Folkways FA 2533. 24, 27, 28, 62.

Frank Luther, *Songs and Stories about America,* Vocalion 73728. 14, 22, 28, 62.

Ed McCurdy, *Songs of the West,* Tradition TLP 2061. 28, 64, 85.

Nevada Slim, *Songs of the Wild West,* 1, Rural Rhythm RRNS 162. 5, 49, 85, 99.

———, *Songs of the Wild West,* 2, Rural Rhythm RRNS 163. 22, 23, 56, 62, 63, 98.

———, *Songs of the Wild West,* 3, Rural Rhythm RRNS 164. 13, 27.

Glenn Ohrlin, *The Hell-Bound Train,* University of Illinois Campus Folksong Club CFC 301. 1, 5, 6, 8, 9, 15, 24, 42, 45, 54, 62, 64.

Ray Oman, *Trail Dust 'n' Saddle Leather,* Ace Recordings. 22, 27.

Stone County Singing, Shoestring Tape SGB-1. 46, 57, 62, 99.

Roger Welsch, *Sweet Nebraska Land,* Folkways FH 5337. 9, 19, 59.

F. Electrical transcriptions

These entries list the performer's name, song title (if different from Glenn's), and any label and release number assigned.

1. My Home's in Montana

Henry M. Halvorson, former editor-in-chief at Ginn and Company, told Judith McCulloh that Christine Turner Curtis, who wrote many music lyrics for Ginn, paraphrased the words of Larkin's "The Cowboy's Lament" for use in *Singing Days* (World of Music Series), a one-book course designed for use in one-room rural schools. The song was included on the first of thirteen 78 rpm records pressed by Victor to accompany *Singing Days;* it was sung by Olive Kline, soprano, with piano accompaniment by Myrtle C. Eaver.

A. Larkin, pp. 14-15 (for the model on which Glenn's text was built).
Lingenfelter, pp. 426-27 (for the tune only).

C. Marguerite V. Hood, Glenn Gildersleeve, and Helen S. Leavitt, *Singing Days* (Boston: Ginn and Co., 1936), p. 18.
Janet E. Tobitt, *The Ditty Bag* (New York: Tobitt, 1946), p. 50.

D. Olive Kline (1935), "The Cowboy," Victor 25300.

E. Glenn Ohrlin, *The Hell-Bound Train,* University of Illinois Campus Folksong Club CFC 301. The text is transcribed in Austin E. Fife and Alta S. Fife, *Songs of the Cowboys by N. Howard ("Jack") Thorp* (New York: Clarkson N. Potter, 1966), p. 170.

———, "Montana Is My Home," *Traditional Music at Newport, 1964,* part 2, Vanguard VRS 79183.

2. My Friends and Relations

Dane Coolidge was born in Natick, Massachusetts, but at an early age moved to Riverside, California, where he spent his early life on his father's orange ranch. He enjoyed hunting and trapping in the mountains, and when he entered Stanford University he obtained a position as field collector. After leaving Stanford he did postgraduate work at Harvard. He wrote many western novels. However, his best works are his short stories (which often escape the influence of Zane Grey's romances that mars his novels) and his nonfiction books. Coolidge's books of nonfiction include *Fighting Men of the West* (1932), *Death Valley Prospectors* (1937), *Texas Cowboys* (1937), *Arizona Cowboys* (1938), and *Old California Cowboys* (1939). With Mary Roberts Coolidge he wrote *The Navajo Indians* (1930) and *The Last of the Seris* (1939).

A. Coolidge, pp. 98-104.

3. The Mowing Machine

For information about Charlie Marshall, see the liner notes to his Ikon LP.

D. Charlie Marshall (1934), "The Mowin' Machine," Vocalion 03045. Reissued on *Those Fabulous, Those Original, Those Authentic "Beverly Hill Billies,"* 2, Rar-Arts Records WLP 1001.

4. Cowboy Jack

A. Laws (1964) (B 24), p. 144.
   Lomax (1938), p. 230.
B. Clark (1932), p. 15.
   Clark (1937), p. 62.
   Clark (1940), p. 46.
   Hobo News, p. 18.
   Lair, p. 77.
   Robison, p. 51.
   Sires, pp. 12-13.
   Williams, p. 10.
C. Jan Harold Brunvand, "Folk Song Studies in Idaho," *Western Folklore,* 24 (Oct., 1965), 238.
   James F. Leisy, *Let's All Sing* (New York and Nashville: Abingdon Press, 1959), pp. 53-54.
   H. D. Munal, *The Songs of Long Ago* (Privately published, 1933), p. 27.
D. Callahan Brothers (1936), Banner 6-09-53, Columbia 20212, Columbia 37613, Melotone 6-09-53, Okeh 03171, Oriole 6-09-53, Perfect 6-09-53, Romeo 6-09-53, Vocalion 03171.
   Carter Family (1934), Bluebird 8167, Montgomery Ward 4545. Reissued on *'Mid the Green Fields of Virginia,* RCA Victor LPM 2772.
   Esmereldy and Dick Thomas, Musicraft 298. Reissued on *Esmereldy and Dick Thomas,* Sutton SU 284.
   Girls of the Golden West [Millie and Dollie Good] (1934), Bluebird 5719.
   Peg Moreland (1929), Victor 23593.
   Arkansas Woodchopper [Luther Ossenbrink] (1930), Conqueror 7882.
   Ranch Boys (ca. 1938), Decca 2645 (in album A-65, *Cowboy Songs*).
   Marc Williams (ca. 1931), Brunswick 430.
E. Don Cleary, *Don Cleary Sings Traditional Cowboy Songs,* Palomino 302.
   Girls of the Golden West, *Songs for You Old and New,* 1, Bluebonnet BL 106.
   Utah Cowboy [J. R. Hall], "Ode to Cowboy Jack," *The Utah Cowboy Sings Again,* Bluebonnet BL 115.
   Harry Jackson, *The Cowboy,* Folkways FH 5723.
   Merrick Jarrett, *The Old Chisholm Trail,* Riverside RLP 12-631, and *Songs of the Old West,* Washington WLP 725.
   Stonewall Jackson, *Great Old Songs,* Columbia CS 9708.

The probable antecedent of "Cowboy Jack" is "Your Mother Still Prays for You, Jack":

C. Cowboy Loye and Just Plain John, *Old Time Ballads and Cowboy Songs* (n.p., n.d.), pp. 13-14.

D. Carter Family (1935), Banner 33462, Melotone 13429, Oriole 5481, Perfect 13152, Romeo 8481, Conqueror 8530.

Billy McGinty's Oklahoma Cowboy Band, Gennett 6387, Champion 15446, Silvertone 8159 (as Grace Means), Supertone 9244 (as Grace Means).

Wade Mainer (ca. 1939), Bluebird 8137, Montgomery Ward 7563.

Jack Mathis (1928), Columbia 15344-D.

Norwood Tew (1937), Montgomery Ward 7233.

E. Cecil Gill, *The Yodeling Country Boy,* Bluebonnet BL 101.

5. Windy Bill

A. Allen, pp. 140-42.

Fife (1969), pp. 204-5.

Larkin, pp. 58-59.

Laws (1964) (dB 41), p. 260.

Lingenfelter, pp. 354-55.

Lomax (1916), pp. 381-82.

Lomax (1938), pp. 113-15.

Thorp (1908), pp. 11-12.

Thorp (1921), pp. 168-70.

B. American, pp. 58-59.

Clark (1934), pp. 50-51.

German (1929), n.p.

Goodwin, p. 59.

Lee (1936a), pp. 34-35.

Patterson, pp. 40-41.

Sires, pp. 28-29.

C. J. Frank Dobie, *The Longhorns* (New York: Little, Brown and Co., 1941), p. 320.

D. Bill Bender, Varsity. Reissued on *Traditional Songs of the Old West,* Stinson SLP 37.

J. D. Farley (1929), "Bill Was a Texas Lad," Victor 40269, Montgomery Ward 4300. Reissued on *Authentic Cowboys and Their Western Folksongs,* RCA-Victor LPV 522.

Powder River Jack and Kitty Lee (1930), "Old Black Steer," Bluebird 5298, Electradisk 2169, Sunrise 3379.

E. Slim Critchlow, *The Crooked Trail to Holbrook,* Arhoolie 5007.

Harry Jackson, *The Cowboy,* Folkways FH 5723.

Nevada Slim, *Nevada Slim Sings Songs of the Wild West,* 1, Rural Rhythm RRNS 162.

Glenn Ohrlin, *The Hell-Bound Train,* University of Illinois Campus Folksong Club CFC 301.

————, University of Illinois Press MAL 731.

6. Ten Thousand Cattle

A. Larkin, p. 151.

Lomax (1938), pp. 128-31.

B. American, p. 6.

Clark (1932), p. 27.

Clark (1937), p. 47.

C. Charles Wellington Furlong, *Let 'er Buck* (New York: G. P. Putnam's Sons, 1921), p. 225.

Norman Luboff and Win Stracke, *Songs of Man* (Englewood Cliffs, N.J.: Prentice-Hall; New York: Walton Music Corp., 1965), p. 48.

John I. White, "Owen Wister, Song Writer," *Western Folklore,* 26 (Oct., 1967),

269-71. A revised version of this article appears in White's book on cowboy and western songs (Urbana: University of Illinois Press, forthcoming).

———, "The Virginian," *Montana, the Magazine of Western History,* 16 (Oct., 1966), 2-11.

Owen Wister, "Ten Thousand Cattle Straying (Dead Broke)" (sheet music) (New York: M. Witmark and Sons, 1904).

E. Ed McCurdy, *The Badmen,* Columbia 1011.

Glenn Ohrlin, *The Hell-Bound Train,* University of Illinois Campus Folksong Club CFC 301.

7. Cowboy in Church

A. Fife (1970), pp. 86-88.
Lomax (1910), pp. 246-48.
Lomax (1916), pp. 246-48.
Lomax (1938), pp. 272-75.
Thorp (1921), pp. 31-34.

B. Clark (1932), p. 14.
Clark (1937), p. 58.
Hobo News, p. 33.

D. Carl T. Sprague (1929), Bluebird 6258.

8. The Swede from North Dakota

A. Lingenfelter, p. 493.

E. Glenn Ohrlin, *The Hell-Bound Train,* University of Illinois Campus Folksong Club CFC 301.

9. Dakota Land

This song and the one that follows are parodies of the familiar gospel hymn "Beulah Land." The melody was written by John R. Sweney, a professor of music at the Pennsylvania Music Academy, who gained fame as a camp-meeting song leader and compiler of gospel song books. Other well-known compositions by Sweney include "Will There Be Any Stars in My Crown?" "Tell Me the Story of Jesus," "More about Jesus," "There Is Sunshine in My Soul," and "I Shall Know Him." Edgar Page Stites, who wrote the words of "Beulah Land" in 1875, used the pseudonym Edgar Page for his hymns. He spent some time as a Methodist missionary in Dakota territory, but a direct connection with this parody of his hymn has not been found.

A. Fife (1969), pp. 62-64.
Lingenfelter, pp. 462-63.
Lomax (1938), pp. 410-12.
Pound, p. 28.
Silber, pp. 233-35.

B. Davis, p. 14.

C. Jan Harold Brunvand, "Folk Song Studies in Idaho," *Western Folklore,* 24 (Oct., 1965), 239.

Edith Fowke, "Labor and Industrial Protest Songs in Canada," *Journal of American Folklore,* 82 (Jan.-Mar., 1969), 43.

Jay Monaghan, *The Book of the American West* (New York: Julian Messner, 1963), p. 556.

Allie B. Wallace, *Frontier Life in Oklahoma* (Washington, D.C.: Public Affairs Press, 1964), p. 101.

Roger Welsch, *Sod Walls* (Broken Bow, Nebr.: Purcells, 1968), pp. 181-84.

———, *A Treasury of Nebraska Pioneer Folklore* (Lincoln: University of Nebraska Press, 1966), pp. 48-49.

Wild West Weekly, 105, no. 1 (Sept. 12, 1936), 123-24.

E. Glenn Ohrlin, *The Hell-Bound Train,* University of Illinois Campus Folksong Club CFC 301.

Roger Welsch, "Sweet Nebraska Land," *Sweet Nebraska Land,* Folkways FH 5337.

10. Saskatchewan

C. Edith Fowke, "Labor and Industrial Protest Songs in Canada," *Journal of American Folklore,* 82 (Jan.-Mar., 1969), 43.

———— and Alan Mills, *Canada's Story in Song* (Toronto: W. J. Gage, 1960), pp. 208-11.

Margaret A. MacLeod, *Songs of Old Manitoba* (Toronto: Ryerson Press, 1960).

E. Alan Mills, *Canada's Story in Song,* Folkways FW 3000.

————, *O Canada,* Folkways FP 3001.

Jim Young, *Folksongs of Saskatchewan,* Folkways FE 4312.

11. Wonderful Watford

W. Lee O'Daniel and the Light Crust Doughboys recorded "Beautiful Texas" in 1933 on Vocalion 02621. O'Daniel used it as a campaign song when he ran for governor of Texas in 1938. For an LP recording see *Girls of the Golden West,* 3, Bluebonnet BL 110.

12. Bonny Black Bess

In *Injun Summer* Bill Walker gives one verse of "Bonny Black Bess" and tells a fanciful tale of how the song was written as a tribute to Billy the Kid's horse, which was killed in a melodramatic escape from a posse. This is a good example of a narrative which has been built around a folksong.

A. Coolidge, pp. 115-18.

Fife (1969), pp. 15-17.

Laws (1957) (L 9), p. 170.

Lomax (1910), pp. 194-96.

Lomax (1916), pp. 194-96.

Lomax (1938), pp. 217-20.

Moore, pp. 155-56.

Randolph, 2, 152-55.

C. William Walker and Daisy F. Baber, *Injun Summer* (Caldwell, Idaho: Caxton Printers, 1952), pp. 118-21.

E. Tom Brandon, *"The Rambling Irishman,"* Folk-Legacy FSC 10.

Lawrence Older, *Adirondack Songs, Ballads and Fiddle Tunes,* Folk-Legacy FSA 15.

13. Hallelujah, I'm a Bum

Harry McClintock wrote many stories and articles for *Railroad Magazine.* "Twilight of the Boomers," in the October, 1939, issue, contains a great deal of autobiographical information.

"Hallelujah, I'm a Bum" appeared in the little red song book of the IWW in 1909. The song was published in sheet music in 1928 by Villa Moret (San Francisco), with no explicit claim of authorship. This sheet music reads "as originally arranged and sung by Harry McClintock, 'Mac,'" whereas the sheet music of "The Bum Song No. 2," which was published during the same year by the same firm, states "words and music by Harry McClintock, 'Mac.'"

The tune of "Hallelujah, I'm a Bum" was composed by John J. Husband early in the nineteenth century. In 1875, P. P. Bliss and Ira D. Sankey used it in *Gospel Hymns and Sacred Songs* as the tune for "Rejoice and Be Glad," by Horatius Bonar. "Revive Us Again," which was written in 1863 by William P. Mackey, was printed below "Rejoice and Be Glad" as an alternate text. Later collections discarded Bonar's text and instead used Mackey's lyrics with Husband's tune. The chorus of "Hallelujah, I'm a Bum" parodies the chorus of Mackey's song:

> Hallelujah! Thine the glory, Hallelujah! amen.
> Hallelujah! Thine the glory, revive us again.

However, the verses of "Hallelujah, I'm a Bum" are parodies of the verses of Bonar's song:

> Rejoice and be glad! The Redeemer has come!
> Go look on His cradle, His cross, and His tomb.

A. Lingenfelter, p. 529.
B. Colby, p. 15.
   Hobo News, p. 30.
   Robison, p. 7.
   Smith, p. 56.
C. Reginald Nettel, *A Social History of Traditional Song* (New York: Augustus M. Kelley, 1969), pp. 221-22.
   J. Barre Toelken, "Northwest Traditional Ballads: A Collector's Dilemma," *Northwest Review,* 5 (1962), p. 15.
D. George Anthony (ca. 1929), Madison 50006.
   John Bennett (ca. 1929), Madison 1642.
   Vernon Dalhart (1928), Columbia 1488-D.
   Arthur Fields [Abe Finklestein] (1928), Grey Gull 4228, Radiex 4228.
   Jack Golding (1928), Gennett 6715.
   Frank Luther (1928), Brunswick 4029, Brunswick 254.
   Lazy Larry [Luther] (1928), Cameo 8296, Lincoln 2944.
   Weary Willie [Luther] (1928), Pathe 32382, Perfect 12461.
   "Mac" (Harry McClintock) (1928), Victor 21343, Bluebird 11083.
   George Olsen and His Music (1933), Victor 24221.
   Hobo Jack Turner (1928), Diva 2705, Harmony 705, Velvet Tone 1705.
E. John Greenway, *The Great American Bum,* Riverside RLP 12-619, and *The Big Rock Candy Mountain,* Washington 710.
   Harry McClintock, *Harry K. McClintock: "Haywire Mac,"* Folkways FD 5272.
   Nevada Slim, *Songs of the Wild West,* 3, Rural Rhythm RRNS 164.
   Pete Seeger, *American Favorite Ballads,* Folkways FA 2445.
   Riley Shephard, *Old Time Comedy Favorites,* Rural Rhythm RR 1166.
   Pick Temple, *The Pick of the Crop,* Prestige 13008.
   Jim Wall, *Old Time Songs,* Rural Rhythm RR 1168.

In the Harry McClintock discography which follows, the numbers in parentheses after the master numbers refer to alternate takes. All 78 rpm releases are on Victor. Some were released later on Bluebird and Montgomery Ward.

Master No.	Title	Release No.

Oakland, Calif. Mar. 1, 1928. Acc. by own guitar; and by Virgi Ward, violin, where noted (*).

Master No.	Title	Release No.
42041	Git Along Little Dogies*	40016
42042	Cowboy's Lament*	21761
42043	Goodbye, Old Paint*	21761
42044	The Texas Ranger	21487
42045	Sam Bass	21420

Oakland, Calif. Mar. 9, 1928. Acc. by own guitar.

42073	Jesse James	21420
42074	The Trail to Mexico	
42075	Sweet Betsy from Pike	23704
42076 (1,2)	Billy Venero	
42077	My Dad's Dinner Pail	21521

Master No.	Title	Release No.

Oakland, Calif. Mar. 16, 1928. Acc. by own guitar; with speech by H. O'Neill where noted (*).

42094	The Bum's Song*	21343
42095	The Man on the Flying Trapeze	21567
42096	Jerry, Go Ile That Car	21521

Oakland, Calif. Mar. 22, 1928. Acc. by his Haywire Orchestra (violin, harmonica, guitar).

42113	The Old Chisholm Trail	21421
42114	My Last Dollar	23690
42115	Bald Top Mountain	23829

Oakland, Calif. Mar. 23, 1928. Acc. by his Haywire Orchestra.

42119	Cowboy's Lament	
42120	Goodbye, Old Paint	
42121	The Trail to Mexico	40016

Oakland, Calif. Mar. 27, 1928. Acc. by his Haywire Orchestra.

42128	Red River Valley	21421

Oakland, Calif. Mar. 31, 1928. Acc. by his Haywire Orchestra where noted (*).

42076 (3,4)	Billy Venero	21487
42129	The Circus Days*	21567
42137	Hallelujah! I'm a Bum	21343

Hollywood, Calif. Sept. 5, 1928. Acc. by own guitar.

46452	Ain't We Crazy	40101

Hollywood, Calif. Sept. 6, 1928. Acc. by own guitar.

46453	Bum Song No. 2	21704
46454	Big Rock Candy Mountain	21704

Hollywood, Calif. Apr. 30, 1929. Acc. by own guitar.

50878	Hobo's Spring Song	40112
		(as Radio Mac)
50879	If I Had My Druthers	40112
		(as Radio Mac)
50880	The Broken Tambourine	
50881	His Parents Haven't Seen Him Since	23586
		(as Pipe Major S. McKinnon)

Culver City, Calif. Dec. 13, 1929. Acc. by his Haywire Orchestra (2 guitars, 2 violins, harmonica, banjo).

54531	He Sure Can Play a Harmoniky	23586
		(as Pipe Major S. McKinnon)
54532	Home-Spun Gal	23510
		(as Radio Mac)
54533	Can I Sleep in Your Barn?	40264
		(as Radio Mac)

Culver City, Calif. Dec. 15, 1929. Acc. by his Haywire Orchestra.

54534	Roamin'	40264
		(as Radio Mac)
54535	Fireman, Save My Child	40234
		(as Radio Mac)
54536	The Trusty Lariat	40234
		(as Radio Mac)

San Francisco, Calif. Oct. 15, 1931. Acc. by violin, accordion, guitar, drums.

68325	Fifty Years from Now	22845
		(as Radio Mac)
68326	When It's Time to Shear the Sheep I'm Coming Back	22845
		(as Radio Mac)

San Pedro, Calif. 1951. *Harry K. McClintock: "Haywire Mac,"* Folkways FD 5272. Acc. by own guitar.

Hallelujah, I'm a Bum

Big Rock Candy Mountains (also issued on *Railroad Songs and Ballads,* Library of Congress Archive of Folk Song AFS L 61)

Long Haired Preachers

Casey Jones (I.W.W. version)

Anecdote on Joe Hill

Tale: Marcus Daly Enters Heaven

Subic

Casey Jones (Saunders's original version)

Jordan Am a Hard Road to Travel

Poor Boy

Paddy Clancy

Utah Carl

Uncle Jim's "Rebel Soldier"

Anecdote on Pete Wells, Canal Boat Fireman

14. My Love Is a Rider

  A. Allen, pp. 157-58.

    Fife (1969), pp. 165-66.

    Larkin, pp. 46-47.

    Laws (1964) (B 15), p. 140.

    Lingenfelter, p. 401.

    Lomax (1910), p. 251.

    Lomax (1916), pp. 251, 367-68.

    Lomax (1938), pp. 267-68.

    Randolph, 2, 228-30.

    Thorp (1908), pp. 26-27.

    Thorp (1921), pp. 14-15.

  B. Clark (1932), p. 7.

    Clark (1937), p. 9.

    Clark (1940), p. 26.

    Davis, p. 10.

    Goodwin, p. 60.

    Lee (1936a), pp. 42-43.

    Lee (1937), pp. 12-13.

    Sires, pp. 40-41.

  C. Stewart Edward White, "The Rawhide," *McClure's Magazine,* 24 (Dec., 1904), 175-76.

  D. Girls of the Golden West (1934), "Bucking Broncho," Bluebird 5752, Montgomery Ward 7204. Reissued on *Authentic Cowboys and Their Western Folksongs,* RCA Victor LPV 522.

    Powder River Jack and Kitty Lee (1930), "My Love Is a Cowboy," Bluebird 5298, Electradisk 2169, Sunrise 3379.

  E. Oscar Brand, *Bawdy Western Songs,* Audio Fidelity AFLP 1920.

    ———, *Courting Songs,* Elektra EKL 22.

    Slim Critchlow, "Bucking Broncho," *The Crooked Trail to Holbrook,* Arhoolie 5007.

    Lonesome Valley Singers, "Belle Starr," *Songs of the Trail,* Diplomat D 2627, (as Bob Jones and the Ranch Hands) "Belle Starr," *Bob Jones,* Coronet CX 281, (as Billy Bond) "Buckin' Broncho," *Music of the Wild Wild West,* Crown 5500.

    Frank Luther, "Bucking Bronco," *Songs and Stories about America,* Vocalion 73738.

Hermes Nye, "Bucking Bronco," *Texas Folk Songs,* Folkways FA 2128.
F. Tom Glazer, Keystone KBS 100.

15. The Hell-Bound Train

A. Fife (1969), pp. 336-37.
  Fife (1970), pp. 91-94.
  Finger (1927), pp. 110-13.
  Lomax (1916), pp. 345-47.
  Lomax (1938), pp. 236-38.
  Randolph, 4, 23-24.
  Thorp (1921), pp. 79-81.
B. Hobo News, p. 42.
  Robison, p. 60.
  Sherwin, n.p.
C. Earl C. Beck, *Lore of the Lumber Camps* (Ann Arbor: University of Michigan
  Press, 1948), pp. 261-62.
  Charles O'Brien Kennedy, *American Ballads* (New York: Fawcett Publica-
  tions, 1952), pp. 93-95.
  ———, *A Treasury of American Ballads* (New York: McBride Co., 1954), pp.
  268-70.
  Alan Lomax, *Folk Songs of North America* (Garden City, N.Y.: Doubleday,
  1960), pp. 393, 402.
  Frank Lynn, *Songs for Swinging House Mothers* (San Francisco: Chandler
  Publishing Co., 1961), pp. 208-9.
  Frank Shay, *More Pious Friends and Drunken Companions* (1928; reprinted,
  New York: Dover Publications, 1961), pp. 168-70.
D. Frank Hutchinson (1928), Okeh 45452.
  Smilin' Ed McConnell (1933), Bluebird 5140, Electradisk 2046, Sunrise 3221.
E. Chuck Berry, "Down-Bound Train," *After School Session,* Chess 1426.
  Billy Faier, *Travelin' Man,* Riverside RLP 12-657.
  Glenn Ohrlin, *The Hell-Bound Train,* University of Illinois Campus Folksong
  Club CFC 301.
  Martin Yarbrough, *The Martin Yarbrough Showcase,* Argo LP 4029.

16. The Gol-Darned Wheel

Colonel Will L. Visscher wrote a poem telling of a battle resembling the one in
this song which Captain Jack Crawford ("The Poet Scout") had with a wheel.
Crawford included Visscher's humorous piece in his book *Lariattes* (Sigourney,
Iowa: William A. Bell Publisher, 1904).

A. Coolidge, pp. 104-8.
  Finger (1923), pp. 29-31.
  Laws (1964) (dB 38), p. 260.
  Lomax (1910), pp. 190-93.
  Lomax (1916), pp. 190-93.
  Lomax (1938), pp. 269-72.
  Thorp (1921), pp. 71-74.
B. German (1929), n.p.
  Lee (1936a), pp. 24-25.
  Lee (1937), pp. 40-41.
C. Ruth A. Barnes, *I Hear America Singing* (New York: Junior Literary Guild,
  1937), pp. 67-70.
E. Van Holyoak, "The Gol-Durned Wheel," *Cowboy Songs,* 2, Arizona Friends of
  Folklore AFF 33-2.
  Glenn Ohrlin, University of Illinois Press MAL 731.

17. Old-Time Cowboy

A. Lingenfelter, pp. 340-41.
  Lomax (1910), pp. 263-64.
  Lomax (1916), pp. 263-64, 365-66.
  Lomax (1938), pp. 220-21.
  Thorp (1908), pp. 40-41.
  Thorp (1921), pp. 121-22.
B. Lee (1936a), p. 11.
  Lee (1937), p. 8.

18. The Old Scout's Lament

A. Finger (1923), pp. 32-33.
  Lomax (1910), pp. 117-18.
  Lomax (1916), pp. 117-18, 348-49.
  Lomax (1938), pp. 354-55.

19. Cowboy's Life

This song, written by D. J. O'Malley, first appeared in the Miles City, Montana, *Stock Growers' Journal,* February 3, 1894, under the title "D-2 Horse Wrangler." The January 23, 1932, issue of Street and Smith's *Western Story Magazine* printed a letter from O'Malley complaining about the claims of R. O. Mack, who had copyrighted O'Malley's song "When the Work's All Done This Fall" in 1929. John I. White saw O'Malley's letter and investigated. White's diligent research confirmed that O'Malley wrote "When the Work's All Done This Fall," as well as other well-known cowboy songs. The history of this important cowboy poet will be well documented in White's forthcoming book (Urbana: University of Illinois Press).

A. Allen, pp. 89-90.
  Coolidge, pp. 126-27.
  Fife (1969), pp. 197-98.
  Laws (1964) (B 27), p. 145.
  Lingenfelter, pp. 338-39.
  Lomax (1910), pp. 136-38.
  Lomax (1916), pp. 136-38.
  Lomax (1938), pp. 119-22.
  Pound, pp. 29-30.
  Thorp (1908), pp. 13-14.
  Thorp (1921), pp. 146-48.
B. American, pp. 44-45.
  Clark (1932), p. 58.
  Davis, p. 52.
  German (1929), n.p.
  Goodwin, p. 26.
  Klickman, pp. 38-39.
  Sires, pp. 2-3.
  Smith, pp. 28-29.
  White (1929), pp. 46-48.
  White (1934), n.p.
C. Ruth A. Barnes, *I Hear America Singing* (New York: Junior Literary Guild, 1937), pp. 126-27.
  Jan Harold Brunvand, "Folk Song Studies in Idaho," *Western Folklore,* 24 (Oct., 1965), 238.
  ———, *A Guide for Collectors of Folklore in Utah* (Salt Lake City: University of Utah Press, 1971), pp. 70-71.

Jay Monaghan, *The Book of the American West* (New York: Julian Messner, 1963), pp. 548-49.

James Warner, *Songs That Made America* (New York: Grossman Publishers, 1972), pp. 67-69.

Roger Welsch, *A Treasury of Nebraska Pioneer Folklore* (Lincoln: University of Nebraska Press, 1966), pp. 22-24.

John I. White, "A Cowboy Poet," *Frontier Times* (Bandera, Tex.), 11 (Feb., 1934), 190-92.

———, "D. J. 'Kid' O'Malley," *Montana, the Magazine of Western History*, 17, no. 3 (July, 1967), 60-73.

———, *D. J. O'Malley: Cowboy Poet* (Westfield, N.J., 1934). John I. White wrote and printed this twenty-page pamphlet and gave most of the copies to O'Malley, who gave them to old friends at the golden jubilee celebration at Miles City, Montana, in the summer of 1934.

———, "A Montana Cowboy Poet," *Journal of American Folklore,* 80 (Apr.-June, 1967), 113-29.

D. Bill Bender (1939), "The Tenderfoot," Varsity 5148.

Tony Kraber (ca. 1945), "The Tenderfoot," Keynote 506. Reissued on *The Old Chisholm Trail,* Mercury MG 20008.

E. Oscar Brand, "The Tenderfoot," *Pie in the Sky,* Tradition TLP 1022.

Slim Critchlow, "The D-Bar-2 Horse Wrangler," *The Crooked Trail to Holbrook,* Arhoolie 5007.

Frances Roberts, "The Tenderfoot," *Cowboy Songs,* 2, Arizona Friends of Folklore AFF 33-2.

Roger Welsch, "Horse Wrangler," *Sweet Nebraska Land,* Folkways FH 5337.

F. Romaine Lowdermilk, "The Tenderfoot," Audio Records of Arizona.

20. Roundup in the Spring

Vernon Dalhart recorded "Roundup in the Spring" on November 1, 1926. My copy of this record gives composer credit to Copeland, although it is possible this was added at a later pressing. The song was first printed in sheet music copyrighted in 1927 by Lou Fishback (Fort Worth, Tex.); Carl Copeland and Jack Williams were listed as co-writers. The following year, the Texas Folklore Society printed an article by J. Frank Dobie, who claimed it was an old song he had obtained from Andy Adams.

A. Lomax (1938), pp. 321-22.

B. Clark (1932), p. 40.

Clark (1934), pp. 22-23.

Davis, p. 22.

Eckstein, pp. 19-20.

Patterson, pp. 21-23.

Smith, pp. 2-3.

C. J. Frank Dobie, "Ballads and Folksongs of the Frontier Folk," *Texas and Southwestern Lore,* Publications of the Texas Folklore Society, 6 (Austin: Southern Methodist University Press, 1927), pp. 161-63.

D. Vernon Dalhart (1926), "I'd Like to Be in Texas When They Round-up in the Spring," Columbia 15131-D.

——— (1926), "I'd Like to Be in Texas When They Round-up in the Spring," Vocalion 5044.

Martin and Roberts (1933), Banner 32747, Oriole 8226, Romeo 5226, Perfect 12906, Conqueror 8206, Melotone 12675, Vocalion 5496 (as Glen Fox and Joe Wilson), (Australian) Regal Zonophone 22247.

Texas Jim Robertson (ca. 1941), *'Round the Campfire,* Victor album P-84.

E. Slim Critchlow, "I'd Like to Be in Texas," *The Crooked Trail to Holbrook,* Arhoolie 5007.

21. Moonlight and Skies

A Jimmie Rodgers discography may be obtained from Don Cleary, P.O. Box 31, Bloomingdale, New Jersey 07403.

A. Laws (1964) (dE 36), p. 267.
   Randolph, 2, 162.
D. Gene Autry (1932), Conqueror 8002.
   Jimmie Rodgers (1930), Victor 23574, Bluebird 5000, Electradisk 1830, Electradisk 1958, Montgomery Ward 4720. Reissued on *Short but Brilliant Life*, RCA Victor LPM 2634, and *Best of the Legendary Jimmie Rodgers*, RCA Victor LSP 3315.
E. Yodeling Slim Clark, *Sings Jimmie Rodgers*, Palamino 300.
   Red River Dave, *The Singing Yodeling Cowboy*, 2, Bluebonnet 122.
   Stanley G. Triggs, *Bunkhouse and Forecastle Songs of the Northwest*, Folkways FG 3569.

Derivatives of "Moonlight and Skies" include:

D. Jimmie Davis (1936), "Moonlight and Skies No. 2," Decca 5104.
E. Jack Guthrie, "New Moonlight and Skies," *Jack Guthrie and His Greatest Hits*, Capitol T 2456.

22. Zebra Dun

A. Allen, pp. 159-61.
   Fife (1969), pp. 194-95.
   Larkin, pp. 36-38.
   Laws (1964) (B 16), pp. 17, 140-41.
   Lingenfelter, pp. 402-3.
   Lomax (1910), pp. 154-57.
   Lomax (1916), pp. 154-57.
   Lomax (1938), pp. 78-81.
   Randolph, 2, 244-45.
   Silber, pp. 262-64.
   Thorp (1908), pp. 27-29.
   Thorp (1921), pp. 171-74.
B. American, pp. 46-47.
   Asch (1964), p. 69.
   Clark (1932), pp. 68-69.
   Colby, p. 8.
   German (1929), n.p.
   Goodwin, p. 11.
   Lee (1936a), pp. 32-33.
   Maynard, pp. 28-30.
   Patterson, pp. 56-57.
   White (1934), n.p.
   Williams, pp. 26-27.
C. MacEdward Leach, *The Book of Ballads* (Mt. Vernon, N.Y.: George Macy Companies, 1967), pp. 166-68, 205.
   H. D. Munal, *The Songs of Long Ago* (Privately published, 1933), pp. 12-13.
   Sam Savitt, *Rodeo* (Garden City, N.Y.: Doubleday and Co., 1963), p. 10.
   John I. White, "The Zebra Dun," *Arizona Republic* (Phoenix), March 9, 1969.
D. Jules Allen (1928), Victor 40022. Reissued on *Authentic Cowboys and Their Western Folksongs*, RCA Victor LPV 522.
   Tex Fletcher (1938), Decca 5302.
   Frank Luther (1939), Decca 1428 (in album K-14).

257

E. Cisco Houston, *Cisco Sings,* Folkways FA 2346.

Harry Jackson, *The Cowboy,* Folkways FH 5723.

Frank Luther, *Git Along Little Dogies,* Decca DL 5035.

———, *Songs and Stories about America,* Vocalion 73738.

Nevada Slim, "Z-Bar Dunn," *Nevada Slim Sings Songs of the Wild West,* 2, Rural Rhythm RRNS 163.

Joan O'Bryant, *Folksongs and Ballads of Kansas,* Folkways FA 2134.

Ray Oman, *Trail Dust 'n' Saddle Leather,* Ace Recordings.

Frances Roberts, *Cowboy Songs,* Arizona Friends of Folklore AFF 33-1.

Dean Turner, *Dean Turner and His Guitar,* Bluebonnet BL 102.

J. M. Wandell, *Cowboy Songs, Ballads, and Cattle Calls from Texas,* Library of Congress Archive of Folk Song AAFS L 28.

F. Romaine Lowdermilk, Audio Records of Arizona.

23. Platonia

A. Fife (1969), pp. 184-85.

Larkin, pp. 112-13.

Laws (1964) (B 12), pp. 138-39.

Lingenfelter, pp. 264-65.

Lomax (1938), pp. 356-58.

Randolph, 2, 242-43.

B. Lee (1936b), pp. 28-29.

Lee (1937), pp. 6-7.

C. Harold W. Felton, *Cowboy Jamboree* (New York: Alfred A. Knopf, 1951), pp. 80-83.

H. D. Munal, *The Songs of Long Ago* (Privately published, 1933), p. 17.

Robert C. Pooley et al., *Sing Out America* (Chicago: Scott, Foresman, 1950), pp. 20-21.

E. Green Valley Singers, "Patanio," *Twenty Golden Moments of Country Music,* Diplomat DS 2422.

Jim Greer and the Mac-O-Chee Valley Folks, "Patonia," *Stars of the WWVA Jamboree,* Rural Rhythm RRJG 161.

Lonesome Valley Singers, "Patanino," *Songs of the Trail,* Diplomat D 2627, (as Billy Bond) "Patonia," *Music of the Wild Wild West,* Crown CLP 5500.

Nevada Slim, "The Story of Patonio," *Songs of the Wild West,* 2, Rural Rhythm RRNS 163.

Hank Snow, "Patonio, the Pride of the Plain," *Heart Break Trail,* RCA Victor LSP 3471.

24. Walking John

The author of "Walking John," Henry Herbert Knibbs, was born in Clifton, Ontario, but spent the latter part of his life in the western United States. At one time he belonged to a group of western writers who met once a month at the University Club in Los Angeles. Will Rogers, Charles M. Russell, Eugene Manlove Rhodes, and E. A. Brininstool were other members. It is interesting that Glenn, who admires Russell, should include two songs from each of his friends Brininstool (nos. 77, 98) and Knibbs (nos. 24, 46) without knowing of their connection with Russell. Knibbs wrote several good western novels. His books of verse include *First Poems* (1908), *Songs of the Outlands* (1914), *Riders of the Stars* (1916), *Songs of the Trail* (1920), and *Saddle Songs and Other Verse* (1922).

A. Larkin, pp. 69-72.

B. Lee (1936b), pp. 14-15.

Lee (1937), p. 9.

C. Henry Herbert Knibbs, *Songs of the Last Frontier* (Boston: Houghton Mifflin, 1930), pp. 64-66.

258

E. George Gillespie, *Cow Camp Songs of the Old West,* Thorne TR 200.

Peter LaFarge, *Peter LaFarge Sings of the Cowboys,* Folkways FA 2533.

Glenn Ohrlin, *The Hell-Bound Train,* University of Illinois Campus Folksong Club CFC 301.

25. Pride of the Prairie

Tunesmiths of Tin Pan Alley often produce "cowboy" songs that appeal to real cowboys. The words of "Pride of the Prairie" were written by Henry J. Breen. George Botsford wrote the music. The song was first published in 1907 by Jerome H. Remick and Company, New York.

B. Clark (1932), p. 86.

German (1929), n.p.

German (1932), n.p.

Remick, pp. 8-9.

D. Tex Owens (1936), Decca 5015.

Texas Ruby and Zeke (ca. 1937), Decca 5364.

E. Slim Berry, "Pride of the Prairie Mary," *Abilene and Other Western Hits,* Viking VK 621.

J. E. Mainer, *The Legendary J. E. Mainer,* 11, Rural Rhythm RRJEM 230.

26. Charlie Quantrell, Oh

The Lomax reference below is the only one related to the "Quantrell" form of this ballad; I have not found any recordings of it. However, another song about Quantrill has been recorded by Paul Clayton, Ed McCurdy, and several others; for examples in print, see Laws (1964) (dE 33), p. 266, and Lingenfelter, pp. 314-15. For the "Brennan" form of Glenn's song, see Laws (1957).

A. Laws (1957) (L 7), p. 169.

Lomax (1938), pp. 144-46.

27. The Sierry Petes

A history of this song and of Gail Gardner, who wrote it in 1917, will be included in John I. White's book on cowboy and western songs (Urbana: University of Illinois Press, forthcoming).

A. Fife (1969), pp. 201-3.

Larkin, p. 66.

Laws (1964) (B 17), pp. 17, 141.

Lingenfelter, pp. 358-59.

Silber, pp. 283-85.

B. German (1929), n.p.

German (1932), n.p.

Lee (1936a), pp. 12-13.

Lee (1937), p. 20.

C. Ira W. Ford, *Traditional Music of America* (1940; reprinted, Hatboro, Pa.: Folklore Associates, 1965), pp. 367-69.

Gail I. Gardner, *Orejana Bull: For Cowboys Only* (Prescott, Ariz.: Privately published, 1935), pp. 6-7.

————, *Wild West Weekly,* Nov. 5, 1932.

Powder River Jack H. Lee, *West of Powder River* (New York: Huntington Press, 1933), pp. 166-69.

————, *The Stampede and Other Tales of the Far West* (Greensburg, Pa.: Standardized Press, n.d.), pp. 149-52.

Arthur Loesser, *Humor in American Song* (New York: Howell, Soskin, 1942), p. 200.

J. Barre Toelken, "Northwest Traditional Ballads: A Collector's Dilemma," *Northwest Review,* 5 (1962), 12-13.

John I. White, "Gail Gardner — Poet Lariat," *Arizona Republic* (Phoenix), May 7, 1967.

Wild West Weekly, July 23, 1932.

D. Cisco Houston, "Tying a Knot on the Devil's Tail," Disc 608.

Powder River Jack and Kitty Lee (1930), "Tying a Knot in the Devil's Tail," Victor 23527, Montgomery Ward 4462. Reissued on *Authentic Cowboys and Their Western Folksongs,* RCA Victor LPV 522.

E. Sam Agins, "Sirree Peaks," *Singin' Sam's Saddlebag of Songs,* Haywire ARA 6419.

Wilf Carter, "Tying a Knot in the Devil's Tail," *Calgary Horseman's Hall of Fame,* (Canadian) Camden CAL 943.

Gail Gardner, *Cowboy Songs,* Arizona Friends of Folklore AFF 33-1.

George Gillespie, *Cow Camp Songs of the Old West,* Thorne TR 200.

John Greenway, "Tying Knots in the Devil's Tail," *The Cat Came Back,* Prestige 13011.

Frank Hamilton, "Knots on the Devil's Tail," *The Folksingers' Folksinger,* Concert-Disc CS 54.

Sam Hinton, "Sierra Peaks," *Singing across the Land,* Decca DL 8108.

Cisco Houston, "Tying a Knot on the Devil's Tail," *Traditional Songs of the Old West,* Stinson SLP 37, and *Cowboy Ballads,* Folkways FA 2022.

Harry Jackson, *The Cowboy,* Folkways FH 5723.

Peter LaFarge, "Sirey Peaks (The Devil Song)," *Peter LaFarge Sings of the Cowboys,* Folkways FA 2533.

Nevada Slim, "Tying a Knot on the Devil's Tail," *Songs of the Wild West,* 3, Rural Rhythm RRNS 164.

Ray Oman, *Trail Dust 'n' Saddle Leather,* Ace Recordings.

Rosalie Sorrels, "Tying Knots in the Devil's Tail," *Folksongs of Idaho and Utah,* Folkways FH 5343.

F. Romaine Lowdermilk, "Tying a Knot in the Devil's Tail," Audio Records of Arizona.

28. The Strawberry Roan

In his 1936 song book listed below, Powder River Jack Lee claimed that Frank B. Chamberlain wrote "The Strawberry Roan" as a recitation in 1894. However, the vernacular of Lee's text conforms better to the rodeo speech of Curley Fletcher's day.

A. Fife (1969), pp. 186-89.

Laws (1964) (B 18), p. 141.

Lomax (1938), pp. 99-102. The song was dropped from later printings of this edition.

Randolph, 2, 232-34.

B. German (1929), n.p.

Lee (1936a), pp. 6-7.

Patterson, pp. 49-50.

C. Dick Best and Beth Best, *Song Fest* (New York: Crown Publishers, 1948), pp. 120-21.

B. A. Botkin, *A Treasury of Western Folklore* (New York: Crown Publishers, 1951), pp. 757-58.

Jan Harold Brunvand, "Folk Song Studies in Idaho," *Western Folklore,* 24 (Oct., 1965), 238.

Austin E. Fife, "The Strawberry Roan and His Progeny," *John Edwards Memorial Foundation Quarterly,* 8 (Autumn, 1972), 149-65 (includes extensive biblio-discography).

Frank Lynn, *Songs for Swinging House Mothers* (San Francisco: Chandler, 1961), pp. 298-99.

H. D. Munal, *The Songs of Long Ago* (Privately published, 1933), p. 29.

Sam Savitt, *Rodeo* (Garden City, N.Y.: Doubleday and Co., 1963), p. 10.

John I. White, "The Strange Career of 'The Strawberry Roan,'" *Arizona and the West*, 11 (Winter, 1969), 359-65.

D. Ames Brothers (ca. 1951), Coral 60888.

Beverly Hillbillies (1932), Brunswick 514, Supertone 2263.

Bill Boyd and His Cowboy Ramblers (ca. 1936), Bluebird 5667, Montgomery Ward 4778.

W. C. Childers (1931), Champion 16467, Champion 45103, Montgomery Ward 4957, Superior 2722 (as Enos Wanner).

Cowboy Rogers [Edward L. Crane] (ca. 1933), Continental 3013.

Paul Hamblen (1930), Victor 40260.

Rex Kelly (1931), Paramount 569, Broadway 8331.

Frank Luther (ca. 1939), Decca 1429 (in album K-14).

Bob Miller (1931), Columbia 15677-D (as Bob Ferguson).

―――― (1931), Okeh 45531 (as Bob Kackley).

Ranch Boys (1936), Decca 5074, Decca 2642 (in album A-65).

John White (1931), Conqueror 7753.

―――― (1931), Oriole 8066, Perfect 12712, Romeo 1629, Romeo 5066.

E. Sam Agins, *Singin' Sam's Saddlebag of Songs*, Haywire ARA 6419.

Bob Atcher, *Songs of the Saddle*, Columbia HL 9013.

Buckskins, *Let's Go West*, Coronet CX 202.

Montana Slim [Wilf Carter], *No Letter Today*, RCA Camden CAS 2171.

Lew Childre, *Country Music Hall of Fame*, 2, Starday S-9-190, and *Old Time Get-Together*, Starday SLP 153.

Pat Foster, *Our Singing Heritage*, 1, Elektra EKL 151.

George Gillespie, *Cow Camp Songs of the Old West*, Thorne TR 200.

Stuart Hamblen, *Remember Me*, Coral 57254.

Cisco Houston, "Outlaw Horse," *Traditional Songs of the Old West*, Stinson SLP 37.

Harry Jackson, *The Cowboy*, Folkways FH 5723, and *Frontiers*, Folkways FR 10003.

Merrick Jarrett, *The Old Chisholm Trail*, Riverside RLP 12-631, and *Songs of the Old West*, Washington WLP 725.

Peter LaFarge, *Peter LaFarge Sings of the Cowboys*, Folkways FA 2533.

Frank Luther, *Git Along Little Dogies*, Decca DL 5035.

――――, *Songs and Stories about America*, Vocalion 73738.

Ed McCurdy, *Songs of the West*, Tradition 2061.

Red River Dave [McEnery], *Red River Dave Album No. 2*, Bluebonnet BL 122.

Lee Moore, *Everybody's Favorite*, Rural Rhythm RRLM 202.

Marty Robbins, *Gunfighter Ballads*, Columbia CS 8158, and *Marty Robbins Country*, Columbia GP 16.

Sons of the Pioneers, *Legends of the West*, RCA Victor LSP 3351.

Wesley Tuttle, *Songs of the Panhandle*, Camay CA 3018.

Willis Brothers, *The Code of the West*, Starday SLP 229.

F. [Art] Dickson's Melody Mustangs, Lang Worth WES 29A.

29. He Rode the Strawberry Roan

Don Cleary (P.O. Box 31, Bloomingdale, N.J. 07403) has compiled a Wilf Carter ("Montana Slim") discography.

C. Austin E. Fife, "The Strawberry Roan and His Progeny," *John Edwards Memorial Foundation Quarterly*, 8 (Autumn, 1972), 156-57, 165.

261

D. Wilf Carter (ca. 1937), (Canadian) Bluebird 4974.

E. Wilf Carter, *Songs of the Calgary Stampede,* (Canadian) Apex AL 1615.

30. The Fate of Old Strawberry Roan

C. Austin E. Fife, "The Strawberry Roan and His Progeny," *John Edwards Memorial Foundation Quarterly,* 8 (Autumn, 1972), 154-55, 165.

D. Wilf Carter (1936), (Canadian) Bluebird 4602, Montgomery Ward 7186, Bluebird 8389 (as Montana Slim). Reissued on *Reminiscing with Montana Slim,* RCA Camden CAL 668.

32. Pete Knight, the King of the Cowboys

C. Wilf Carter, *More Cowboy Songs,* 2 (Toronto: Gordon V. Thompson, 1937), p. 16.

D. Wilf Carter (ca. 1937), (Canadian) Bluebird 4989.

E. Wilf Carter, *Songs of the Calgary Stampede,* (Canadian) Apex AL 1615.

33. Pete Knight's Last Ride

C. Wilf Carter, *Cowboy Songs,* 3 (Toronto: Gordon V. Thompson, 1938), pp. 14-15.

D. Wilf Carter, Victor 27785 (in album P-114), (Canadian) Bluebird 4623.

34. Paddy Ryan

C. Helen Clark, "Paddy Ryan," *Western Horseman,* 29, no. 5 (May, 1964), 34-35, 116-19.

35. Fritz Truan, a Great Cowboy

C. Larry Finley, *Hoofs and Horns* (further data unavailable).

36. Heelin' Bill

C. *Hoofs and Horns,* February, 1951, p. 2.

Willard H. Porter, *13 Flat* (South Brunswick, N.J.: A. S. Barnes and Co., 1967), p. 185.

37. Kenny Madland

C. Lois Green, *The Buckboard,* June, 1950.

38. Powder River Jack

C. Colorado Bill, *Hoofs and Horns* (further data unavailable).

40. Powder River, Let 'er Buck

For the use of "Powder River!" as an ornamental call to enliven square dances, see Ira W. Ford, *Traditional Music of America* (1940; reprinted, Hatboro, Pa.: Folklore Associates, 1965), p. 199.

B. Lee (1936b), pp. 32-34.

Lee (1937), pp. 4-5.

C. Duncan Emrich, *It's an Old Wild West Custom* (New York: Vanguard Press, 1949), pp. 237-41.

Powder River Jack H. Lee, *West of Powder River* (New York: Huntington Press, 1933), pp. 17-20.

D. Powder River Jack and Kitty Lee (1930), Victor 23527, Montgomery Ward 4462. Reissued on *Authentic Cowboys and Their Western Folksongs,* RCA Victor LPV 522.

Powder River Jack and Kitty Lee made the commercial recordings listed below. Abbreviations: B = Bluebird, E = Electradisk, MW = Montgomery Ward, S = Sunrise, V = Victor.

Master No.	Title	Release Nos.

Hollywood, Calif. Nov. 3, 1930. Acc. by own guitars.

61049	Tying a Knot in the Devil's Tail	V-23527, MW-4462
61050	The Old Black Steer	B-5298, S-3379, E-2169
61051	My Love Is a Cowboy	B-5298, S-3379, E-2169
61052	Powder River Let 'er Buck	V-23527, MW-4462

41. A Tale of the Trail

We are indebted to Bob Cook, the editor of *Bar North,* for the information that this poem was written by James W. Foley and appeared in his 1914 book of western sketches and poems.

C. *50 Years in the Saddle: Looking down the Back Trail* (Boston: Meador Press, 1963).

James W. Foley, *Bar North,* January, 1958.

————, *Tales of the Trail* (New York: E. P. Dutton and Co., 1914).

42. Sam's "Waiting for a Train"

In view of the great number of recordings derived from the Jimmie Rodgers version of "Waiting for a Train," only 78 rpm records issued before 1930 and a sampling of current LPs of this version are included in the following discography. A definitive study of this song, with a complete discography, will be included in Norm Cohen's book on railroad songs (Urbana: University of Illinois Press, forthcoming).

A. Laws (1964) (H 2), pp. 230-31.
  Randolph, 4, 360.
B. Asch (1965), p. 34.
D. Bill Baker with Bob Miller's Hinker Dinkers (1930), "Wild and Reckless Hobo," Brunswick 445, Supertone 2059.
  Dock Boggs (1927), "Danville Girl," Brunswick 132.
  Britt and Ford (1935), "Free Wheelin' Hobo," Melotone 13293.
  Burnett and Rutherford (1927), "Rambling Reckless Hobo," Columbia 15240-D, Clarion 5436 (as Clayton and Parker), Velvet Tone 2496.
  Cliff Carlisle (ca. 1938), "Waiting for a Ride," Bluebird 7094, Montgomery Ward 7032, Montgomery Ward 7365. Reissued on *Cliff Carlisle,* 1, Old Timey LP 103.
  Carter Family (1930), "Western Hobo," Victor 40255, Bluebird 6223, Montgomery Ward 7147.
  Cofer Brothers (1927), "Georgia Hobo," Okeh 45099.
  Vernon Dalhart (1925), "Wild and Reckless Hobo," Brunswick 2942, Supertone 2005.
  Jeff Calhoun [Vernon Dalhart] (1927), "Wild and Reckless Hobo," Grey Gull 4140, Radiex 4140.
  Morgan Dennon (ca. 1928), "Wild and Reckless Hobo," Okeh 45327.
  Dixon Brothers (ca. 1936), "The Girl I Left in Danville," Bluebird 7674, Montgomery Ward 7337. Reissued on *Babies in the Mill,* Testament T 3301.
  Richard Eustis (1927), "Wild and Reckless Hobo," Madison 5073, Van Dyke 5073.
  Jimson Brothers [Frank Luther and Carson Robison] (ca. 1929), "Waiting for a Train," Edison 52578.
  Clayton McMichen (1933), "Free Wheeling Hobo," Varsity 5075 (from Crown master).

Frankie Marvin (ca. 1938), "A Thousand Miles from Home," Varsity 5109.

Bill Palmer [Bob Miller], "Free Wheelin' Hobo," Electradisk 1908, Bluebird 5010, Sunrise 3110.

Bob Ferguson [Bob Miller] (1930), "Wild and Reckless Hobo," Columbia 15616-D.

Pie Plant Pete [Claude D. Moye] (ca. 1930), "Waiting for a Train," Gennett 7167, Champion 45093, Supertone 9668, Champion 15970 (as Asparagus Joe), Superior 2577 (as Jerry Wallace).

Riley Puckett (1929), "Waiting for a Train," Columbia 15408-D.

George Reneau [with Gene Austin] (1925), "Wild and Reckless Hobo," Vocalion 14999.

Hoke Rice (ca. 1929), "Waiting for a Train," Gennett 6839, QRS R 9012, Champion 15767 (as Lee Landon), Supertone 9496 (as Duke Lane).

Fred Richards (1929), "Danville Blues," Columbia 15483-D.

Jimmie Rodgers (1929), "Waiting for a Train," Victor 40014, Bluebird 5161, Montgomery Ward 8109, Sunrise 3244, RCA Victor 21-0175, RCA Victor 27-0104. Reissued on *Never No Mo' Blues*, RCA Victor LPM 1232, and *Best of the Legendary Jimmie Rodgers*, RCA Victor LPM 3315.

Virginia Mountain Boomers (ca. 1928), "Rambling Reckless Hobo," Gennett 6567, Supertone 9305, Champion 15610 (as Blue Mountain Ramblers).

Ed "Jake" West (1929), "Waiting for a Train," Banner 6370, Broadway 8109, Cameo 9219, Challenge 813, Conqueror 7348, Jewel 5586, Oriole 1561, Regal 8775, Romeo 1021 (as Jimmy Price), Romeo 3821 (as Jimmy Price), Cameo 9219 (as Jimmy Price).

E. Elton Britt, "Waiting for a Train," *The Jimmie Rodgers Blues*, RCA Camden CAS 2295.

Johnny Cash, "Waiting for a Train," *Blood, Sweat and Tears*, Columbia CL 1930.

Yodeling Slim Clark, "Waiting for a Train," *Yodeling Slim Clark Sings Jimmie Rodgers*, Palamino 306.

Merle Haggard, "Waiting for a Train," *Same Train, a Different Time*, Capitol SWBB 223.

Grandpa Jones, "Waiting for a Train," *Yodeling Hits*, Monument 8001.

Glenn Ohrlin, *The Hell-Bound Train*, University of Illinois Campus Folksong Club CFC 301.

Jim Reeves, "Waiting for a Train," *Country Side*, RCA Camden S 686.

Hank Snow, "Waiting for a Train," *Railroad Man*, RCA Victor LSP 2705.

Billy Walker, "Waiting for a Train," *Billy Walker Salutes the Country Music Hall of Fame*, Monument 18101.

43. Paddy on the Turnpike

This song appears to be an amalgamation of several popular songs. For instance, in 1928 Jimmie Rodgers recorded the third verse as part of "Brakeman's Blues" (Victor 21291, reissued on *My Rough and Rowdy Ways*, RCA Victor LPM 2112).

44. Let Old Nellie Stay

C. Dick Best and Beth Best, *The New Song Fest* (New York: Crown Publishers, 1955), p. 64.

Richard A. Reuss, "An Annotated Field Collection of Songs from the American College Student Oral Tradition" (thesis, Indiana University, 1965), pp. 289-92.

45. Put Your Little Foot

C. Lawrence (Bud) Bol, *The Square Dance* (Chicago: Chicago Park District, 1950), pp. 244-46.

264

Ira W. Ford, *Traditional Music of America* (1940; reprinted, Hatboro, Pa.: Folklore Associates, 1965), p. 151.

Lloyd Shaw, *Cowboy Dances,* rev. ed. (Caldwell, Idaho: Caxton Printers, 1950), pp. 78-90, 392.

D. Bluebird Band (ca. 1939), "Varsoviana," Bluebird 7721.

Bill Boyd and His Cowboy Ramblers (ca. 1950), "Varsoviana," RCA Victor 21-0071.

Jimmie Clossin's Blue Bonnet Playboys, "Varsouvienne," *Texas Square Dances,* Imperial Album FD 17.

Conway's Band (1917), "Varsoviana (See My New Shoes)," Victor 35535.

Henry Ford's Old-Fashioned Dance Orchestra (ca. 1927), "Varsovienne," Columbia 683-D.

Henry Ford's Old-Time Dance Orchestra (1925), "Varsoviana," Victor 19910, Bluebird 5449, and "Hungarian Varsovienne," Columbia 936-D.

Les Gotcher, "Varsouvienna," MacGregor album 2.

Ken Griffin (ca. 1949), "Put Your Little Foot Right Out," Columbia 39711.

Harry Harden's Orchestra (ca. 1947), "Put Your Little Foot Right Out," Decca 2926.

"Hungarian Varsouvienne," Henry Ford 103-A.

Sammy Kaye and His Orchestra (ca. 1949), "Put Your Little Foot Right Out," RCA Victor 20-1812.

Pee Wee King and His Golden West Cowboys (ca. 1950), "Varsoviana," RCA Victor 20-4971, Bluebird 58-0266. Reissued on *Pee Wee King's Biggest Hits,* RCA Camden CAS 2460.

Louie and His Old Time Band, Globe 5002.

Harley Luse and His Blue Ridge Mountain Boys, "Varsouvianna," *Square Dances,* Imperial album FD 8.

Louise Massey and the Westerners (1935), "Varsovienna," Banner 33328.

——— (ca. 1939), "Put Your Little Foot Right Out," Columbia 20718, Okeh 05425.

Plainsmen, "Varsoviana," Coast 225.

Frank Quinn and John Muller (ca. 1926), "Varsuviana," Gennett 5074.

Frank Quinn and Joe McGuire (1927), "Varsouviana," Columbia 33234-F.

Dick Robertson's Orchestra (1948), "Put Your Little Foot Right Out," Decca 3131.

Bob Skyle's Four Old Timers (1928), "Varsouvienne," Okeh 45243.

Cliffie Stone (1950), "Varsouvianna (Put Your Little Foot)," Capitol 1109.

Bud Udick with Cactus Tait's Orchestra, "La Varsouvianna," Pikes Peak Records.

Byron Wolfe's Orchestra (ca. 1946), "Varsouvienne," Decca 2092.

E. Los Charros (Francisco Vallejos and Rafael Martinez), "La Varsouviana," *Bailes de Taos,* Taos TRP 6.

Pee Wee King, "Varsoviana," *Golden Olde Tyme Tunes,* Briar M 102.

Glenn Ohrlin, *The Hell-Bound Train,* University of Illinois Campus Folksong Club CFC 301.

Earl Robinson, "Varsovienne," *Hootenanny Tonight,* Folkways FH 2511.

Tex-i-an Boys, *Songs of Texas,* Folkways FH 5328.

46. Jake and Roanie

C. Henry Herbert Knibbs, *Songs of the Last Frontier* (New York: Houghton Mifflin, 1930), p. 73.

Charles M. Russell, *Trails Plowed Under* (Garden City, N.Y.: Doubleday, Page, and Co., 1927), pp. 82-84 (anecdote).

E. Sam Agins, "Jake and Rony," *Singin' Sam's Saddlebag of Songs,* Haywire ARA 6419.

Glenn Ohrlin, "Jake and Roaney and the Bald Faced Steer," *Folk Festival of the Smokies,* 2, Traditional Records FFS 529.

———, *Stone County Singing,* Shoestring Tape SGB 1.

Frances Roberts, "Boskey Steer," *Cowboy Songs,* Arizona Friends of Folklore AFF 33-1.

F. Romaine Lowdermilk, Audio Records of Arizona.

47. Lee's Ferry

During the 1910s and 1920s, Romaine Lowdermilk wrote some of the most realistic short stories published about the American West. However, when publishers began to demand the type of romance made popular by Zane Grey, an Ohio dentist, Lowdermilk quit writing and became the manager of dude ranches.

C. John I. White, "And That's How a Folksong Was Born," *Arizona Republic* (Phoenix), August 13, 1967. The article describes another Romaine Lowdermilk composition, "The Big Corral."

E. Glenn Ohrlin, University of Illinois Press MAL 731.

F. Romaine Lowdermilk, Audio Records of Arizona.

49. High Chin Bob

A. Fife (1969), pp. 333-35.
Fife (1970), pp. 40-42.
Lingenfelter, pp. 360-61.
Lomax (1919), pp. 30-35.
Thorp (1921), pp. 81-83.

C. Ruth A. Barnes, *I Hear America Singing* (New York: Junior Literary Guild, 1937), pp. 62-64.
Charles Badger Clark, *Sun and Saddle Leather* (1915; revised, Stockton, California: Westerners Foundation, 1962), pp. 77-80. (Published by Westerners International, University Station Box 3941, Tucson, Arizona 85710.)
Satis N. Coleman and Adolph Bergman, *Songs of American Folks* (New York: John Day and Co., 1942), pp. 48-50.
John I. White, "Badger Clark: Poet of Yesterday's West," *Arizona Highways,* 45, no. 2 (Feb., 1969), 30-32, 34.

E. George Gillespie, *Cow Camp Songs of the Old West,* Thorne TR 200.
Merrick Jarrett, *The Old Chisholm Trail,* Riverside RLP 12-631, and *Songs of the Old West,* Washington WLP 725.
Nevada Slim, "The Cowboy and the Lion," *Songs of the Wild West,* Rural Rhythm RRNS 162.

51. The Cowman's Prayer

Unlike many collections of folksongs, which are limited to popular antiquities, Glenn Ohrlin's songbag is filled with live songs. They are an important part of his everyday life and change as circumstances change. In this song, the price of beef, a vital matter to ranchers, rises to meet inflation. When Carl T. Sprague recorded "The Cowman's Prayer" in 1927, he had the cowman pray for beef to bring five cents a pound. Glenn changed the price to thirty cents a pound when he compiled this collection of songs in 1969. In 1972 he made it forty cents, and when federal price controls went into effect in June, 1973, four months after he recorded the LP which accompanies this book, he said he wished he had prayed for sixty-cent beef.

A. Allen, pp. 132-33.
Fife (1969), pp. 338-39.
Fife (1970), pp. 83-84.
Lomax (1910), p. 24.
Lomax (1916), p. 24.
Lomax (1938), pp. 329-30.

Thorp (1921), p. 52.
B. Davis, p. 43.
Patterson, pp. 8-9.
C. *Ace High Magazine* (New York), 62 (Aug. 28, 1931), 474.
    Norman Luboff and Win Stracke, *Songs of Man* (Englewood Cliffs, N.J.:
        Prentice-Hall; New York: Walton Music Corp., 1965), p. 334.
    Socorro Bullion (Socorro, N.Mex.), Oct. 30, 1886.
    Clifford P. Westermeier, *Trailing the Cowboy* (Caldwell, Idaho: Caxton
        Printers, 1955), pp. 265-66.
    John I. White, "Carl T. Sprague: The Original 'Singing Cowboy,'" *John
        Edwards Memorial Foundation Quarterly,* 6 (Spring, 1970), 32-34.
D. Carl T. Sprague (1927), Victor 21402.
E. Glenn Ohrlin, University of Illinois Press MAL 731.

52. The Dying Ranger

A. Allen, pp. 80-83.
    Coolidge, pp. 109-13.
    Finger (1927), pp. 170-73.
    Laws (1964) (A 14), pp. 14, 125-26.
    Lingenfelter, pp. 270-71.
    Lomax (1910), pp. 214-18.
    Lomax (1916), pp. 214-18.
    Lomax (1938), pp. 366-68.
    Moore, pp. 316-19.
    Randolph, 2, 196-99, 264-65.
B. American, pp. 20-21.
    Clark (1932), p. 30.
    Clark (1937), p. 44.
    Davis, p. 47.
    Goodwin, p. 54.
    Lee (1936b), pp. 28-29.
    Lee (1937), p. 42.
    Williams, pp. 16-17.
C. Roger D. Abrahams, *A Singer and Her Songs* (Baton Rouge: Louisiana State
        University Press, 1970), pp. 31-33.
    Jan Harold Brunvand, "Folk Song Studies in Idaho," *Western Folklore,* 24
        (Oct., 1965), 238.
    Shelby Darnell [Bob Miller], *Jake and Carl the Original Night Hawks Favorite
        Cowboy Song Book,* 2 (New York: Bob Miller, 1939), 49.
    Patrick B. Mullen, "Folk Songs and Family Traditions," *Observations and Re-
        flections on Texas Folklore,* Publications of the Texas Folklore Society, 37
        (Austin: Encino Press, 1972), pp. 55-56.
    Frank Shay, *More Pious Friends and Drunken Companions* (1928; reprinted,
        New York: Dover Publications, 1961), pp. 202-5.
D. Cartwright Brothers (1929), Victor 40198, Bluebird 5355, Montgomery Ward
        4460.
    Marc Williams (1932), Brunswick 497.
E. Dock Boggs, *Dock Boggs,* 3, Asch AH 3903.
    Johnny Prude, *Cowboy Songs, Ballads, and Cattle Calls from Texas,* Library
        of Congress Archive of Folk Song AAFS L 28.
    Spark Gap Wonder Boys, *"Cluck Old Hen,"* Rounder 0002.

53. The Texas Rangers

A. Laws (1964) (A 8), pp. 37-38, 52, 70, 111, 123.
    Lingenfelter, pp. 266-67.

267

Lomax (1910), pp. 44-46.

Lomax (1916), pp. 44-46.

Lomax (1938), pp. 359-61.

Moore, pp. 312-14.

Pound, pp. 28-29.

Randolph, 2, 169-73.

B. Clark (1932), pp. 59-60.

Famous, p. 39.

Hobo News, p. 36.

Maynard, pp. 16-17.

C. Roger D. Abrahams, *A Singer and Her Songs* (Baton Rouge: Louisiana State University Press, 1970), pp. 14-15.

Finlay Adams, *Hootenanny*, 1, no. 3 (May,.1964), 40.

H. M. Belden, "Balladry in America," *Journal of American Folklore*, 25 (1912), 14-15.

The Frank C. Brown Collection of North Carolina Folklore, 4: *The Music of the Ballads*, ed. Jan P. Schinhan (Durham, N.C.: Duke University Press, 1957), pp. 276-77.

Jan Harold Brunvand, "Folk Song Studies in Idaho," *Western Folklore*, 24 (Oct., 1965), 238.

Michael E. Bush, *Folk Songs of Central West Virginia* (Ravenswood, W.Va.: Custom Printing Co., 1969), pp. 45-47.

John Cohen and Mike Seeger, *The New Lost City Ramblers Song Book* (New York: Oak Publications, 1964), p. 150.

Josiah H. Combs, *Folk-Songs of the Southern United States*, ed. D. K. Wilgus (Austin: University of Texas Press, 1967), p. 208.

Mary O. Eddy, *Ballads and Songs from Ohio* (1939; reprinted, Hatboro, Pa.: Folklore Associates, 1964), pp. 291-93.

Emelyn Elizabeth Gardner and Geraldine Jencks Chickering, *Ballads and Songs of Southern Michigan* (1939; reprinted, Hatboro, Pa.: Folklore Associates, 1967), pp. 239-40.

MacEdward Leach, *The Book of Ballads* (Mt. Vernon, N.Y.: George Macy Companies, 1967), pp. 138-39, 201.

Frank Shay, *More Pious Friends and Drunken Companions* (1928; reprinted, New York: Dover Publications, 1961), pp. 152-53.

Roger Welsch, *A Treasury of Nebraska Pioneer Folklore* (Lincoln: University of Nebraska Press, 1966), pp. 31-32.

D. Cartwright Brothers (1929), Victor 40198, Bluebird 5355, Montgomery Ward 4460. Reissued on *Authentic Cowboys and Their Western Folksongs*, RCA Victor LPV 522.

"Mac" (Harry McClintock) (1929), Victor 21487, Montgomery Ward 4784 (as Radio Mac).

Lester McFarland and Robert A. Gardner (1928), Brunswick 168, Vocalion 5177.

Ernest V. Stoneman (1926), Okeh 45054.

E. Paul Clayton, *Cumberland Mountain Folksongs*, Folkways FA 2007.

Sam Eskin, *Songs of All Times*, Cook Laboratories 1020.

Leo Gooley, *Ontario Ballads and Folksongs*, Prestige International INT 25014.

Sara Grey, *Sara Grey*, Folk-Legacy FSI 38.

Paul Joines, "Roving Ranger," *Ballads and Songs of the Blue Ridge Mountains: Persistence and Change*, Asch AH 3831.

Sloan Matthews, *Cowboy Songs, Ballads, and Cattle Calls from Texas*, Library of Congress Archive of Folk Song AAFS L 28.

New Lost City Ramblers, *New Lost City Ramblers*, 2, Folkways FA 2397.

Norris, *Folk and Bluegrass at Neusüdende, 1971-72,* part 2, Folk Variety FV
12003.

Hermes Nye, "Longstreet's Rangers," *Ballads of the Civil War,* Folkways
FA 2188.

Joan O'Bryant, *American Ballads and Folksongs,* Folkways FA 2338.

A discography of the Cartwright brothers follows. All songs are accompanied by
violin and guitar. Abbreviations: B = Bluebird, C = Columbia, V = Victor,
MW = Montgomery Ward.

Master No.	Title	Release Nos.
Dallas, Tex. Dec. 2, 1927.		
W145300	Kelly Waltz	C-15220-D
W145301	Honeymoon Waltz	C-15220-D
Dallas, Tex. Dec. 6, 1928.		
W147577	When the Work's All Done This Fall	C-15346-D
W147578	On the Old Chisholm Trail	C-15346-D
W147579	Get Along Little Dogies	C-15410-D
W147580	Utah Carrol	C-15410-D
Dallas, Tex. Aug. 11, 1929.		
55334	The Dying Ranger	V-40198, B-5355, MW-4460
55335	Texas Ranger	V-40198, B-5355, MW-4460
55336	San Antonio Waltz	V-40147
55337	Zacatecas March	V-40147
Dallas, Tex. Oct. 16, 1929.		
56394	Mammy's Little Black Eyed Boy	V-23512
56395	Pickaninny Lullaby	V-23512
56396	Pretty Little Doggies	V-40247
56397	The Wandering Cowboy	V-40247

See also "The Cartwright Brothers' Story," by Bill Rattray with Jack Cartwright,
in *Old Time Music,* 9 (Summer, 1973), 10-14.

54. Bull Riders in the Sky

E. Glenn Ohrlin, *The Hell-Bound Train,* University of Illinois Campus Folksong
Club CFC 301.

Glenn's model, "Riders in the Sky," is represented in this sampling:

D. Burl Ives (1949), Columbia 38445.
Spike Jones (ca. 1950), RCA Victor 20-3741.
Vaughn Monroe (1949), RCA Victor 20-3411. Reissued on *Vaughn Monroe's
Caravan,* RCA Victor LPM 3048.
Sons of the Pioneers (ca. 1951), RCA Victor 48-0060. Reissued on *Cool Water,*
RCA Victor LSP 2118, and *The Sons of the Pioneers' Best,* RCA Victor
LSP 3476.

E. Eddy Arnold, *Thereby Hangs a Tale,* RCA Victor LSP 2036.
Morton Gould and His Orchestra, *Wagon Wheels,* Columbia ML 4858.
Robert Horton, *Man Called Shenandoah,* Columbia CS 9208.

55. Backward, Turn Backward

This song and the one which follows are derived from "Rock Me to Sleep Again,
Mother," which was copyrighted in 1860 by G. D. Russell of Boston. Elizabeth
Akers wrote the lyrics under the pseudonym Florence Percy; the music is credited

to Ernest Leslie. John H. Hewitt and Edward Johnson also composed tunes for Miss Akers's text.

A. Pound, p. 67.

Other versions of Miss Akers's song include:

E. Pee Wee King, *Country Barn Dance,* RCA Camden S-876.
Slim Whitman, *I'm a Lonely Wanderer,* Imperial 12226, and *Unchain Your Heart,* Sunset 5112.

56. Make Me a Cowboy Again

In his 1932 song book George German credits this parody to Joe and Zack Miller of 101 ranch Wild West show fame.

A. Allen, pp. 143-47.
Fife (1969), pp. 311-13.
B. Clark (1934), pp. 28-29.
German (1932), n.p.
Patterson, pp. 34-35.
C. J. Evetts Haley, "Cowboy Songs Again," *Texas and Southwestern Lore,* Publications of the Texas Folklore Society, 6 (Austin: Southern Methodist University Press, 1927), pp. 203-4.
D. Peg Moreland (1929), Victor 40272.
E. Nevada Slim, *Songs of the Wild West,* 2, Rural Rhythm RRNS 163.
Dean Turner, "Make Me a Cowboy Again for a Day," *Dean Turner and His Guitar,* Bluebonnet BL 102.

57. Sporting Cowboy

A. Laws (1964) (E 17), pp. 75-79, 184.
Lomax (1938), pp. 161-63.
Randolph, 2, 33.
B. Goodwin, p. 21.
C. *The Frank C. Brown Collection of North Carolina Folklore,* 4: *The Music of the Ballads,* ed. Jan P. Schinhan (Durham, N.C.: Duke University Press, 1957), pp. 354-55.
Wild West Weekly, 107, no. 6 (Jan. 9, 1937), 123.
D. Allen Brothers (1928), "The Prisoner's Dream," Victor 40210.
Riley Puckett (1928), "The Moonshiner's Dream," Columbia 15324. Reissued on *Old Time Greats,* 1, GHP LP 902.
Tenneva Ramblers (1928), "Seven Long Years in Prison," Victor 21406. Reissued on *Native American Ballads,* RCA Victor LPV 548, and *Tenneva Ramblers,* Puritan 3001.
Watts and Wilson (1927), Paramount 3006, Broadway 8113 (as Weaver and Wiggins). Reissued on *Old Time Ballads from the Southern Mountains,* County 522.
Frank Welling (1930), "The Moundsville Prisoner," Superior 2585 (as Walter Ragan), Conqueror 7273 (as Joe Summers).
E. Glenn Ohrlin, *Stone County Singing,* Shoestring Tape SGB 1.

58. Come All Ye Western Cowboys

A. Randolph, 2, 175-77.
D. Buell Kazee (1927), "The Roving Cowboy," Brunswick 156.

59. Cole Younger

See John Q. Anderson's recent case study of this ballad for additional bibliodiscography.

A. Fife (1969), pp. 261-62.
  Finger (1923), pp. 20-21.
  Laws (1964) (E 3), pp. 20, 177.
  Lingenfelter, pp. 321-22.
  Lomax (1910), pp. 106-7.
  Lomax (1916), pp. 106-7.
  Moore, pp. 345-47.
  Randolph, 2, 12-16.
B. Sherwin, n.p.
C. John Q. Anderson, "Another Texas Variant of 'Cole Younger,' Ballad of a
  Badman," *Western Folklore,* 31 (Apr., 1972), 103-15.
  Jan Harold Brunvand, "Folk Song Studies in Idaho," *Western Folklore,* 24
  (Oct., 1965), 238.
  Josh Dunson and Ethel Raim, *Anthology of American Folk Music* (New York:
  Oak Publications, 1973), pp. 46-47.
  Roger Welsch, *A Treasury of Nebraska Pioneer Folklore* (Lincoln: University
  of Nebraska Press, 1966), pp. 40-41.
D. Edward L. Crane (1931), "Bandit Cole Younger," Columbia 15710-D. Reissued
  on *American Folk Music,* 1, Folkways FA 2951.
  Cowboy Ed Crane (1932), "Bandit Cole Younger," Conqueror 8010.
  Marc Williams (1932), Brunswick 544.
E. Dock Boggs, *Dock Boggs,* 2, Folkways FA 2392.
  Paul Clayton, *Wanted for Murder,* Riverside RLP 12-640.
  Roger Welsch, *Sweet Nebraska Land,* Folkways FH 5337.

60. The Cowboy's Christmas Ball

Larry Chittenden was born in Montclair, New Jersey. He owned a ranch at Anson,
Texas, for a while but returned east and founded the Christmas Cove, Maine,
autograph library.

A. Finger (1923), pp. 21-24.
  Lingenfelter, pp. 350-52.
  Lomax (1916), pp. 335-39.
  Lomax (1919), pp. 112-16.
  Lomax (1938), pp. 246-49.
  Thorp (1908), pp. 35-36.
  Thorp (1921), pp. 35-39.
B. Clark (1932), pp. 70-71.
  Clark (1937), p. 42.
  Clark (1940), p. 32.
  Lee (1936a), pp. 20-21.
  Sires, pp. 38-39.
C. W. L. Chittenden, *Ranch Verses* (New York: G. P. Putnam's Sons, 1893),
  pp. 12-17.
  Dayton Kelley, "Cowboy's Christmas Ball," *Western Horseman,* 24, no. 12
  (Dec., 1959), 31, 66-67. This article accompanies one of the many annual
  reprintings of Larry Chittenden's poem.

61. The Stray

C. Pecos the Ridgerunner, "The Estrays," *Bit and Spur,* 1948 (further data unavailable).

62. Trail to Mexico

A. Allen, pp. 72-73.
  Fife (1969), pp. 179-82.

Larkin, pp. 49-51.

Laws (1964) (B 13), p. 139. See also Laws (1957), p. 180, "Early, Early in the Spring" (M 1).

Lingenfelter, pp. 394-95.

Lomax (1910), pp. 132-35.

Lomax (1916), pp. 132-35.

Lomax (1938), pp. 52-56.

Moore, pp. 285-89.

Silber, pp. 187-91.

B. American, pp. 52-53.

Clark (1932), pp. 62-63.

Clark (1937), pp. 20-21.

Davis, p. 53.

Goodwin, p. 20.

Lair, p. 35.

Lee (1936b), p. 25.

Lee (1937), p. 50.

White (1929), pp. 24-25.

C. Ruth A. Barnes, *I Hear America Singing* (New York: Junior Literary Guild, 1937), pp. 64-67.

Cowboys and Cattle Country (New York: American Heritage Publishing Co., 1961), p. 146.

Archibald T. Davison, Katherine K. Davis, and Frederic W. Kempf, *Songs of Freedom* (Boston: Houghton Mifflin Co.; Cambridge, Mass.: Riverside Press, 1942), pp. 58-59.

Glenn Gildersleeve and Julia Smith, *Living Songs* (New York: Carl Fischer, 1940), pp. 5-6.

Ruth Heller, *Our Singing Nation* (Chicago: Hall and McCreary Co., 1955), p. 133.

Frank Luther, *Americans and Their Songs* (New York: Harper and Brothers, 1942), p. 264.

Katharine Stanley-Brown, *The Song Book of the American Spirit* (New York and London: Harper and Brothers Publishers, 1927), p. 27.

Henry Whitter, *Familiar Folk Songs as Sung by Henry Whitter* (Privately published, n.d.), n.p.

D. Jules Allen (1929), "Cow Trail to Mexico," Victor 23757.

Frank Luther (ca. 1939), Decca 1429 (in album K-14).

"Mac" (Harry McClintock) (1928), Victor 40016, Montgomery Ward 4469.

Westerners (Massey Family) (ca. 1934), Conqueror 8205.

Len Nash and His Country Boys (ca. 1930), Brunswick 354, Supertone 2069.

Carl T. Sprague (1925), "Following the Cow Trail," Victor 20067, Montgomery Ward 4468. Reissued on *Authentic Cowboys and Their Western Folksongs,* RCA Victor LPV 522.

Texas Rangers (ca. 1936), Decca 5183.

Leslie York, "New Trail to Mexico," Mellow 1633.

E. Bill Bender, *Traditional Songs of the Old West,* Stinson SLP 37.

Slim Critchlow, *The Crooked Trail to Holbrook,* Arhoolie 5007.

Charles Ingenthron, *Songs of the Mormons and Songs of the West,* Library of Congress Archive of Folk Song AAFS L 30.

Peter LaFarge, *Peter LaFarge Sings of the Cowboys,* Folkways FA 2533.

Frank Luther, *Git Along Little Dogies,* Decca DL 5035.

———, *Songs and Stories about America,* Vocalion 73738.

Ed McCurdy, *Songs of the Old West,* Elektra EKL 112.

Nevada Slim, *Songs of the Wild West,* 2, Rural Rhythm RRNS 163.

Joan O'Bryant, *American Ballads and Folksongs,* Folkways FA 2338.

Glenn Ohrlin, *The Hell-Bound Train,* University of Illinois Campus Folksong Club CFC 301.

————, *Stone County Singing,* Shoestring Tape SGB 1.

Pete Seeger, *Frontier Ballads,* Folkways FA 2175.

Carl T. Sprague, "Following the Cow Trail," *The First Popular Singing Cowboy,* Folk Variety FV 12001.

Roger Wagner Chorale, *Folksongs of the Frontier,* Capitol P 8332.

Melvin Wrinkle, *Music of the Ozarks,* National Geographic Society 703.

63. Utah Carol

A. Allen, pp. 96-98.
   Fife (1969), pp. 217-19.
   Larkin, pp. 116-18.
   Laws (1964) (B 4), pp. 16, 111, 135.
   Lingenfelter, p. 436.
   Lomax (1910), pp. 66-68.
   Lomax (1916), pp. 66-68.
   Lomax (1938), pp. 125-28.
   Moore, pp. 325-27.
   Randolph, 2, 239-41.
   Silber, pp. 197-99.
B. American, pp. 70-71.
   Clark (1932), pp. 48-49.
   Famous, p. 40.
   German (1929), n.p.
   Hobo News, p. 48.
   Lee (1936b), pp. 6-7.
   Maynard, pp. 12-13.
   Patterson, pp. 52-55.
   Sires, pp. 6-7.
C. Roger D. Abrahams, *A Singer and Her Songs* (Baton Rouge: Louisiana State University Press, 1970), p. 182.
   Jan Harold Brunvand, "Folk Song Studies in Idaho," *Western Folklore,* 24 (Oct., 1965), 238.
   H. D. Munal, *The Songs of Long Ago* (Privately published, 1933), p. 14.
D. Cartwright Brothers (1928), "Utah Carroll," Columbia 15410.
   Carl T. Sprague (1927), "Utah Carroll," Victor 21194. Reissued on *Authentic Cowboys and Their Western Folksongs,* RCA Victor LPV 522.
   Frank Wheeler and Monroe Lamb (1929), "Utah Carl's Last Ride," Victor 40169, Montgomery Ward 4470.
   Marc Williams (ca. 1929), "Utah Carroll," Brunswick 304.
E. Cecil Gill, "Utah Carroll," *The Yodeling Country Boy,* Bluebonnet BL 101.
   Van Holyoak, "Utah Carl," *Cowboy Songs,* 2, Arizona Friends of Folklore AFF 33-2.
   Harry Jackson, "Utah Carroll," *The Cowboy,* Folkways FH 5723.
   Merrick Jarrett, "Utah Carroll," *The Old Chisholm Trail,* Riverside RLP 12-631, and *Songs of the Old West,* Washington WLP 725.
   Lucy Johnson, "Utah Carl," *Music of the Ozarks,* National Geographic Society 703.
   Harry McClintock, "Utah Carl," *Harry K. McClintock: "Haywire Mac,"* Folkways FD 5272.
   Nevada Slim, "Utah Carl's Last Ride," *Songs of the Wild West,* 2, Rural Rhythm RRNS 163.
   Marty Robbins, *Gunfighter Ballads,* Columbia CS 8158.

273

64. The Cowboy #1

The works of Shakespeare were included among the premiums smokers could get by collecting Bull Durham tobacco coupons. W. C. Tuttle and other western writers often referred to Shakespeare in their stories. The tall tales that were told about "Bill Shakespeare," Sheriff Henry's inebriated rooster, are a high spot of Tuttle's popular stories about "The Shame of Arizona." A good example of Tuttle's use of Shakespeare can be found in "When Hamlet Hit Dogieville," *Argosy,* July 18, 1936.

In *The Complete Rancher* (revised, Minneapolis: T. S. Denison and Co., 1965), a guide to ranching that covers everything from breeds of cattle to kinds of grass, Russell H. Bennett comments on Shakespeare's popularity: "On a farm or ranch the abundant metaphor of the more classic writers comes alive. This is because the reader shares the experiences upon which so many of the metaphors are based and from which they take their color" (p. 175).

A. Allen, pp. 69-71.
  Fife (1969), pp. 331-33.
  Fife (1970), pp. 11-15.
  Larkin, pp. 130-32.
  Lingenfelter, pp. 342-43.
  Lomax (1910), pp. 96-99.
  Lomax (1916), pp. 96-99.
  Lomax (1938), pp. 67-70.
  Thorp (1921), pp. 4-6.
B. Clark (1932), p. 7.
  Clark (1937), p. 22.
  Clark (1940), p. 33.
  German (1929), n.p.
  German (1932), n.p.
  Goodwin, p. 56.
  Patterson, pp. 12-14.
C. Harold W. Felton, *Cowboy Jamboree* (New York: Alfred A. Knopf, 1951), pp. 88-92.
  Alan McCandless, "The Cowboy's Soliloquy," *Wild West Weekly,* 111, no. 4 (June 12, 1937), 127.
D. Carl T. Sprague (1927), Victor 21402, Montgomery Ward 4465.
E. Merrick Jarrett, "All Day on the Prairie," *The Old Chisholm Trail,* Riverside RLP 12-631, and *Songs of the Old West,* Washington WLP 725.
  Ed McCurdy, *Songs of the West,* Tradition 2061.
  Glenn Ohrlin, *The Hell-Bound Train,* University of Illinois Campus Folksong Club CFC 301.

65. The Cowboy #2

A. Fife (1969), p. 85.
  Lomax (1938), p. 139.
B. American, p. 15.
  Clark (1932), p. 69.
  Davis, p. 40.
  White (1929), p. 11.

66. Franklin Slaughter Ranch

A. Fife (1969), pp. 241-43.
  Larkin, pp. 144-45.
  Laws (1964) (B 7), p. 136.
  Lomax (1938), pp. 124-25.
  Randolph, 2, 204.

C. Van Holyoak, "Lone and Painted Cottage," *AFFword,* 1, no. 3 (Oct., 1971), 24-25.
D. Arthur Miles (1929), "The Lonely Cowboy," Victor 40156.
E. Dave Fredrickson, "Frenchman's Ranch," *Songs of the West,* Folkways FH 5259.

68. Tipperary
C. Joe Killer, "Tex Fletcher, Rodeo's Songster," *Hoofs and Horns,* 23, no. 10 (Apr., 1954), 3.

69. Little Joe the Wrangler's Sister Nell
A. Laws (1964) (dB 36), p. 260.
    Randolph, 2, 236.
B. Clark (1934), pp. 20-21.
E. Harry Jackson, *The Cowboy,* Folkways FH 5723.
    Eddie Nesbitt, *Lost Treasures,* Bluebonnet BL 116.

70. Windy Bill's Famous Ride
B. German (1929), n.p.

71. I Learned about Horses from Him
This song is modeled on Kipling's "The Ladies," which Frank Crumit set to music and recorded as "I Learned about Women from Her." Crumit's tune resembles the one commonly associated with "The Blue Velvet Band" and "Bury Me out on the Prairie."
B. German (1932), n.p.
C. D. K. Wilgus, " 'I Learned about Women from Her,' " *Journal of American Folklore,* 86 (Apr.-June, 1973), 179-80.
D. Frank Crumit (1928), "I Learned about Women from Her," Victor 21735.
    Goebel Reeves (1929), "I Learned about Women from Her," Okeh 45381.

72. Button Willow Tree
The many relatives of this song include the popular hit "A Guy Is a Guy" (Doris Day, Columbia 39673) and the bawdy song "A Gob Is a Slob" (Oscar Brand, *Bawdy Songs and Backroom Ballads,* 2, Audio Fidelity AFLP 1806).
A. Laws (1957) (K 43), pp. 162-63.
C. Frank Shay, *American Sea Songs and Chanteys* (New York: W. W. Norton and Co., 1948), pp. 144-45.
    Laura Alexandrine Smith, *The Music of the Waters* (1888; reprinted, Detroit: Singing Tree Press, 1969), pp. 25-27.
    Ken Stubbs, *The Life of a Man* (London: English Folk Dance Society, 1970), pp. 54-55.
E. Alan Mills, "Home, Dearie, Home," *Songs of the Sea,* Folkways FA 2312.
    Glenn Ohrlin, University of Illinois Press MAL 731.

The chorus, or a variant of it, has appeared with other ballads and tunes. See, for example, the following:
C. Archibald T. Davison, Katherine K. Davis, and Frederic W. Kempf, *Songs of Freedom* (Boston: Houghton Mifflin Co.; Cambridge, Mass.: Riverside Press, 1942), pp. 108-9.
    Margaret Dean-Smith, *A Guide to English Folk Song Collections* (Liverpool: University Press of Liverpool in association with the English Folk Dance and Song Society, 1954), p. 94.
    Claude M. Simpson, *The British Broadside Ballad and Its Music* (New Brunswick, N.J.: Rutgers University Press, 1966), pp. 351-53.

74. Tell Your Horse's Age

C. *Bit and Spur,* 1948 (further data unavailable).

77. The Cowboy's Prayer

Many songs of the American West are the products of scholars of national repute. Earl Alonzo Brininstool, who wrote this song as well as "The Chuck Wagon's Stuck" (no. 98), was one of the first historians to explode the Custer myth. His works on western history include *A Trooper with Custer* (1925), *Capture and Death of Crazy Horse* (1929), *Captain Benteen's Story of the Custer Fight* (1933), and *Troopers with Custer* (1952). Other examples of such songs are "The Santa Fe Trail" (no. 85), by James Grafton Rogers, and "The Railroad Corral," by historian Joseph Mills Hanson, who is probably best known for *The Conquest of the Missouri* (1909).

A. Fife (1970), pp. 78-81.

C. E. A. Brininstool, *Trail Dust of a Maverick* (New York: Dodd Mead, 1914), pp. 43-44.

80. Midnight

A photograph of the epitaph at Midnight's grave appears in the Ainsworth book. Savitt prints a variant of this verse, attributing it to Otis Cusack, senator from Colorado.

C. Ed Ainsworth, *The Cowboy in Art* (New York: Crown Publishers, Bonanza Books, 1968), p. 180.

Sam Savitt, *Rodeo* (Garden City, N.Y.: Doubleday and Co., 1963), p. 51.

81. Starlight

C. Noah Henry, *Hoofs and Horns,* 27, no. 11 (May, 1958), 18.

83. My Stetson Hat

C. *Hoofs and Horns,* 23, no. 5 (Nov., 1953), 8. Reprinted from *Hoofs and Horns* for June, 1935; the poem was sent in by Harry Woods.

Western Horseman, 29, no. 5 (May, 1964), 76.

E. Glenn Ohrlin, University of Illinois Press MAL 731.

For a recent list of variants of the tune to which this text is set, see the following:

C. Alan Jabbour, *American Fiddle Tunes,* Library of Congress Archive of Folk Song AFS L 62, brochure notes for "French Four," pp. 2-5.

84. The Girl I Left in Missouri

A. Laws (1957) (P 1B), pp. 248-49.

Lingenfelter, pp. 392-93.

Lomax (1910), pp. 244-45.

Lomax (1916), pp. 244-45.

Lomax (1938), pp. 192-94.

Moore, pp. 202-5.

B. German (1929), n.p.

C. Jan Harold Brunvand, "Folk Song Studies in Idaho," *Western Folklore,* 24 (Oct., 1965), 238.

Thomas G. Burton and Ambrose N. Manning, *Collection of Folklore: Folksongs* (Johnson City: East Tennessee State University, 1967), pp. 59-60.

Josiah H. Combs, *Folk-Songs of the Southern United States,* ed. D. K. Wilgus (Austin: University of Texas Press, 1967), p. 214.

D. Dick Reinhart, "Girl I Left Behind," Brunswick 59001 (in album B-1024).

Buell Kazee (1927), "The Roving Cowboy," Brunswick 156.

E. Roger Abrahams, "The Girl I Left behind Me," *Make Me a Pallet on the Floor*, Prestige International INT 13034.

Dock Boggs, "Peggy Walker," *Dock Boggs*, 3, Asch AH 3903.

Dave Fredrickson, "Girl I Left Behind," *Songs of the West*, Folkways FH 5259

Clint Howard, "Maggie Walker Blues," *Old Time Music at Clarence Ashley's*, Folkways FA 2355.

Harry Jackson, "The Gal I Left Behind," *The Cowboy*, Folkways FH 5723.

Pleaz Mobley, "My Parents Raised Me Tenderly," *Anglo-American Songs and Ballads*, Library of Congress Archive of Folk Song AAFS L12.

Spencer Moore, "The Girl I Left Behind," *Southern Journey*, 4: *Banjo Songs, Ballads and Reels from the Southern Mountains*, Prestige International INT 25004.

Obray Ramsey, "The Roaming Boy," *Folksongs from the Gateways to the Great Smokies*, Prestige International INT 13030.

Jean Ritchie, "The Girl I Left Behind," *Kentucky Mountain Songs*, Elektra EKL 25.

For a sampling of the related "Joe Bowers," see:

A. Laws (1964) (B 14), pp. 139-40.
Lingenfelter, pp. 96-97.

B. Asch (1964), pp. 60-61.
Famous, p. 23.
Hobo News, p. 5.

C. John Quincy Wolf, "Who Wrote 'Joe Bowers'?" *Western Folklore*, 29 (Apr., 1970), 77-89.

85. 'Longside of the Santa Fe Trail

I am indebted to John I. White for the information that James Grafton Rogers, a former dean of the University of Colorado Law School, wrote the words of this song, which he titled "The Santa Fe Trail." J. H. Gower wrote the music. Comet Publishing Company of Denver published the sheet music in 1911.

A. Allen, pp. 137-39.
Lomax (1938), pp. 308-11.

B. Colby, p. 17.
Lee (1936a), pp. 18-19.
Lee (1937), pp. 28-29.

D. Jules Allen (1929), Victor 40118, Montgomery Ward 4780.
Westerners (Massey Family) (1936), "Santa Fe Trail," Melotone 6-03-58, Oriole 6-03-58, Perfect 6-03-58, Conqueror 8434, Romeo 6-03-58.

E. George Gillespie, "The Santa Fe Trail," *Cow Camp Songs of the Old West*, Thorne TR 200.

Girls of the Golden West, "Santa Fe Trail," *Girls of the Golden West*, 1, Bluebonnet BL 106.

Ed McCurdy, "Along Side the Santa Fe Trail," *Songs of the West*, Tradition 2061.

Nevada Slim, "Santa Fe Trail," *Songs of the Wild West*, 1, Rural Rhythm RRNS 162.

F. Beverly Hillbillies, "Santa Fe Trail," MacGregor 2550.

A discography of recordings by Jules Allen, who was the first to record this song, is given below. Numbers in parentheses after the master numbers refer to alternate takes. Abbreviations: V = Victor, MW = Montgomery Ward.

Master No.	Title	Release Nos.
El Paso, Tex. Apr. 21, 1928. Acc. by own guitar.		
42193	Little Joe the Wrangler	V-21470, MW-4344
42194	Jack o' Diamonds	V-21470, MW-4464
42195 (1)	Po' Mourner	

Master No.	Title	Release Nos.

El Paso, Tex. Apr. 24, 1928. Acc. by own guitar.

42195 (2)	Po' Mourner	V-23834
42211	Somebody, But You Don't Mean Me	V-23598
42212	The Days of Forty-nine	V-21627, MW-4463
42213	Home on the Range	V-21627, MW-4343

El Paso, Tex. Apr. 30, 1928. Acc. by own guitar; and by D. A. Champaigne, harmonica (*) and unknown violin (†).

42254	The Texas Cowboy*	V-40068
42255	A Prisoner for Life†	V-40068
42256	The Gal I Left behind Me*†	V-40022
42257	Zebra Dun	V-40022, MW-4464

Hollywood, Calif. Mar. 28, 1929. Acc. by own guitar.

50567	The Cow Trail to Mexico	V-23757
50568	When the Work's All Done This Fall (Chisholm Trail)	V-40167, MW-4463
50569	Cowboy's Love Song	V-40167, MW-4104
50570	Sweetie Dear	V-23598

Los Angeles, Calif. Apr. 8, 1929. Acc. by own guitar and by Charles Coffey, violin.

50594	'Long Side the Santa Fe Trail	V-40118, MW-4344
50595	Two Fragments	V-40118
50596	The Cowboy's Dream	V-40178
50597	Cowboy's Lament	V-40178, MW-4099
50598	Little Old Sod Shanty	V-23757
50599	The Dying Cowboy	

See also "Jules Verne Allen: 'The Original Singing Cowboy,' " by William Koon and Carol Collins, in *Old Time Music,* 10 (Autumn, 1973), 17-18, 23.

87. The Sweeter the Breeze #2

C. Glenn Ohrlin, *The Hell-Bound Train* (University of Illinois Campus Folksong Club CFC 301), brochure notes, p. 5 (verse and line drawing).

88. Keep Your Saddle Tight

A. Lingenfelter, pp. 387-88.

B. Sires, pp. 42-43.

D. Carl T. Sprague (1926), "If Your Saddle Is Good and Tight," Victor 40066.

For a sketch of Sprague by a fellow recording artist, see John I. White, "Carl T. Sprague: The Original 'Singing Cowboy,' " *John Edwards Memorial Foundation Quarterly,* 6 (Spring, 1970), 32-34. A discography of Sprague's recordings follows. Numbers in parentheses after the master numbers refer to alternate takes. Abbreviations: V = Victor, MW = Montgomery Ward, B = Bluebird.

Master No.	Title	Release Nos.

Camden, N.J. Aug. 3, 1925. Acc. by own guitar.

33124 (1,2,3)	Kisses	
33125 (1,2,3)	When the Work Is All Done This Fall	

Camden, N.J. Aug. 4, 1925. Acc. by own guitar.

33139	Bad Companions	V-19747
33140	Chicken	
33141	Sarah Jane	

Camden, N.J. Aug. 5, 1925. Acc. by own guitar.

33125 (4,5,6)	When the Work's All Done This Fall	V-19747, MW-8060
33143	Following the Cow Trail	V-20067, MW-4468
33144	The Kicking Mule	

Master No.	Title	Release Nos.
33145	Cowboy Love Song	V-20067
33146	The Last Great Round-up	
33147	The Club Meeting	V-19813

Camden, N.J. June 21, 1926. Acc. by own guitar; and by C. R. Dockum and H. J. McKenzie, violins, where noted (*).

35193 (1,2,3)	Here's to the Texas Rangers*	
35194	If Your Saddle Is Good and Tight	V-40066
35539 (1,2,3)	The Boston Burglar*	
35540	The Gambler	V-20534

Camden, N.J. June 22, 1926. Acc. by own guitar; and by C. R. Dockum and H. J. McKenzie, violins, where noted (*).

33124 (4,5)	Kisses	V-19813
35541 (1,2,3)	O Bury Me Not on the Lone Prairie (The Dying Cowboy)*	
35542	The Cowboy's Dream*	V-20122, MW-4343

Camden, N.J. June 23, 1926. Acc. by own guitar and by C. R. Dockum and H. J. McKenzie, violins.

35193 (4,5,6)	Here's to the Texas Rangers	V-40066
35539 (4,5)	The Boston Burglar	
35541 (4,5,6)	The Dying Cowboy (O Bury Me Not on the Lone Prairie)	V-20122, MW-4099

Camden, N.J. June 24, 1926. Acc. by own guitar and by C. R. Dockum and H. J. McKenzie, violins.

35539 (6,7,8)	The Boston Burglar	V-20534

Savannah, Ga. Aug. 24, 1927. Acc. by own guitar and by Olie Olsen and Joe Mintz, violins.

39838	Rounded Up in Glory	V-20932, MW-4466
39839	The Last Great Roundup	V-20932, MW-4466
39840	The Cowman's Prayer	V-21402
39841	The Cowboy	V-21402
39842	Utah Carroll	V-21194
39843	The Two Soldiers	V-21194

Dallas, Tex. Oct. 13, 1929. Acc. by own guitar.

56374	The Wayward Daughter	V-40246
56375	The Prisoner's Meditation	B-6258
56376	The Cowboy's Meditation	V-40197
56377	The Last Longhorn	V-40197
56378	The Cowboy at Church	B-6258
56379	The Mormon Cowboy	V-40246

Bryan, Tex. Mar. 2-20, 1972. *Carl T. Sprague: The First Popular Singing Cowboy*, Folk Variety FV 12001. Acc. by own guitar; and by Craig Davis, second guitar, where noted (*).

Home on the Range
It Is No Secret
Following the Cow Trail
The Girl I Loved in Sunny Tennessee
When the Work's All Done This Fall
Kissing
The Club Meeting
Bad Companions
Rounded Up in Glory*
Red River Valley*

Roll On Little Dogies*
The Last Great Roundup
The Last Fierce Charge
The Gambler

93. Circuit Rider's Home

E. Johnny Baker, *Songs of the Rodeo,* Audio Arts 705.

94. Average Rein

E. Johnny Baker, *Songs of the Rodeo,* Audio Arts 705.

95. Ballad of Billy the Bull Rider

E. Johnny Baker, *Songs of the Rodeo,* Audio Arts 705.

96. Blue Bell Bull

E. Johnny Baker, *Songs of the Rodeo,* Audio Arts 705.

97. Trading-out Blues

E. Johnny Baker, *Songs of the Rodeo,* Audio Arts 705.

98. The Chuck Wagon's Stuck

E. A. Brininstool, who wrote this song, titled it "Trouble for the Range Cook."

B. German (1929), n.p.
German (1932), n.p.
White (1929), pp. 12-13.
C. E. A. Brininstool, *Trail Dust of a Maverick* (New York: Dodd Mead, 1914),
pp. 164-65.
E. Nevada Slim, "Trouble at the Chuck Wagon," *Songs of the Wild West,* 2,
Rural Rhythm RRNS 163.

99. Billy Venero

"Billy Venero" is derived from a poem by Eben E. Rexford, "The Ride of Paul
Venarez," which first appeared in the *Youth's Companion.* Lingenfelter gives this
text, from its reprinting in Phineas Garrett's *One Hundred Choice Selections No.
21* (Philadelphia, 1910). Rexford, a long-time garden editor of the *Ladies Home
Journal,* is best known as the writer of "Silver Threads among the Gold."

A. Coolidge, pp. 118-23.
Fife (1969), pp. 129-31.
Larkin, p. 27.
Laws (1964) (B 6), pp. 16, 136.
Lingenfelter, pp. 262-63.
Lomax (1910), pp. 299-302.
Lomax (1916), pp. 299-302.
Lomax (1938), pp. 197-200.
Randolph, 2, 222-27.
B. American, pp. 28-29.
Clark (1932), pp. 60-61.
German (1929), n.p.
Goodwin, p. 28.
Maynard, pp. 6-8.
C. *Ace High Magazine* (New York), 66, no. 1 (Mar. 4, 1932).
B. A. Botkin, *A Treasury of Western Folklore* (New York: Crown Publishers,
1951), pp. 759-60.
Jan Harold Brunvand, "Folk Song Studies in Idaho," *Western Folklore,* 24
(Oct., 1965), 238.

Eben E. Rexford, "The Ride of Paul Venarez," *Youth's Companion,* 54 (Dec. 29, 1881), 502.
D. Billie Maxwell (1929), Victor 40148.
   "Mac" (Harry McClintock) (1928), Victor 21487.
E. Elton Britt, "The Legend of Rocky Run," *I Heard a Forest Praying,* ABC Paramount ABC 331.
   Don Cleary, *Don Cleary Sings Traditional Cowboy Songs,* Palomino 302.
   Nevada Slim, *Songs of the Wild West,* 1, Rural Rhythm RRNS 162.
   Glenn Ohrlin, *Stone County Singing,* Shoestring Tape SGB 1.
   Joe and Benny Rodriguez, *Cowboy Songs,* Arizona Friends of Folklore AFF 33-1.
   Luther Royce, "Billy Vanero," *Folk Music from Wisconsin,* Library of Congress Archive of Folk Song L55.
   Texas Old Timers, *Playing and Singing the Old Hits,* Bluebonnet BL 104.

One of the rewards for doing a biblio-discography of this sort is the chance to express thanks to the many gracious people who have contributed their time and knowledge. Judith McCulloh has put an immense amount of work and patience into these notes. Joe Dan Boyd, James Bratcher, Leland D. Case, Norm Cohen, Bob Cook, Austin and Alta Fife, Ed Frost, Gail I. Gardner, Archie Green, Joseph C. Hickerson, Glenn Ohrlin, Margaret Pead, Page Stephens, and John I. White have also given valued assistance. A sincere thank-you is offered to all.

HARLAN DANIEL

Index

Page numbers for main appearances of the songs are given in **boldface;** for first lines, in *italics.*

284

285

McElroy, Lacey, 182, 185
McElroy, Shane, 182, 184, 185
McGonigal, Clay, 91
Mack, Roy, 38, 179, 202
Mackey, William P., 250-51
McNab, Jim, 193
McWiggins, Zack, 48
Madland, Kenny, 93
Madsen, Anders, 28
Magee, 13
"Make Me a Cowboy Again" (no. 56), **136-37**, 270
Malpais, 13
"Map of Chihuahua" brand, 73
Marshall, Charlie, 8
Martin, Dutch, 207
Marty (Ekalaka bartender), 166
Marty, Bill, 166
Marty, Ed, 164, 166
Maynard, Ken, 130
Meathead (bucking bull), 229
Mefford, Buddy, 86
Midnight (bucking horse), 193
"Midnight" (no. 80), **193**, 276
Miller, Charlie, 97
Miller, Joe, 136, 159, 270
Miller, Ruth, 123
Miller, Zack, 136, 159, 270
Mill Iron ranch, 161
"Montana Slim." *See* Carter, Wilf
"Moonlight and Skies" (no. 21), **52-53,** 257
Moreland, Peg, 136
Morris, Chip, 86, 99, 165, 205, 206
Morris, Pee Wee, 205
"Moundsville Prisoner," 138
"The Mowing Machine" (no. 3), **8-9,** 16, 247
Mulkey, Burel, 80
Mullin (ranch owner), 97
"My Friends and Relations" (no. 2), **6-7,** 246-47
"My friends and relations they live in the the Nations," 7
"My Harding County Home" (no. 67), **161-63**
"My Home's in Montana" (no. 1), **3-5,** 6, 10, 246
"My home's in Montana, I wear a bandana," 5
"My Love Is a Rider" (no. 14), **34-35,** 253-54
"My love is a rider, wild broncos he breaks," 34
"My Old Pinto Pal" (no. 89), **211-12**
"My parents treated me kindly, having no one but me," *200*
"My Stetson Hat" (no. 83), **198-99,** 276

Nix, Bill, 91
Nixon, Alan, 25
North Dakota Stockmen's Association, 102

"Not so many years ago I left old Buffalo," *163*
Number Three (bucking bull), 229

O'Daniel, W. Lee, 250
"Oh, come hear my story of heartaches and sighs," *53*
"Oh, down in the tules, a-wranglin' around," *183*
"Oh, I'm a Swede from Nort Dakota," *21*
"Oh, once in the saddle I used to go dashing," *9*
"Oh, she rode up to the wagon, the sun was sinking low," *170*
"Oh, why don't you work like other men do?" *32*
"Oh, Windy Bill was a Texas boy, and he could rope, you bet," *13*
Ohrlin, Alma, 149, 182
Ohrlin, Bert, 20, 30
Ohrlin, Glenn: early riding experiences, 3-4; boyhood, 3-4, 30, 149; first rodeo, 4, 206-7; on cowboys' work, 6, 13, 148-49; later rodeos, 12, 25, 49, 54, 81, 86, 93, 106-7, 110-11, 132, 135, 148, 165, 172, 174, 196, 205; as author or songwriter, 18, 117, 120, 132, 146, 198, 206, 240; as announcer, 25, 86, 173, 213; as singer, 36, 48-49, 99, 106, 109, 129, 132, 142, 148, 153; as cowboy, 61-62, 97, 110-11, 113; as collector, 64, 69, 82, 86, 104, 136, 161, 166, 173, 187, 196, 211, 237, 241; on cowboy values, 88-89; on price of beef, 125, 266
Ohrlin, Kay, 86, 166, 173, 211
"An old cowpoke went riding to a rodeo one day," *133*
"The Old Jail Song," 138
"The Old Scout's Lament" (no. 18), **43-44,** 45, 255
"Old-Time Cowboy" (no. 17), **41-42,** 45, 255
Old Time Cowboys Association, 190
Olmstead brothers, 48
"O Lord, please lend to me thine ear," *125*
Olson, Carl, 48
O'Malley, D. J., 45, 255
101 ranch, 136, 159
"On the wild and woolly prairie," *65*
Orejana Bull: For Cowboys Only, 69
O'Rourke, Frank L., 190
Orr, Gail "Boston Blackie," 207
"Outlaw Dunny" (no. 75), **185-86**
"Outlaw Tom," 6
"Over the divide a great cowboy did go," *90*
Owens, Mitch, 80, 81, 194
Ozark Folksongs, 30, 140, 142, 159

"Paddy on the Turnpike" (no. 43), **106-8,** 264
"Paddy Ryan" (no. 34), **86-87,** 166, 262

287

288

289

Books in the Series Music in American Life

Only a Miner: Studies in Recorded Coal-Mining Songs
Archie Green

Great Day Coming: Folk Music and the American Left
R. Serge Denisoff

John Philip Sousa: A Descriptive Catalog of His Works
Paul E. Bierley

The Hell-Bound Train: A Cowboy Songbook
Glenn Ohrlin

Oh, Didn't He Ramble: The Life Story of Lee Collins as Told to Mary Collins
Frank J. Gillis and John W. Miner, Editors

American Labor Songs of the Nineteenth Century
Philip S. Foner

Stars of Country Music: Uncle Dave Macon to Johnny Rodriguez
Bill C. Malone and Judith McCulloh, Editors

Git Along, Little Dogies: Songs and Songmakers of the American West
John I. White

A Texas-Mexican *Cancionero*: Folksongs of the Lower Border
Américo Paredes

San Antonio Rose: The Life and Music of Bob Wills
Charles R. Townsend

Early Downhome Blues: A Musical and Cultural Analysis
Jeff Todd Titon

An Ives Celebration: Papers and Panels of the Charles Ives
Centennial Festival-Conference
H. Wiley Hitchcock and Vivian Perlis, Editors

Sinful Tunes and Spirituals: Black Folk Music to the Civil War
Dena J. Epstein

Joe Scott, the Woodsman-Songmaker
Edward D. Ives

Jimmie Rodgers: The Life and Times of America's Blue Yodeler
Nolan Porterfield

Early American Music Engraving and Printing: A History
of Music Publishing in America from 1787 to 1825
with Commentary on Earlier and Later Practices
Richard J. Wolfe

Sing a Sad Song: The Life of Hank Williams
Roger M. Williams

Long Steel Rail: The Railroad in American Folksong
Norm Cohen

Resources of American Music History: A Directory of Source Materials
from Colonial Times to World War II
D. W. Krummel, Jean Geil, Doris J. Dyen, and Deane L. Root

Tenement Songs: The Popular Music of the Jewish Immigrants
Mark Slobin

Ozark Folksongs
Vance Randolph; Edited and Abridged by Norm Cohen

Oscar Sonneck and American Music
Edited by William Lichtenwanger

Bluegrass Breakdown: The Making of the Old Southern Sound
Robert Cantwell

Bluegrass: A History
Neil V. Rosenberg

Music at the White House: A History of the American Spirit
Elise K. Kirk

Red River Blues: The Blues Tradition in the Southeast
Bruce Bastin

Good Friends and Bad Enemies: Robert Winslow Gordon
and the Study of American Folksong
Debora Kodish

Fiddlin' Georgia Crazy: Fiddlin' John Carson, His Real World,
and the World of His Songs
Gene Wiggins

America's Music: From the Pilgrims to the Present
Revised Third Edition
Gilbert Chase

Secular Music in Colonial Annapolis: The Tuesday Club, 1745-56
John Barry Talley

Bibliographical Handbook of American Music
D. W. Krummel

Goin' to Kansas City
Nathan W. Pearson, Jr.

"Susanna," "Jeanie," and "The Old Folks at Home": The Songs of
Stephen C. Foster from His Time to Ours
Second Edition
William W. Austin

Songprints: The Musical Experience of Five Shoshone Women
Judith Vander

"Happy in the Service of the Lord": Afro-American Gospel Quartets
in Memphis
Kip Lornell